Deep Brain Learning

evidence-based essentials in education,

treatment, and youth development

To Graham

Courage!

Larry Brendtro

Larry K. Brendtro & Martin L. Mitchell

ISBN: 978-0-9961591-0-4

Action Research and contributed features include excerpts from the following articles published in the journal Reclaiming and other publications copyrighted by Starr Commonwealth: Ch. 1: Brokenleg, 2012; James & Lunday, 2014. Ch. 2: Jackson, 2014a. Ch. 3: Seita, 2014b. Ch. 4: Fecser, 2015. Ch. 5: Tate, Copas, & Wasmund, 2012; Kreisle, 2012. Ch. 6: Laursen, 2014. Ch. 7: Anglin, 2014. Ch. 8: Bath, 2015; Steele & Kuban, 2014. Ch. 9: Hatter, 2014; Van Bockern & McDonald, 2012; Woodland Hills Youth, 2008; Quigley, 2014. Ch. 10: Peterson, 2013b; Larson, 2014; Ponds, 2014; Longhurst & Brown, 2013.

The following are trademarks of Starr Commonwealth: Autism Assets™, Circle of Courage®, CLEAR®, Cultures of Respect™, Deep Brain Learning®, Designer Genes®, Developmental Audit®, Glasswing®, Positive Peer Culture®, Reclaiming Children and Youth®, Response Ability Pathways®, SITCAP®, TherapyWise®, Three Pillars of TraumaWise Care®, The National Institute for Trauma and Loss in Children®, and Rolling with Resilience™.

Preface

This book identifies Evidence-Based Essentials for creating positive environments where all can thrive. These principles apply across diverse settings including education, treatment, juvenile justice, child and youth care, and family and community-based programs. Ours is a team project drawing on the experience of many colleagues and the children and families we serve. We are grateful to those whose creativity is seen in these pages or acknowledged in the bibliography. A unique feature of this book is that all chapters contain research and practice features from the *Reclaiming* journal.

What do we mean by *Deep Brain Learning*? John Dewey coined the term "habitudes" to describe deeply embedded habits and attitudes that shape what kind of person one becomes. He defined habitudes as those enduring learnings "formed in the constant give and take of our relationships with others."[a] *Deep Brain Learning* is not a book on neuroscience, but it includes relevant brain research which informs our goal of making deep, lasting change in individuals and society.

This is a Circle of Courage publication produced by Starr Commonwealth, now in its second century of service. Starr provides research, training, and publications through the Circle of Courage Network, a global alliance of practitioners, researchers, and advocates working to build strong families, schools, and communities.

The chapters are organized into three sections. Part I introduces cultural and scientific perspectives on *searching for solutions* to problems faced by modern youth. Part II documents *evidence-based essentials* for positive change and growth. Part III explores the challenges of *delivering what works* in the real world. Finally, we point the reader to further resources for professional development.

---

a Dewey, 1916, p. 22.

Contents

PART III: DELIVERING WHAT WORKS

1

Cultural Wisdom

Martin Brokenleg, Larry K. Brendtro, & Martin Mitchell[a]

Let us build communities and families in which our children and youth, especially those who are most troubled, can belong. Let us build a country in which our children and youth can learn to care for and respect others. [1]

Nelson Mandela

Until recently, research on child and youth development largely reflected perspectives from middle class communities in Europe and North America.[2] Anthropologists who first studied children from Native tribes in the Americas described them as radiantly happy, courageous, and highly respectful of elders. Similar observations have been made about other indigenous nations worldwide.[3] Yet only recently has knowledge from these traditional systems of child development been seen as relevant to modern times.

Cultures which deeply respect children share a strong commonality—they all see children as sacred.[4] The Lakota word for child literally translates as sacred being. The Maori refer to a child as a gift of God. The descriptor for children in the Nigerian Ibo tongue means what wonders has God wrought! Across all social groups in India, the newborn child is regarded as God's gift to the family.[5] The Zulu concept of children describes feelings of joy they elicit in adults.

Zululand University sociologist Herbert Vilakazi observed that much knowledge about human nature predates Western science. The notion that indigenous people did not have serious theories of child psychology was wildly in error. In fact, societies that deeply valued children built their cultural wisdom around caring for and educating the young. Vilakazi describes African elders having highly nuanced theories of child development.

a **Martin Brokenleg, EdD,** *co-author of this chapter, is Professor Emeritus at Augustana College in South Dakota and most recently was Director of Native Ministries and Professor of Native American Theology and Ministries at the Vancouver School of Theology in Vancouver, British Columbia. He is an enrolled member of the Rosebud Sioux Tribe.*

I know of no people more concerned about child psychology,
and very meticulous and systematic in their consideration for children….
The old African men and women, particularly the old women,
were consummate child psychologists.[6]

The challenge for modern society according to Vilakazi is to reclaim this lost wisdom to solve the problems facing modern youth.

Cultural practices in many traditional societies were well-matched to this task. Mothers in Mayan tribes of Guatemala, like those in tribal cultures of India, are much more responsive to the needs of children than is common in Western child rearing. Small children in Polynesia watch others work and then pitch in to help as soon as they master simple skills.[7] In all of the world's indigenous cultures, children grow to maturity immersed in interactions with adults and older peers as caregivers. Traditional kinship systems worldwide ensure that children have many mothers, fathers, and grandparents.

In the nineteenth century, children in Euro-American cultures were separated by age for efficiency in running factory schools. From toddler days, they are shunted off to age-graded schools. By adolescence, peer relationships trump family and community ties. Elsewhere in the world, most children's groups include a full range of ages, and children spend only about ten percent of their time with same-age peers.[8] Today, children are confined to artificial cliques of the immature and are deprived of mature adult and peer models.

Harsh discipline is rare—and also quite unnecessary—in cultures where children and adults live in mutual respect. The attachment instinct motivates the child to emulate elders, not disobey them. In turn, the warmth of children activates the tending instinct in adults. So it has been throughout the history of humanity. Such is the lost truth we must now rediscover. We begin that search as Martin Brokenleg shares from his experience growing up in a traditional Native American culture.

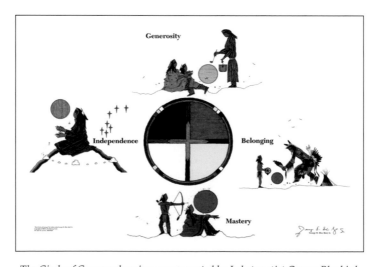

The Circle of Courage drawings were created by Lakota artist George Bluebird.

Circles of Courage

I learned that courage was not the absence of fear, but the triumph over it.[9]

Nelson Mandela

I grew up on the Rosebud Reservation in South Dakota. In my Lakota tongue, children are called Wakan, which literally means sacred. Our book *Reclaiming Youth at Risk*[10] introduced the Circle of Courage which blends traditional Native child and youth care philosophy with research and best practice from the Western tradition. That work described four universal growth needs which form the foundation of resilience and positive youth development: Belonging, Mastery, Independence, and Generosity. When these needs are met, children thrive. When not, they experience pain and trauma. Trauma is closely intertwined with *resilience* which is defined as "the capacity for adapting successfully and functioning competently, despite experiencing chronic stress or adversity following exposure to prolonged or severe trauma."[11]

One of the great exemplars of surmounting trauma with resilience is Nelson Mandela who led his nation from apartheid to democracy. The first time I went to South Africa, I asked to visit the grave of Steve Biko. He courageously fought for equality under apartheid but was killed while in police custody. Biko often declared that the most powerful tool of an oppressor is the mind of the oppressed. The worst kind of oppression is internalized. Once in someone's head, it is hard to remove. If someone can convince us that we are not good enough, not smart enough, and not capable enough, then oppression can become permanent inside our heads.

Traumatic experiences are cumulative. If one generation does not heal, problems are transmitted to subsequent generations. This is particularly apparent in how trauma affects Native persons worldwide who were ripped from their cultural moorings. Trauma sculpts how we think, how we respond emotionally, our social dynamics, and, at the deepest level, our spirituality. Trauma has wounded many of us deeply. There were times in my life when I wondered, "Is there something wrong with me? Is there something wrong with our people? What did we do to cause all of this to happen?" The truth is there is nothing wrong with traumatized *people*—they are struggling to cope with an abnormal *experience*.

Today we see a society-wide disregard of our young who are treated as if they really do not matter. When visiting a community, I often ask teenagers how far across their city or town they could walk before someone would speak to them. Some say they could walk all the way across without being greeted. The biggest threat to many modern youth is the lack of significant caring relationships. Oddly, we "friend" on Facebook and we can twitter and tweet and cheep and chirp. But we are missing the eyeball to eyeball contact that keeps us strong.

An exciting dynamic in youth development is the focus on positive psychology and resilience. The Circle of Courage model is unique in that it creates a synergy of separate fields of knowledge: contemporary psychology and traditional Native child rearing. These are well matched. Native grandmothers knew exactly what they were doing, drawing knowledge from centuries of experience in cultures that deeply valued children. Resilience science helps us understand the power of these human connections. Resiliency is being able to get up again when life knocks us down. So adults should be teaching young people resiliency. Our schools are much better at dispensing facts than helping youth flourish. *Knowledge* describes training of the mind, and we are in a mad race to do this with the goal of high test scores. But there is another kind of learning which Aristotle called *capacities*. We seek to reach their heart, to teach their spirit, to nurture the inner life.

One cannot teach resiliency with posters or words or workbooks. What we need are transformative experiences. Here are four simple examples of the match between findings of eminent researcher in self-worth Stanley Coopersmith[12] and the four Circle of Courage growth needs:

> *Significance:* Realizing that one matters to others creates enormous inner strength. This describes the spirit of *Belonging.*

> *Competence:* A capable person can learn, solve problems, and develop talents. Such is the joy that comes from *Mastery.*

> *Power:* Personal power is the ability to control one's emotions and act with responsibility. This is genuine *Independence.*

> *Virtue:* The ultimate proof of one's worth is to be of value to others. This is the spirit of *Generosity.*

Let me share an event from my youth which captures the spirit of belonging. My parents were traditional Lakota people and seldom would go anywhere without their children. The first time I was ever going to be away from my family was in grade eleven. To this day I do not know where I got this idea, but I asked my parents, if I could go to a boys' military school. So it happened that I enrolled in a boarding school in another state. I proudly wore my uniform and marched around from September to December. Then it was home to the Rosebud Reservation for the holiday furlough. After a wonderful time with my family, Christmas vacation came to an end. The winter weather was threatening so my father decided it best that I fly back to school. As we drove toward Rapid City, the radio warned of a blizzard. My father left me at the downtown hotel and he hurried back to the reservation.

I got up early the next morning when it was still dark. The snow was blowing sideways, and I could not even see the ground. I phoned the hotel desk and found that the 6 AM flight was still scheduled. As I sat in the lobby near the window, snow was blowing everywhere. It let up for an instant and I could see a shadow passing under the street light. Someone was leaning into the wind heading toward the hotel. The person was all wrapped up and came inside. She shook the snow off her Pendleton blanket and I saw that she was one of my relatives who lived a couple miles away. She had no car but had walked to see me before I departed. She put her arms around me and said, "Son, I heard you were going back to school today and I wanted to come see you. How is your mother and how is your father?" We sat down and talked until the shuttle arrived. As we stood to leave, she put her arms around me. She said, "I want you to know that I am proud of you for staying in school. Someone in our family should have an education. You learn everything you can. I will think about you and pray for you every day." She wrapped herself in the blanket and walked out into the blowing snow.

When someone cares for us amidst the blizzards of life, we know we are significant. This cannot be taught in words but is communicated to others in how we treat them. Our students will forget most of what we say to them but they will never forget how we make them feel. That is the difference between learning in the head and deep learning in the heart. Belonging, Mastery, Independence, and Generosity are the vital signs of positive youth development. These are a birthright of Native people, but also a precious gift for children of any culture which values its young. We have put these around a medicine wheel which we call the Circle of Courage because the result is becoming courageous in surmounting the challenges of life.

Rituals of Respect

From the moment I entered their village, I was captivated by their respectful behavior, self-confident demeanor, and astonishing creativity.[13]

Inge Bolin

Indigenous cultures offer unique models of positive youth development because they immerse children in what Inge Bolin has called *rituals of respect.*[14] Bolin is a German-born Canadian anthropologist who has lived with the Quechua people from isolated mountain villages in highland Peru. While cut off from the supposed benefits of modern civilization, Bolin observes that children combine politeness and responsibility toward family and surprising scholastic abilities. Per the Circle of Courage model, children from all cultures have needs for Belonging, Mastery, Independence, and Generosity. When these needs are met, children thrive. The examples below are drawn from Bolin's study, *Growing Up in a Culture of Respect.*

Belonging

Respect for others is the most deeply ingrained value that guides all thought and action. In the Quechua culture, child rearing is the responsibility of the entire village. Bolin offers this example of the intimate bonds between generations in the High Andes of Peru:

> *Evenings are a time of fun, laughter, and storytelling. The girls sing and the boys and men sometimes play their instruments. Children are the center of attention before they retire to their sleeping corners. They are played with, joked with and tickled. They are never neglected, regardless of how tired parents and grandparents may be. Since loneliness is considered the saddest of states, everyone makes sure that no one lacks attention…. at home and, if at all possible, in school, children are listened to and have the right to speak out for themselves.* [15]

Attachment to adults is a prerequisite to learning from them. For millennia, the image of education was a group of children gathered around a respected elder. Children crave such guidance.

Mastery

The desire for competition is inborn but cultures shape its practice. There are two contrasting models: we either *compete with* or we *compete against* others. In hierarchical cultures, the goal is to fight hard and to beat an opponent—note the combat metaphors. But many tribal cultures are horizontal rather than hierarchical. Thus when children of the Andes compete in activities or in school, they give their best without creating a status of winners and losers. Bolin explains:

> *There is a difference between wanting to win to be better than others and using the "challenge" of others to give one's best. The former is a negative, aggressive approach to competition, and the latter is a positive constructive, developmental approach…. The satisfaction is not in winning but in seeing improvement in oneself over time.*[16]

Children are taught not to flaunt their superiority. Physical and mental differences are accepted without prejudice. Young people banter and joke continuously, but never does this escalate into insults or fights. Work well done is appreciated, but none are praised to the detriment of others. Nor do children brag of their achievements. When the talents of all are cultivated, all become winners.

Independence

Cultures of respect treat children as young citizens and responsible members of society. From age three, children of the Andes begin doing all sorts of little jobs, like running errands and holding the bottle for a baby. They proudly learn adult tasks and eagerly join in songs and dances. Adolescence is seen as a wonderful period of life as youth take on many of the rights and responsibilities of adults.[17] Instead of demanding obedience, discipline is based on powerful bonds between the young and the old.

> *I have never seen a small child being spanked, yelled at, or treated in a rough way. Yet children do not turn out to be spoiled. They soon learn about the behavioral norms that are accepted by family and community and demonstrated by adults and older siblings. At a young age they are introduced to the unwritten law of reciprocity, the hallmark of Andean life. This requires that respect be given and received in an eternal cycle that maintains their lives in balance.[18]*

Forcing a child to do something for which he or she is not yet ready is considered disrespectful.[19] This principle is embodied in the discipline practices of many tribal cultures. Problems are solved as children engage in respectful conversations with elders.

Generosity

Cultures of respect immerse young people in service to the community. Adolescents are given apprenticeships and are always present at village meetings where processes of decision making are transparent. Cross-age positive networks provide opportunities to take care of one another, creating positive peer cultures. Ancient ways of teaching respect are passed on to each new generation.

> *Children of Highland Peru participate in rituals, tending to their elders with food, drink, and courtesies. They care for younger children, who in turn idolize them. They are challenged by meaningful activities that contribute to the community. As they approach adulthood, they join formal groups to help police their neighborhood and solve social and community problems.*

As children learn to show respect for others and all life, they are well on their way to being full contributing members of a community. Remarkably, the Quechua language has no word for respect. This is because respect is expected at all times, it is the central value pervading all thought and action.[20]

Cultural Brains

Ego and empathy, self-interest and other interest
are key features in our personal and social behavior.[21]

Gerald Cory, Jr.

The human brain has two distinct systems to meet needs: one is designed for personal survival and self-preservation; the other is for empathy and concern for others.[22] Both brain-based programs are necessary to flourish, but sometimes they conflict. Of course, individuals and societies vary in egocentric or altruistic values.

Why does the human brain take over twenty years to fully mature? To download a complex culture. The social brain theory first advanced by Robin Dunbar[23] described how an oversized neocortex enables humans to live in complex social networks. Homo sapiens naturally thrive in larger social groups than any primate, 150 individuals—which is called Dunbar's number.[24] Our extinct cousins, the Neanderthals, were physically stronger and in "survival of the fittest" terms, should have prevailed. But they had less social brain capacity and had to live in much smaller groups.[25]

A long period of brain development enables humans to build neural circuits to become socialized into a society. The neocortex is involved in conscious thought, language, emotional, and behavioral regulation, empathy, and the theory of mind—the ability to read the feelings and intentions of others.[26] Humans are the most social of beings, which has been the basis of our success as a species.

Universal Needs

Since humans can only survive in social communities, our entire system of brain-based needs are designed for this purpose. Thus, we experience reward from mutual social interactions and sensations of pain when we are rejected or excluded. The social brain underpins the science of human motivation. Pioneer anthropologist Bronisław Malinowski (1884-1942) observed that the ultimate purpose of any culture is to satisfy biological needs.[27] Even our so called higher needs are rooted in survival.[28] Humans join together for security and support, and we learn to solve problems and cope with challenges in the environment.

The strength of a culture ultimately depends on the successful socialization of its young. Ironically, cultural research shows that supposedly less "developed" hunter-gatherer cultures are more focused on nurturing needs of children than many supposedly "advanced" civilizations. Specifically, this means being responsive to the needs of children and treating them with great respect.[29]

New Zealand psychiatrist Peter Gluckman and UK biologist Mark Hanson contend that modern society is grossly mismatched with the way humans are genetically designed.[30] For many thousands of years, humans lived in close kinship groups that provided strong social support. But the depersonalized and transient relationships in modern society result in breakdowns in physical health, emotional adjustment, and social stability. While we cannot trade in our genes, we can build healthier environments that are more responsive to the needs of children.

Philosophers and scientists have long pondered the question of what humans need to meet their potential. The most enduring and parsimonious answer was put forth by Abraham Maslow.[31] More than seven decades after publishing his hierarchy of needs, Maslow is still the world's most cited psychologist of human motivation.[32] What gave his model staying power was its simplicity. While others produced exhaustive lists,[33] Maslow sought to describe the core human needs tied to well-being and survival.

At the lowest level are the physiological needs, which keep the body in balance, followed by safety needs. Once these survival needs are met, belongingness, esteem, and self-actualization needs come into play. This latter term met two major criticisms. First, the focus on the self was biased toward individualistic Western society. Second, it enshrined selfishness at the top of human motivation.[34] Near the end of his life, Maslow corrected this oversight, adding a higher level called self-transcendence—commitment to a person or cause beyond oneself.[35] Ironically, many textbooks are still stuck on the selfish version.

At the core of all emotional and behavioral problems are unmet needs.[36] Yet it is often difficult to recognize or respond to these needs because disruptive behavior seems to call for "extreme interventions." Maslow proposed that thwarting basic needs leads to psychopathology. Emotional disorders are more than "a bag of symptoms"[37] but should be seen as "an understandable coping mechanism and as a reasonable (though stupid and fearful) effort to satisfy the needs of a deeper-lying, more intrinsic, biological self."[38]

The Healthy Society

Maslow's studies of tribal cultures in Canada profoundly influenced his view of healthy human development. He was particularly struck with the generosity of Blackfoot Indians and believed that this contributed to their superior mental health. Like Malinowski, Maslow saw the purpose of any culture as satisfying human needs. This principle forms the blueprint for positive development as well as restorative interventions. The healthy society "permits man's highest purposes to emerge by satisfying all his prepotent basic needs."[39]

Maslow estimated that 80 percent of members of the Blackfoot tribe were high in emotional security in contrast to perhaps 10 percent in the dominant society.[40] He studied their child rearing philosophy, but publishers were not interested in this anthropological research. Decades later, he was disheartened to learn that the healthy culture he observed in the 1930s had been devastated by government policies of colonial domination.[41]

As seen in Table 1, there is a correspondence between growth needs in Maslow's revised hierarchy and Circle of Courage.

Table 1. Two Models of Positive Development

Maslow's Hierarchy of Needs	Circle of Courage Needs
Self-Transcendence	Generosity
Self-Actualization	Independence
Esteem	Mastery
Belongingness	Belonging

In fact, researchers have found a consilience around these simple core constructs which, with semantic variations, are embodied in virtually every theory of child and youth development.[42]

Indigenous Science

Adrienne Brant James

The old are dedicated to the service of the young as their teachers and advisors, and the young in turn regard them with love and reverence.[43]

Ohiyesa, 1911

Ohiyesa is the Dakota name of Charles Eastman, MD, who tended the survivors of the Wounded Knee massacre. This tragedy launched a life-long quest to share the wisdom of his culture and to transform how children are reared in modern society. The author of many books reflecting Native life, Eastman also was instrumental in forming the Boy Scouts, Campfire Girls, and YMCA programs. He was part of a progressive global movement in education and youth work.[44]

For thousands of years, children in traditional cultures have bonded closely with elders and internalized shared values, beliefs, and practices. Today, kinship is fractured as one or two parents struggle to rear children without a network of support. A century ago, the vision of "education for democracy" motivated reformers like John Dewey[45] and Maria Montessori.[46] Today, the goal of educating young citizens gives way to training a workforce for a global economy, and schools mutate into test prep centers in the "race to the top." Computers can enrich learning, but warped priorities spawn for-profit "virtual schools" barren of human interaction. Youth who are alienated from family, school, and community gravitate to other disconnected peers.

Cultural historian Riane Eisler has identified two principal types of societies: dominator cultures and cultures of respect.[47] Cultures that respect children are designed to meet their growth needs.[48] But materialistic, dominator societies stifle learning and generate social, emotional, and behavioral problems. The core values driving each of these cultures are contrasted in Table 2.

Table 2. Values of Dominator and Democratic Cultures

Dominator Values	Democratic Values
Egocentrism—individualism supplants community bonds	**Belonging**—joining in a community of mutual support
Superiority—competing to win in order to appear better than others	**Mastery**—cooperating to learn and develop competence
Intimidation—using power and rank to subjugate others	**Independence**—respecting each person's right to autonomy
Privilege—pursuing "the good life" in self-centered materialism	**Generosity**—demonstrating care and concern for others

Nowhere is this disconnection more dramatic than with those whose cultures were degraded or demolished by slavery or colonial domination. Children of color and indigenous students world-wide demonstrate a lag in academic achievement and a lack of enthusiasm for schooling in its conventional colonial form.[49] They drop out at high rates and are subjected to disciplinary push out, which becomes a pipeline into the justice system.[50] Research points to the need for new approaches that build on strengths of all students.

According to the Search Institute, a majority of today's children have less than half of the "developmental assets" necessary for them to achieve their full potential.[51] Ironically, anthropological studies of indigenous peoples reveal that these cultures were intentionally organized to successfully socialize children.[52] All children have a cultural birthright to be reared in environments that enable them to thrive and flourish.

Traditional peoples shared a worldview grounded in respect for all life. At the core of Native science are *the natural laws of interdependence.*[53] In contrast to this ecological view, modern research moves toward reductionism, measuring isolated variables. As Dakota scholar Vine Deloria, Jr., observes, Western science tries to force nature to reveal its secrets, while traditional peoples simply petition nature for friendship.[54] Living in harmony requires a relational—not linear—worldview.[55]

From the Americas to Australasia and Africa, the subjugation of indigenous peoples ripped families from their cultural moorings. The dominator view was that children were born evil and required harsh discipline in order to learn. This cultural myth was exported globally as seen in the autocratic model of schooling imposed on India, the apartheid education of South Africa, and the stolen generation of Australia. In nineteenth century North America, "education for extinction" was built upon the motto "kill the Indian to save the man."[56] Vestiges of hierarchical education still persist, preventing students from reaching their full potentials.

The arc of human history is marked by the universal quest for freedom. Creating harmony and social equity requires sophisticated systems for sharing power, resolving conflicts, and seeking consensus. Western civilization was rich with knowledge but employed this for power rather than the moral good.[57] In contrast, democratic processes were well established in many indigenous societies, for example, *The Great Law of Peace* of the Iroquois Confederacy.[58] First codified in 1100 AD, these principles inspired framers of the U.S. constitution in designing their fledgling democracy.

Contemporary psychology also has been influenced by indigenous philosophies. Carl Jung's encounter with a Taos Pueblo elder had a profound effect on his writings. He noted that this experience made him aware of his imprisonment "in the cultural consciousness of the white man."[59] Erik Erikson formulated his developmental stages drawing from observations of Sioux and Yurok child-rearing.[60] Abraham Maslow's hierarchy of needs was shaped by his field work with a Blackfoot tribe in Canada whose community ethos he called an oasis in the desert.[61]

There is now renewed recognition of the value of indigenous science and wisdom concerning rearing children in cultures of respect.[62] The Circle of Courage principles bridge Native and Western knowledge. The universal values of Belonging, Mastery, Independence, and Generosity are the foundation for positive youth development and wellness in any culture.[63] These needs are designed in the human brain. They are celebrated by cultures that honor children. As Goethe once said, everything important has been thought of before, the difficulty is to think of it again.

1. Mandela, 2003, p. 418.
2. Rogoff, 2003.
3. Rogoff, 2003.
4. Brokenleg, 1998.
5. Anandalakshmy, 2010, p. 27.
6. Vilakazi, 1993, p. 37.
7. Martini & Kirkpatrick, 1992.
8. Rogoff, 2003.
9. Mandela, 2012, p. 18.
10. Brendtro, Brokenleg, & Van Bockern, 1990/2002.
11. Cicchetti & Valentino, 2006, p. 165.
12. Coopersmith, 1967.
13. Bolin, 2006, p. 33.
14. Bolin, 1998.
15. Bolin, 2006, p. 56.
16. Bolin, 2006, p. 154.
17. Bolin, 2006.
18. Bolin, 2006, p. 152.
19. Bolin, 2006.
20. Bolin, 2006.
21. Cory, Jr., 2000, p. 46.
22. Cory, Jr., 2000.
23. Dunbar, 1998
24. Lieberman, 2013.
25. Hall, 2008.
26. Vrlicka, 2013.
27. Malinowski, 1944.
28. Maslow, 1967.
29. Hewlett & Lamb, 2005
30. Gluckman & Hanson, 2006.
31. Maslow, 1943.
32. Diener, Oishi, & Park, 2014, p. 29.
33. Murray, 1938.
34. Wallach & Wallach, 1983.
35. Koltko-Rivera, 2006.
36. Sternberg, 1999.
37. Hoffman, 1988, p. 109.
38. Maslow 1967, p. 93.
39. Maslow, 1943, p. 394.
40. Hoffman, 1999.
41. Gray, 2011.
42. Jackson, 2014a
43. Eastman, 1911, pp. 23-24.
44. Key, 1909.
45. Dewey, 1916.
46. Montessori, 1912.
47. Eisler, 1998.
48. Rogoff, 2003.
49. Reyhner, Martin, Lockhard, & Gilbert, 2013
50. Skiba, 2014.
51. Benson, 1997.
52. Bolin, 2006; Diamond, 2012; Rogoff, 2003.
53. Cajete, 2000.
54. Deloria, Jr., 2009.
55. Cross, 2012.
56. Adams, 1997; Pratt, 2004.
57. Deloria, Jr., 2009.
58. Cohen, 1942.
59. Jung, 1973, p. 247.
60. Erikson, 1950.
61. Hoffman, 1988.
62. Bolin, 2006; Diamond, 2012.
63. Brendtro, Brokenleg, & Van Bockern, 2002.

2

Searching for Solutions

There are two systems which have been in use through all ages
in educating youth: the preventive and the repressive.[1]

John Bosco, 1816-1888

Cultures differ greatly in how they treat their young. In the well-known book *Centuries of Childhood*, Philippe Aries proposed that parents in medieval Europe widely neglected and abused their children.[2] One wonders how Western society could have survived amidst such barbaric treatment. In fact, recent historic research indicates that most parents showed affection for their children.[3] This is consistent with how deeply empathy and caring are designed within the human brain.[4]

While humans are designed for love, political institutions are not. English common law treated children as chattel—mere property without power or voice. Church doctrine prescribed harsh discipline to drive evil from children presumed to be born in original sin. Schools and courts used oppressive means to exact obedience and punish deviance. Today, different societal forces impede the development of youth. But a thousand years of historic records show that when basic needs go unmet, children display a host of problems.[5]

Pygmalion Pioneers

What we want to achieve in our work with young people is to find and strengthen the positive and healthy elements, no matter how deeply they are hidden.[6]

Karl Wilker

The idealism of early youth work pioneers was exemplified by Dr. Karl Wilker who worked with Berlin's most challenging youth following World War I.[7] For centuries, humanistic reformers from many societies have called for treating all children with dignity and respect. But these ideas did not begin to take hold in Europe until the dawn of democracy when children were first seen as young citizens. In this new spirit, reformers set out to transform education and child rearing.

Great Expectations

Notable nineteenth century visionaries included Swiss educator Johann Pestalozzi and French physician Jean Marc Itard. In 1801, Pestalozzi founded an orphanage school for waifs who wandered the streets of European cities after the Napoleonic wars.[8] He was inspired by French philosopher Rousseau's fictional book *Emile,* which portrayed children as inherently good.[9] Pestalozzi showed that youngsters from the most impoverished backgrounds could thrive in a caring environment. He invented sophisticated teaching techniques but contended that the ultimate goal of education was to develop a moral individual. Experiences of love, trust, and gratitude could lead to success with even the most difficult students.

Also in 1801, Jean Marc Itard penned *The Wild Boy of Aveyron,* the first scientific account of the education and treatment of a child with autism.[10] This youngster had been abandoned with a slit throat but survived in the forests of France until captured by hunters at about age 12. Mute and animal like, he was put on public display and a prominent psychiatrist diagnosed him as an incurable idiot. But young physician Jean Marc Itard believed otherwise and spent five years working with this boy he named Victor. Itard developed creative strategies to teach language and empathy, carefully documenting his successes and frustrations. While Victor never mastered verbal communication, he became an affectionate, helpful companion to his caregivers. Itard established a core principle of individualized education: "To be judged fairly, this young man must be compared only to himself."[11]

In the early 20th century, a spirit of optimism flourished in education and youth work. There was belief that all young people could thrive, even those who had experienced great hardship and adversity. Janusz Korczak, who was called the Polish Pestalozzi, formed a self-governing school for Jewish street kids of Warsaw.[12] In Italy, inspired by Itard, Maria Montessori developed a *scientific pedagogy* to show that poor and disabled students from the slums of Rome had highly absorbent minds.[13] Rabindrinath Tagore built a school for cast-off children in India and won the Nobel Prize for poetry lifting up the oppressed.[14]

The most widely known reformer was John Dewey who sparked the progressive education movement, transforming schools into laboratories for democracy.[15] In Chicago, Jane Addams founded the first juvenile court which was soon adopted by all of the world's democracies.[16] W. E. B. Dubois described the despair and doubt of children of color and worked to liberate their untapped talents.[17] Sadly, such reforms seldom survived the tenure of their charismatic leaders. Global wars, depression, poverty, and racism fueled a sense of powerlessness and pessimism. Schools retreated from progressive ideals and became depersonalized bureaucracies. The juvenile court strayed from the idealism of its founders. And public policy was of little interest to researchers more enraptured with "rigor" than "relevance."[18] What was needed was a new kind of scholar who could employ science to find solutions to real-world problems.

Action Research

Answering this call was Kurt Lewin (1890-1947) who emigrated from Nazi Germany to the United States with a passion to create democratic social change. His brief life was like the arc of a comet lighting the way for generations of researchers who would follow, using science to transform society. In his words: "Research that produces nothing but books will not suffice."[19]

Reared in a Jewish family, Kurt Lewin was active in the Wandervogel youth movement which fought against authoritarian, anti-Semitic practices.[20] After World War I, he completed his doctorate and taught at the University of Berlin. When Hitler came to power, Lewin and his immediate family were traveling in the United States and were able to escape the Holocaust which enveloped their extended family members.

Deeply committed to egalitarian values, Lewin pioneered "action research" to seek practical solutions to societal problems. This included ground-breaking studies of group dynamics, democratic schools, conflict resolution, racial relations, and organizational change. Lewin died in his fifties, but his co-workers would transform the treatment of children. Their studies of discrimination influenced the 1954 U. S. Supreme Court decision on school segregation.[21] His colleagues helped construct the Head Start program for children in poverty. And, their classic research on reclaiming troubled youth influenced thousands of professionals, including authors of this book.[22]

Missing from most current theories is the voice of youth. James Anglin of the University of Victoria conducted qualitative action research with youth at risk and their staff in ten Canadian group care facilities.[23] He was surprised to find that the four-letter word that young people most often used to describe their experience was PAIN. Yet staff labelled them as "disruptive" or "behaviorally disordered." Anglin suggests a more accurate description would be *pain-based behavior.*

What we need are scientific methods matched to the practical challenges of developing young lives.[24] Success requires that we break free not only from folk psychology but also from narrow theories of behavior. Only then can we respond to the needs of youth instead of react to their problems.[25]

Standards of Evidence

Much of the research that guides evidence-based practice is too inaccessible, overwhelming, and removed from practice.[26]

Carol Goodheart

Writing as president of the American Psychological Association, Carol Goodheart described the challenge of identifying core principles underlying effective approaches. This is no small task since Googling evidence-based practices yields millions of hits. The term evidence-based was coined by Canadian medical researchers in the 1990s.[27] Now the search for Evidence-Based Practices (EBP) extends to prevention, education, treatment, and youth justice. But even if a method is listed on some EBP registry, this is no promise of success. The challenge is to *deliver what works* on the front lines of practice.[28] Note this important distinction:

> *Evidence-Based Practices* are based on efficacy research in carefully controlled studies.

> *Practice-Based Evidence* requires evaluation of effectiveness in real-world situations.

Evidence-Based Practices can never be precisely replicated to match the original experimental conditions. In the real world, one must balance *fidelity* to a method with *flexibility* to meet the unique demands of a setting.[29] In fact, fewer than 20 percent of research-based programs are implemented with fidelity.[30] And, while many methods have some measureable impact, studies of empirically validated programs *in the actual community* often show very weak effects.[31] When adjusted for research biases, highly promoted Evidence-Based Practices are often no better than other methods. This is because powerful effect sizes are due to general factors like positive relationships and positive expectations rather than technique or method.[32]

More research does not necessarily lead to more truth. In 1800, there were but a thousand persons in the world who might be considered scientists. Today, millions churn out mountains of research reports. Even technically accurate studies seldom apply to real world problems.[33] We are literally drowning in data.

In the search for solutions, we cannot simply append an off-the-shelf EBP to existing programs. This is particularly true in complex settings like family, school, residential group care, and community programs. The challenge is to merge research with practice expertise to best meet the needs of those we serve.[34]

The preoccupation with Evidence-Based Practice has sparked a "battle of the brands" motivated by a "mine's better" mentality.[35] Much rhetoric about evidence-based approaches is simplistic and even deceptive, driven by politics or profits. Slick science sells drugs as solutions to problems in living.[36] Program advocates spin glowing reports of mundane methods. Cost-cutting officials seek evidence to justify curtailing care, not raising its quality. Blue ribbon lists of approved programs become a passport to funding as methods of every ilk compete to claim the status of being evidence based.

Shaky Science

By definition, Evidence-Based Practice uses the best available research and applied expertise in making decisions.[37] Some argue that the "gold standard" for evidence-based intervention is the random blind trial as used in the drug industry. But even if a treatment has statistical significance, the amount of change may be insignificant. And, as with drugs, any intervention can have unintended side effects. In the quest for an evidence-based method, one can easily lose sight of the big question—what approaches will lead to lasting learning and change in the life of a particular youth?

A leading trauma researcher, Bessel van der Kolk, opposes anointing certain methods as "evidence-based" merely because they prevail in narrow comparative studies. He contends that passing out seals of approval as "treatments of choice" violates the spirit of science:

> *This concern is particularly relevant as long as findings of neuroscience, attachment, and cross-cultural research remain isolated from an increasingly prescriptive approach to intervention and treatment.*[38]

This call for a cross-cultural, bioecological perspective is supported by decades of science. One of the most research-validated principles in the field of psychology was first articulated by Kurt Lewin: *Behavior is a function of both the person and the environment.*[39] Literally thousands of isolated variables have some measureable but trivial effect on a desired outcome. The challenge is to identify *evidence-based essentials,* those powerful factors that lead to lasting change.

There is now a large body of research documenting the weak, faulty, and biased science behind current attempts to identify Evidence-Based Treatments.[40] When various studies are subjected to careful meta-analysis, the predictable finding is that there are no meaningful differences in methods. Three prominent examples drawn from different fields of study are illustrative.

Education. For over a decade, the federal What Works Clearinghouse reported evaluation research to identify effective programs that could be brought to scale. These included a full range of reading and math curricula, social-emotional interventions, and programs for prevention and change of at-risk behavior. This effort yielded so few programs that met its evidence standards that it earned the nickname Nothing Works Clearinghouse.[41]

Trauma Therapy. A Cochrane Review studied outcomes from seven models of trauma treatment for children and adolescents. While all methods had some measurable positive effect, researchers found no clear evidence for the effectiveness of one therapy versus another. Nor was there evidence of whether children with particular types of trauma are more or less likely to respond to therapies. These outcome measures also were limited to 30 days, which is certainly not lasting change.[42]

Community-Based Treatment. The American Psychological Association published a sophisticated meta-analysis of Multisystemic Treatment (MST), a widely promoted alternative to residential treatment for troubled youth.[43] In spite of a profusion of glowing, selective, repetitive endorsements, MST had some impact but was not superior to other methods. Such research challenging sacred cows unleashes a political firestorm of appeals to consensus, hostility, and *ad hominem* responses. These are classic signs of an old paradigm that is collapsing.[44]

Most well-intentioned efforts are better than doing nothing. However, it is time to quit pursuing magic Evidence-Based Practices and to identify instead the powerful Evidence-Based Essentials that drive deep, lasting change. In that regard, science is much stronger since one draws on a consilience of findings from diverse sources.

Consilience: The Test for Truth

Truth cannot contradict truth.[45]

Pope John Paul II

The highest standard for scientific evidence is *consilience* which means that findings from separate areas of knowledge converge to provide strong conclusions. The term consilience was coined by William Whewell, a nineteenth century English wordsmith who also invented better known labels like scientist and physicist.[46] Triple trained in science, architecture, and theology, Whewell was intrigued to discover connections between these dissimilar disciplines. From the time of the earliest universities, scholars saw all knowledge as related and an educated person was expected to master many fields of study. But as science became increasingly specialized, consilience was forgotten.

The concept of consilience was reintroduced by Harvard socio-biologist Edward O. Wilson, who claimed that modern science is captive to its own complexity. Universities chop up knowledge into "a flurry of minor disciplines and specialized courses" and lose sight of the big truths.[47] Consilience links findings from separate fields to discover simpler universal principles. Simple does not mean simplistic, since basic truths can be profound. As Einstein once said, "If you can't explain your theory to a six year old, you probably do not understand it yourself."

Figure 1. Consilience Model

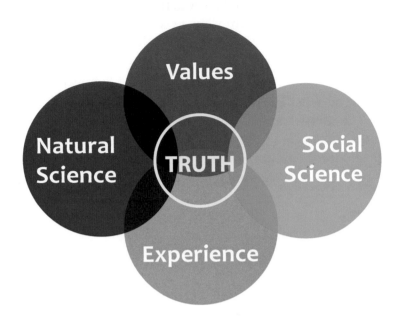

Wilson proposes a model of consilience which brings together relevant findings from natural sciences, social sciences, experience, and values as shown in the accompanying figure.

Values: Respect for the dignity of children, youth, and families.

Experience: Wisdom of practitioners and those we serve.

Natural Science: Research on the brain, body, and behavior.

Social Science: Research about humans in the social ecology.

We are most likely to solve challenging real-world problems by tapping ideas that overlap at the center of the circle. For example, here is consilience of evidence on the power of caring relationships: *Values* of dignity and respect are incompatible with coercive, exclusionary disciplinary practices which rupture relationships. *Experience* includes practice expertise on building trusting relationships with youth and viewing children and families as experts on their own lives. *Natural sciences* document how nurture or neglect can alter gene expression to build brain pathways for either resilient or reactive coping patterns. *Social sciences* show that children thrive with secure attachment, but relational trauma sparks problem behavior.

The coming chapters will explore biosocial foundations of the Evidence-Based Essentials of attachment, achievement, autonomy, and altruism. Our discussion is informed by fields as diverse as psychology, neuroscience, anthropology, sociology, psychiatry, pedagogy, and a rich tradition of values and practice wisdom. One does not need to be an expert in any of these areas to tap the truths they offer. Using the lens of consilience, we are able to focus on building environments where all young people thrive.

The Bioecological Model

The exemplar of consilience in programs for children and youth is the *bio-ecological* model developed across six decades by Urie Bronfenbrenner of Cornell University.[48] Born in Moscow, he came to the U.S. as a boy where his father was a physician in a children's institution. Bronfenbrenner received his Ph.D. from the University of Michigan in 1942 and was immediately inducted into the military service. He was assigned to work under Kurt Lewin in the Office of Strategic Services, the precursor to the CIA. Operating in a secret location, they selected persons to become spies behind enemy lines. They did not rely on formal tests but made candidates adopt an undercover identity and live in a natural group situation without blowing their cover.

Bronfenbrenner conducted research on real-world problems in real-world environments. He once described traditional psychology as the study of "the strange behavior of children in strange situations with strange adults for the briefest possible periods of time."[49] Instead, he studied children in the natural setting, relating to significant persons, across the span of development. A prominent product of such research is the Head Start early childhood program.

Figure 2. Ecology of Childhood

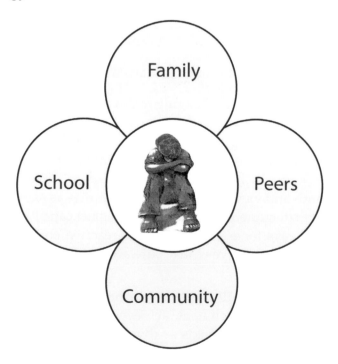

Bronfenbrenner's model of the Ecology of Childhood is illustrated in the accompanying figure.[50] The key circles of influence are family, school, peers, and community.[51] Surrounding this are broader social systems. But the greatest impact comes from the child's immediate life space—namely what happens in one's own home, school, peer group, and neighborhood.

Bronfenbrenner's bioecological model is perhaps the most extensively researched approach to understanding child and youth development. His most basic belief was that trusting bonds with children are the most powerful force in building healthy brains and behavior. He articulated this principle in simple terms: *Every child needs at least one adult who is irrationally crazy about him or her.*[52] Children thrive with caring families, concerned teachers, positive peers, and a supportive community. But those reared in unhealthy ecologies experience a host of emotional, behavioral, and learning problems. Bronfenbrenner believed that debates on *nature versus nurture* were meaningless since both are intertwined. While personal traits are important, behavior is always a *reciprocal transaction* with significant others, not a solo performance. A parent influences a child, but the child also influences the parent. The teacher impacts the student, but the student also has an effect on teacher behavior. Children choose their peers and in turn are influenced by them. Humans live in reciprocity, whether conflict or harmony.

The most significant point about the four worlds of childhood is that these are the realms where a young person's needs are met—or neglected. The Circle of Courage operates at the center of these circles of influence. Family, school, peers, and community all have the potential—and responsibility—to provide opportunities for the development of attachment, achievement, autonomy, and altruism.

Defining Youth Development

William C. Jackson

A consilience of research identifies core principles that foster resilience and positive youth development.

A long-held view in Western society is that adults must civilize youth who by their very nature are disposed to engage in disobedient and destructive behavior.[53] Such notions justify zero tolerance schools,[54] boot camps to shock and humiliate, and "injustice for juveniles."[55] Also, traditional deficit-based diagnosis in mental health casts children's attempts to cope with life challenges as psychiatric disorders.[56] In place of these pessimistic mindsets is a new paradigm of strengths.

Searching for Strengths

Positive psychology and the science of Positive Youth Development are toppling the traditional notion that kids are broken and need to be fixed. Emerging research shows that young people are not passive underlings to be trained by adults. Instead, they are active agents who shape their own subculture.[57] This power of peer influence is not necessarily problematic but can be a positive force. Youth are not risks to manage but resources to be developed.[58] Practitioners are eager to find strategies for building strengths, but complexity confounds the literature on youth development.[59] A Search Institute analysis of the field describes a tangle of overlapping vocabularies, constructs, and objectives.[60] The solution to this confusion is consilience, identifying powerful, simple truths in a mass of data. A growing literature points to the Circle of Courage as a clear, parsimonious, universally applicable model for defining resilience and Positive Youth Development (PYD).[61]

Charles Darwin described two ways scholars classify knowledge. *Splitters* create many categories while *lumpers* look at the big picture.[62] Here are examples from the search to understand youth development.

Peter Benson and researchers from the Search Institute[63] created a list of 40 Developmental Assets which are markers for positive youth development. These include 20 *Internal Assets* lumped into four categories similar to the Circle of Courage strengths. Another 20 *External Assets* enumerate ecological supports that build inner strengths.

Cathann Kress and a national team of 4-H youth development researchers[64] developed a list of eight factors contributing to positive youth development. Subsequently they lumped this list into the four Circle of Courage constructs which they designated as the *4-H Essentials of Youth Development.*

A team from Tufts University[65] extensively studied the Circle of Courage based 4-H Essentials but used synonyms based on the four Cs (connection, competence, confidence, character) introduced by Rick Little of the Kellogg Foundation and elaborated by Karen Pittman.[66] Over time, that list has split into various overlapping, redundant categories and is now being marketed as the seven Cs.[67]

Instead of churning out inflated lists of risk and protective factors, there is a growing consensus that we should focus on a smaller number of elements that foster resilience and positive growth.[68] We turn to consilience to make sense out of the chaos of competing terminology. As shown in Table 1, the bio-social needs of Attachment, Achievement, Autonomy, and Altruism and the Circle of Courage principles correspond to concepts drawn from ten research traditions.[69]

Table 1. The Consilience on Essentials of Positive Youth Development

Bio-Social Needs	Attachment	Achievement	Autonomy	Altruism
Hierarchy of Needs (Maslow, 1943)	Belongingness	Esteem	Self-actualization	Transcendence
Roots of Self Esteem (Coopersmith, 1967)	Significance	Competence	Power	Virtue
Developmental Ecology (Bronfenbrenner, 1979)	Social Bond	Complex Tasks	Increased Power	Reciprocity
Internal Assets (Benson, 1990, 1997)	Social Competence	Investment in Learning	Positive Identity	Positive Values
Youth Development (Little, 1991 in Pittman, 2001)	Connection	Competence	Confidence	Character
School Success (Purkey et al., 1993)	Relating	Coping	Asserting	Investing
Boys Town Model (Peter, 2000)	Relationships	Skills	Empowerment	Spirituality
Spiritual Growth (Larson & Brendtro, 2000)	Trust	Talent	Power	Purpose
Resilience Research (Benard, 2004)	Social Competence	Problem Solving	Autonomy	Purpose
Prepare Curriculum (Goldstein et al., 2014)	Social Skills	Problem Solving	Emotion Control	Moral Values
Universal Values	Belonging	Mastery	Independence	Generosity

Strengths in Action

The Circle of Courage provides a succinct approach to Positive Youth Development grounded in research on Belonging, Mastery, Independence, and Generosity. These growth needs also define resilience factors[70] and character strengths.[71] Professionals worldwide apply Circle of Courage constructs to childcare, education, treatment, juvenile justice, community and faith-based settings, and healthcare.[72]

Schools employ the Circle of Courage to establish positive climates and restorative discipline.[73] Teachers replace coercion with respectful communication.[74] Students with emotional and behavioral problems show reduced incidents of crisis and higher graduation rates.[75] These core principles provide a cross-cultural framework of shared human values rather than polarizing around differences.[76]

The Circle of Courage model is widely applied in treatment and juvenile justice settings. "These vital signs of Positive Youth Development are essential to building strong families, schools, and communities and must inform prevention and intervention."[77] These principles provide a strength-based approach to treatment.[78] They are also essential in healing trauma and post-traumatic growth.[79] Programs to build "Autism Assets" are organized around these core strengths.[80]

In medicine, the Circle of Courage is being used as an integral part of health and wellness assessment.[81] A publication of the American Academy of Pediatrics describes the goal "to raise adolescents' awareness of their developing strengths and to motivate them to take responsibility for the role they can play in their own well-being."[82] Health professionals use the Circle of Courage as a guide to discussions with youth in order to foster well-being.

Socialization research shows that peers are influential in shaping youth culture.[83] Positive Peer Culture (PPC) is an evidence-based program[84] which engages youth in prosocial helping to meet Circle of Courage needs.[85] This peer helping process creates safe environments[86] and develops prosocial thinking, values, and behavior.[87] Negative peer influence is a serious concern[88] which PPC reverses by empowering youth in helping roles.[89] Christoph Steinebach of Switzerland describes Positive Peer Culture as an exemplar of positive psychology.[90]

Until recently, most assessment with challenging youth focused on problems and ignored potentials. Now there are strength-based instruments that measure dimensions similar to Circle of Courage constructs. Most directly, 4-D is an assessment tool based on the four Circle of Courage dimensions.[91] Other scales measure resilience, school connectedness, youth assets, and character strengths.[92] Such research marks a trend from focusing on strengths instead of deficits.

Many so-called evidence-based practices only produce marginal effects but fail to transform young lives.[93] The Circle of Courage highlights those powerful variables that create deep lasting change. Effective programs zero in on what matters most and then measure these outcome variables.[94] A consilience of evidence suggests that policy and practice should focus like a laser on the life-altering outcomes of Belonging, Mastery, Independence, and Generosity.

1. Bosco, 2000.
2. Aries, 1965.
3. Orme, 2003.
4. Perry & Szalavitz, 2010.
5. Sanders, 2011.
6. Wilker, 1921, p. 69.
7. Wilker, 1920.
8. Pestalozzi, 1801.
9. Rousseau, 1762.
10. Itard, 1801.
11. Candland, 1995, p. 31.
12. Brendtro & Hinders, 1990.
13. Montessori, 1912.
14. Tagore, 2007.
15. Dewey, 1916.
16. Addams, 1909.
17. Dubois, 1903.
18. Golati, 2007.
19. Lewin, 1946, p. 35.
20. Gold, 1999.
21. Philogéne, 2004.
22. Morse, 2008.
23. Anglin, 2002.
24. Kazdin & Weisz, 2003.
25. Anglin, 2002.
26. Goodheart, 2010, p. 9.
27. Guyatt, Cairns, & Churchill, 1992.
28. Duncan, Miller, Wampold, & Hubble, 2010.
29. Kendall et al., 2008.
30. Hallfors, Pankratz, & Harrison, 2007.
31. Dishion & Kavanagh, 2008.
32. Duncan, Miller, Wampold, & Hubble, 2010.
33. Lloyd, 2007.
34. APA, 2006.
35. Duncan, Miller, Wampold, & Hubble, 2010.
36. Kirsch, 2010.
37. APA, 2006.
38. van der Kolk, McFarlane, & Weisaeth, 2007, p. xi.
39. Bronfenbrenner, 2005; Lewin, 1936.
40. Duncan, Miller, Wampold, & Hubble, 2010; Wampold & Imel, 2015.
41. Schoenfeld, 2006.
42. Gilles, et al, 2012.
43. Littell, 2010.
44. Kuhn, 2012.
45. Pope John Paul II, 1996.
46. Whewell, 1847.
47. Wilson, 1998, p. 13.
48. Bronfenbrenner, 2005.
49. Bronfenbrenner, 1977, p. 518.
50. Bronfenbrenner, 1986.
51. Phelan, 2004.
52. Bronfenbrenner, 2005.
53. Elder, 1994.
54. APA, 2008.
55. Schwartz, 1987; Brendtro, Ness, & Mitchell, 1983.
56. Frances, 2013.
57. Cosaro, 2011.
58. Damon, 2004.
59. Small & Memmo, 2004.
60. Benson et al., 2006.
61. Jackson, 2014b.
62. Darwin, 1857, p. 438.
63. Leffert, Benson, & Roehlkepartain, 1997.
64. Kress, 2014.
65. Lerner et al., 2013.
66. Pittman et al., 2001.
67. Ginsberg & Kinsmun, 2014.
68. Masten, 2014.
69. First presentation of the Circle of Courage was Brokenleg & Brendtro, 1988.
70. Werner, 2012.
71. Peterson, 2013g.
72. Martin & Martin, 2012.
73. Ashworth, 2008; Espiner & Guild, 2010; Kress & Forrest, 2000; McDonald, 2013; Van Bockern & McDonald, 2012; Villa & Thousand, 2000.
74. Forthun & McCombie, 2007.
75. Shields, Milstein, & Posner, 2010.
76. Kauffman, 2000.
77. Brooks and Roush, 2014, p. 46.
78. Brendtro & Shahbazian, 2003; Pfeifer, 2011.
79. Bath, 2015; Steele & Kuban, 2013.
80. Laursen, Moore, Yazdgerdi, & Milberg, 2013; Laursen & Yazdgerdi, 2012; Sarahan & Copas, 2014.
81. Duncan et al., 2007; Frankowski, Leader, & Duncan, 2009.
82. Frankowski, Brendtro, Van Bockern, & Duncan, 2014, p. 237.
83. Cosaro, 2011.
84. James, 2011.
85. Giacobbe, Traynelis-Yurek, & Laursen, 1999.
86. Gold & Osgood, 1992.
87. Gibbs, 2014.
88. Dodge, Dishion, & Lansford, 2006.
89. Osgood & Briddell, 2006.
90. Steinebach, Jungo, & Zihlmann, 2013.
91. Gilgun, Chalmers, & Kesinen, 2002.
92. Oman et al., 2002; Prince-Embury, 2007.
93. Lyons, 2009.
94. Guskey, 2000.

3

Attachment and Trust

I am good at reading people. Sometimes I use reverse psychology, like if a counselor is getting too close, then I ask him about his life, his problems, and it scares him away. I can tell if a person really cares and wants to help or is just doing a job for the money.[1]

Jonathan

Jonathan does not trust adults so he drives them away. He is caught in a conflict between two competing drives: seek relationships with adults—but also avoid danger. Our brains have inbuilt maps to reach goals shared by all humans. Researchers call these brain programs *prepared learning* or *experience expectant learning.*[2] From birth, humans are prepared to form relationships, learn, control their lives, and help one another. These are basic biosocial needs for *attachment, achievement, autonomy,* and *altruism.* These needs are expressed in universal cultural values for Belonging, Mastery, Independence, and Generosity.

The Need to Belong

Be related, somehow, to everyone you know.[3]

Ella Deloria

The need for trusting relationships is as basic as hunger or thirst. Across all cultures, humans bond together for social support. They prefer to spend much of their time in groups, invest in socializing children, and draw on support from elders. Children develop strong attachment to their primary caregivers, and rejection always has a malignant effect on development.[4]

For centuries, poets, sages, and philosophers have portrayed humankind as a community of persons who support, nurture, and love one another. But only in recent decades has science begun to document this central principle of human existence. In their classic 1995 study *The Need to Belong*, psychologists Roy Baumeister and Mark Leary gathered an impressive array of evidence to support the premise that humans have a universal biosocial motivation to build and maintain interpersonal attachments.[5] There is a major distinction between *needs* and *wants*. Unsatisfied wants may cause temporary distress whereas unsatisfied needs inflict destructive consequences.

The desire for interpersonal attachments—the need to belong—is a fundamental human motivation. People form social bonds readily even under the most adverse conditions, and they resist losing attachments. Abundant evidence attests that the need for belonging shapes emotions and cognition. Secure social attachments produce positive emotions while even subtle threats to social bonds generate unpleasant emotional states. Humans also devote a disproportionate amount of thinking about their relationships.[6]

Deficits in belonging lead to a variety of ill effects—consistent with the principle that this is a need and not a want. Belonging is beneficial and essential for psychological and physical health. Belonging is both an immediate and long-term need. People seek frequent positive interactions with individuals they trust, and these ideally occur in a framework of long-term, stable caring and concern. In terminology from resilience science, these are the principles of connection and continuity.[7]

Many psychological phenomena are impacted by the need to belong. Humans everywhere form groups for support and sustenance. They are often prejudiced against outsiders with whom they have no opportunity to belong. And, although antisocial behavior may seem to disprove belonging, it is readily apparent that such is a sign of thwarting the need to belong. As Baumeister and Leary note:

> *A great deal of neurotic, maladaptive, and destructive behavior seems*
> *to reflect either desperate attempts to establish or maintain relationships*
> *with other people or sheer frustration and purposelessness when one's*
> *need to belong goes unmet.*[8]

Human culture is the framework enabling people to satisfy the need to belong. All important knowledge is conveyed through culture, and values are set and supported. Modern civilizations use prisons to punish norm violators because depriving contact with relationship partners is extremely aversive. Solitary confinement is the most severe form of sanction, rivaling illegal forms of torture.

The political pursuit of power can be seen as a counterfeit substitute for belonging through love.[9] Belonging is also central in religion and patriotism as people connect in community and commit to a cause beyond self. "The desire for interpersonal attachment may well be one of the most far-reaching and integrative constructs currently available to understand human nature."[10]

Powerful Attachments

Bowlby's biosocial theory of attachment and loss[11] laid the foundation for one of the most sophisticated and extensively researched fields of psychology, providing a comprehensive account of both normal and abnormal development.[12] Attachments first formed in infancy with caregivers expand as children develop friendships, kinship bonds, and compassion for others.[13]

The human social brain is the secret of our survival on this planet. We are not physically endowed to compete in the animal kingdom. We lack sharp teeth or claws; we cannot outrun predators, fly away, or hide under water. Instead, our survival depends on living in supportive groups. When under threat, we band together to befriend and protect each other.[14]

From birth, the brains of children are prepared to focus on human faces. "These small areas of skin are the most scrutinized area of the planet."[15] The face is the primary display board for human emotions. The amygdala instantly detects cues of safety or threat through eye contact, facial expressions, gestures, and tone of voice. Children's survival is dependent on adults, and so they continually search for evidence that they are valued. "All I want is some kind of noticement," said Daniel, a troubled boy in a Cleveland alternative school.[16]

The motivation to bond is universal across cultures since it is designed into our DNA. Human attachment is closely intertwined with the need for safety. Attachment involves proximity, and humans feel secure in the presence of trusted persons.[17] Children run to their parents' bedroom in the middle of the night when frightened by a thunderstorm or a bad dream. Neuroscience suggests they are rushing for a dose of oxytocin.

Oxytocin is the hormone for social bonding.[18] It is central to parental, fraternal, sexual, and benevolent relationships.[19] While cortisol is the primary stress hormone that revs up the brain, oxytocin creates trust and calms the brain.[20] Secure, trusting relationships regulate emotion and turn off the stress response.[21]

Other hormones combine with oxytocin in various kinds of relationships involving attraction, attachment, empathy, or lust. Human bonds are maintained over the long haul by these very pleasurable substances in the brain. Love is a many-splendored chemical thing.

Oxytocin makes better partners and parents—in both people and prairie dogs. Only three percent of all mammals form lasting pair bonds. Prairie voles mate for life and both males and females participate in parental care. This is because males, like females, have a rich supply of oxytocin. A relative of the prairie vole is the montane vole, which looks remarkably similar but is oxytocin deficient. These males are promiscuous and ignore their young.[22] Without oxytocin, the animals are fickle partners and deadbeat dads.

In general, females have more oxytocin than males, and males have more vasopressin, which also contributes to social bonding. Both of these closely related chemicals are crucial in tending behavior and loyalty to partners and kin.[23]

>*Oxytocin* helps us let down our guard and trust others. It is released during positive social interactions and permits expression of vulnerable behaviors. Oxytocin also can calm aggression associated with testosterone.

>*Vasopressin* makes us courageous protectors of those we love. It plays a role in vigilance and guarding of mate and offspring, a behavior seen in both sexes but more often associated with males.[24]

These hormones foster trust and are antidotes to painful emotions. Rejection and abandonment trigger fear, anxiety, and shame. Trust turns off the amygdala alarm and calms fear. "Learning anything positive, including love, requires freedom from fear."[25]

Caregivers calm emotions until children learn to do this solo. Until higher brain controls are operative, children must borrow the prefrontal cortex of the adults as a model for their own developing brain. Each time we help children move from agitation to a calm and regulated state, they build pathways for self-control. Ideally, this happens early in life, but if not, this is the goal of teaching and treatment.[26]

Friend or Foe?

The exciting new Polyvagal Theory developed by Stephen Porges[27] shows how trusting social bonds shut down the stress system. *Vagal* means "wandering" and refers to the 10th cranial nerve, a tube containing fibers which wander throughout the body. Vagal nerves connect the brain with the heart and other internal organs. We read cues from eye contact, facial expressions, tone of voice, and physical gestures to form a split-second gut response: Is this friend or foe?

In all animals, the vagus nerve activates the autonomic nervous system to meet challenge or threats. But mammals, and particularly humans, have a much more advanced polyvagal system so that trust can override threat reactions. One branch of the vagal system still triggers reflexive fight or flight while the other uses social engagement to put the brakes on the primitive survival brain. As seen in the accompanying diagram, trust trumps fear.

The *social engagement system* uses emotional cues from sensory information to determine if another person is behaving in a benign or predatory manner. The logical brain adds its assessment of whether the person can be trusted, drawing on past learning. If the person or persons are judged to be safe, responses of tend and befriend ensue, and oxytocin shuts down the stress system. But if threat is detected, the autonomic nervous system triggers fight or flight reactions.

Social engagement is linked to positive emotions and physical health.[28] Recurrent positive emotions nurture the human body, give feelings of belonging, and boost physical health. Over time, this upward spiral to growth becomes self-sustaining.

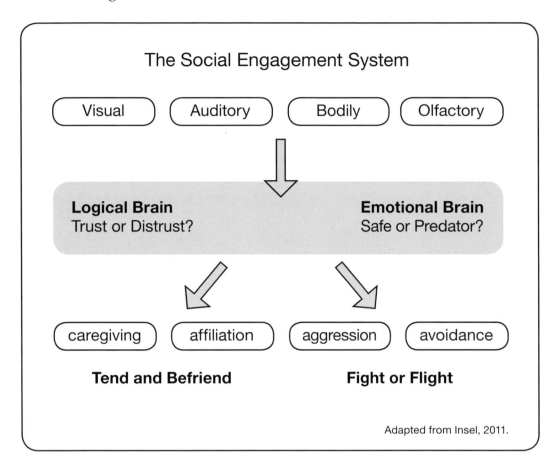

The Social Engagement System

Visual   Auditory   Bodily   Olfactory

Logical Brain
Trust or Distrust?

Emotional Brain
Safe or Predator?

caregiving   affiliation   aggression   avoidance

Tend and Befriend   **Fight or Flight**

Adapted from Insel, 2011.

Broken Bonds

Hate is a reaction to an unsatisfied need for love.[29]

August Aichhorn

A draconian study of love deprivation was conducted in the thirteenth century by Holy Roman Emperor Frederick II. He spoke several languages and hoped to discover if humans had a natural in-born language by raising children who would never hear speech. Nurses were hired to suckle and bathe children, but they were forbidden to speak to them. His experiment ended in disaster as all of the children died before uttering a single word. The Emperor concluded the "children could not live without clapping of the hands and gestures and gladness of countenance and blandishments."[30]

Attachment science shows the powerful impact of human relationships on positive or pathological adjustment.[31] A rich body of research comes from Mary Ainsworth's[32] study of young children left in a strange situation. Separation of a toddler from a caregiver activates the attachment-seeking system, but reunion behavior shows striking individual differences. Based on their response to being left with a stranger, researchers have identified four attachment styles which appear to be related to the parenting practices of the caregiver:

Secure Attachment. Following separation, children eagerly greet their caregivers, seek proximity until calmed, and then return to play. Caregivers of securely-attached children are sensitive and responsive, particularly when the child is distressed.

Avoidant Attachment. These children ignore the caregiver upon reunion, looking or turning away instead of approaching. Their caregivers have been observed to express little emotion and avoid physical contact when their children are upset.

Resistant Attachment. These children may cling but are not easily comforted, showing anger and distress. Their caregivers are thought to be erratic in response to infant distress and more concerned with their own needs than the children's.

Disorganized Attachment. These children exhibit chaotic behaviors and have no stable attachment strategy. Caregivers are likely to be transmitting their own prior trauma experience with unpredictable feelings of helplessness, hostility, or withdrawal.

Dante Cicchetti found that mothers who abused their one-year-old infants had themselves experienced maltreatment and insecure attachments in their own childhoods.[33] Their infants showed significantly higher rates of disorganized attachment. These mothers were randomly assigned to receive either infant-parent psychotherapy, psychoeducational parenting, or typical child protection services.

About a year later at follow-up, children who received either of the specialized treatments showed substantial increases in secure attachment, while disorganized attachment continued to predominate in those who received typical services. This is a dramatic example of the power of targeted early intervention.

Jaak Panksepp has spent decades studying emotions and has identified their corresponding brain circuits.[34] Humans share seven primary emotions with other mammals: *fear, rage, lust, attachment, care, seeking,* and *play.* The emotion most directly related to belonging is *attachment,* which makes touch and proximity to caregivers rewarding while separation distress sparks panic, grief, and behavior that seeks to restore bonds. The corresponding emotion of *care* enables parents to respond to the needs of the child. *Play* further strengthens belonging by teaching cooperation with peers. While sharing these primary emotions with other mammals, we also have a highly-developed sense of self which gives rise to complex social emotions. These include pride and shame, which are related to the approval and love of others.

Love and Hate

Scottish psychiatrist Ian Suttie authored the classic book *The Origins of Love and Hate,* but died two weeks before it was published in 1935.[35] He was influenced by Freud's therapist Sandor Ferenczi whose similar ideas on empathy and love caused both to be banned by the psychoanalytical society. Yet, in time, virtually all of their work was verified by research on attachment and brain science. John Bowlby brought Suttie to prominence by writing the foreword to the 1988 edition.

Suttie[36] wrote of the biology of love and laid the foundation for theories of attachment, separation, and trauma. He described the "taboo on tenderness" of depersonalized professionals. He saw aggression, delinquency, and the search for power as products of thwarted love. He demonstrated that the need to give and receive love is biologically rooted in the early maternal-child bond, and all later relationships build on this foundation.

The withdrawal of love produces feelings of shame and worthlessness.[37] Children find it unbearable to believe they are bad and unloved and may exhibit depression or rage. Emotions triggered by loneliness signal that one's need to belong is not being met. Contrary to popular belief, loneliness occurs more often in young people than in elders and is highest during adolescence.[38]

When social bonding is disrupted by neglect or abuse, children can find other means to stimulate reward pathways in the brain, such as drugs, sex, aggression, and intimidating others. Lacking empathy, they are less constrained by concern about violating trusting relationships.[39]

It is not just overt rejection that is painful. Humans are very alert to subtle signs of dislike or rudeness, whether verbal or nonverbal. These small signs of disrespect are highly toxic, making a person feel that he or she does not belong. Such *microinsults* are a powerful dynamic in racism, sexism, sexual orientation, and other ways that humans devalue an individual.[40]

By design, our brains are hyper sensitive to social rejection and register even small slights as a painful event. The bulk of bullying involves belittling comments instead of physical harm. We all have the need to belong, and signs that others like, admire, and love us are central to well-being.

People on our Mind

Our brain is so social that, when not busy with a specific task, it shifts to its default system—thinking about others, self, and our relations to them. We carry on conversations in our mind, even during dreams. With such constant social cognition, children become amateur psychologists at an early age. In any field, expertise requires 10,000 hours of practice, so most youngsters gain that status by age 10. But those with autism or others deprived of attachment may avoid social thinking, thus curbing development of social intelligence. Whether because of different brain circuitry or relational trauma, they elude social pain by retreating from relationships.[41]

Curiosity is the brain's most pervasive human emotion, and prime brain pathways are dedicated to social curiosity.[42] Humans have profound social interests; while we can discuss any topic imaginable, we mostly talk about people. Daniel Goleman suggests that social intelligence is not just a sideshow in the thinking brain. In fact, general intelligence is an offshoot of social intelligence.[43] The brain's primary design is to negotiate our social world.

In many cultures, *intelligence* is not academic proficiency but interpersonal prowess. Elaborate networks of mirror neurons in the human brain ensure that every generation of children will imitate the behavior of their caregivers. Mirror neurons help us acquire social skills by observation. When the mirror neurons do not operate correctly—as in autism—children experience a host of developmental impairments.

Mirror neurons help us understand the minds of others, not through logical reasoning but by becoming attuned to their brains. Young children are highly attentive to their caregiver's emotions and behavior. Only hours after birth, infants start mirroring adults. Mirror neurons permit them to adjust their turbulent emotions to the mother's calm state. As they mature, children in a group attune to social behavior of one another.[44] Mirror neurons explain why crowd behavior becomes contagious and how we get caught in conflict cycles. And, mirroring can be fun; even adults enjoy activities where all act in unison, whether cheering with the crowd at a sports event or singing in a choral group.

Children have sophisticated skills to read emotion. An Israeli study showed high school students 10-second films of teachers they had not met and rated them on how they would teach. Their judgments correlated with actual ratings from genuine students.[45]

Children also scan their social world to determine what others think of them.[46] The brain is wired to be aware when we are being watched. In one experiment, employees were placed on the honor system to put money for their refreshment breaks in a cash box. This depository for donut money was placed beneath a prominent picture—which alternated weekly between flowers and a pair of watchful eyes. Cash contributions were 2.76 times greater when eyes were looking down at the employees.[47] Our brain reacts powerfully to faces and eye contact, even in pictures.

In traditional cultures, children are under the watchful eye of adult and peer caregivers. From the first year of life, the child is able to detect where the eyes of others are directed. The sense of being watched is a primary behavior control at any age. Parenting language is rich with references like *keep an eye on the kids* or *don't let them out of your sight*. But in elder-deprived cultures, few eyes are on children and almost none on teens.

Bids to Connect

Humans use specific behaviors to make *bids* for connection. Eye contact, smiling, laughter, and touch are all deep-brain invitations to bond. These release oxytocin and create strong feelings of attraction and well-being. Oxytocin has a short half-life and is gone in minutes, but the joy of small signs of affection can connect persons to one another, even during times of trial.

Physical touch can be a powerful means of providing support and soothing stress.[48] Of course, such contact makes one vulnerable so it is only effective when trust is secure. Human touch connects to the core of the social brain and conveys emotional warmth. There are great cultural differences in how much human touch is encouraged or inhibited. The many restrictions on touch in schools and youth programs can work against creating trusting communities.

Laughter also stimulates social bonding. It signals positive intentions and conveys that one is accepted and part of a group. Humans have a brain-based laugh detector, which in turn activates our laughter generator.[49] Children laugh and smile more than adults, probably because their brains are more focused on recruiting relationships. Research by Boys Town found that youth rated joking as one of the most desirable qualities of adults they like.[50] As John Digney of Ireland has shown, tapping into a young person's sense of humor can be key to establishing a trusting connection.[51]

Emotions of delight spring from the lower areas of the brain that regulate approach or avoidance.[52] A spontaneous deep brain laugh is unlike a forced laugh, which is only a superficial motor behavior. Social survival requires spotting the difference between genuine laughter and smiles and contrived versions. Even children can tell authentic enjoyment from polite or false friendliness.

The human face has 43 muscles used for emotional expressions. Smiling is a universal social signal that can be seen at a distance of 100 meters. Nineteenth century French scientist Duchenne identified two very different smiles. The forced smile curves the mouth while the genuine smile mobilizes the whole face. Smiling is easier to detect than other emotions. Authentic smiles are among the most powerful tools in building trust.[53]

Swedish brain scientist Bjorn Merker studied children who had a rare condition of being born without a cortex.[54] Some of the parents had been told by neurologists that their child had a brain *like that of a reptile* and would be vegetative. But when reared in loving families, such children laugh and smile in the uniquely human manner. At the deepest levels, our brain is formatted for friendliness.

The human brain is so tied to the rewards of social contact that persons who are disconnected feel great emptiness. Even their immune systems are compromised. In effect, our brains are oxytocin-addicted to bonds of trust. Ironically, drugs of abuse can mimic this natural high of human bonding. Substance abuse is often an attempt to compensate for the biochemical rush of positive relationships. On the other hand, some psychoactive drugs prescribed to manage behavior actually lower oxytocin levels, perhaps impeding relationships and therapeutic alliances.[55]

Lacking the chemistry of love, many pursue the love of chemicals. Addicts may satisfy their need for intimacy by manipulating the biochemistry of bonding and attachment. Cocaine, ecstasy, and some other drugs are thought to achieve at least some of the brain effects that relationships would otherwise provide.[56] This enchantment with chemicals is a poor substitute for stable trusting bonds.[57]

Powerful Alliances

Every child needs at least one adult who is irrationally crazy about him or her.

Urie Bronfenbrenner

Researchers Junlei Li and Megan Julian[58] describe *developmental relationships* as the active ingredient in success of interventions in family, school, treatment programs, and community settings. To borrow the pharmacy science term, *active ingredient* refers to the critical component that produces desired change (e.g., fluoride in toothpaste). A wide range of evidence from various fields show that *developmental relationships* are the most potent ingredients in effective education of treatment.

The definition of developmental relationships is drawn from Urie Bronfenbrenner's classic research of learning and development, which includes four elements corresponding to essential growth needs as noted below:[a]

A strong emotional attachment [Belonging]

Increasingly more complex tasks [Mastery]

Power shifts to developing person [Independence]

Reciprocity of relationship [Generosity]

Punitive interventions such as behavior control by suspension or exclusion directly impede developmental relationships. Ironically, most attempts to improve schools or youth programs which manipulate *inactive* ingredients (incentives, curricula, accountability) do not produce powerful results. Such is typical

---

[a] This is Bronfenbrenner's citation: "Learning and development are facilitated by the participation of the developing person in *progressively more complex* patterns of *reciprocal activity* with someone with whom that person has developed a *strong and enduring emotional attachment* and when the *balance of power gradually shifts* in favor of the developing person" (1979, p. 60; italics added).

of educational "reforms" such as test-based accountability, merit pay for teachers, paying students for grades, and school choice. In spite of the supposed logic of reinforcement and competition, these behavioristic or economic ingredients do not create consistent, lasting positive effects.[59]

Children are designed to thrive in an environment in which they have at least one close adult relationship. While there are some additional benefits of having more than one supportive relationship, the most powerful difference is between having none and the power of one relationship. This is shown in the accompanying graph.[60]

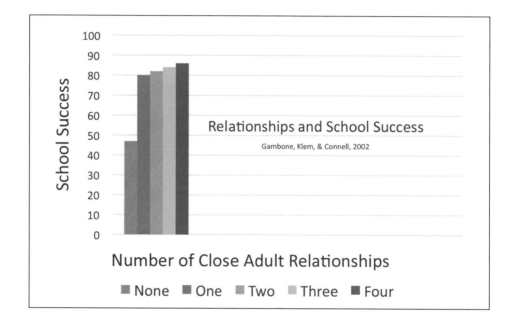

Supportive relationships turn out to be the most powerful force for positive change in school, treatment, and youth development settings.[61] However, many adults do things *to* or *for* youth rather than joining *with* them in alliance.[62]

Respectful Alliances	Resistant Encounters
Trust—the youth believes the adult cares, understands, and is able to help.	**Distrust**—the youth believes the adult will not care, understand, or be able to help.
Cooperation—the youth and adult work together for mutual benefit, e.g., solving a problem.	**Discord**—the youth and adult do not share goals, e.g., adult wants control, youth wants autonomy.
Connection—harmony and respect increase.	**Disconnection**—conflict and avoidance increase.

Researchers investigated the quality of the alliance between teacher-counselors and youth in the Pressley Ridge schools and treatment centers.[63] Youth were likely to resist adults who showed these traits: dominance (bossy), rule conscious (moralistic), perfectionism (compulsive), and privateness (guarded). On the other hand, youth formed alliances with adults demonstrating openness to change (flexibility), emotional stability (calm), and warmth. Youth report that they trust adults who care, help solve problems, and listen to them. This helping alliance is the core of all successful work with youth.

Conclusion

The evidence is abundantly clear: attachment is the linchpin to surviving and thriving. Subsequent chapters will explore achievement, autonomy, and altruism. Each has distinct brain circuits but are closely intertwined. As Maslow first proposed, belonging is the foundation for other higher needs. This now has been validated in a series of experimental studies by Roy Baumeister and colleagues:

> *Attachment and achievement—Social exclusion reduces the capacity for rational thought.* Children learn from those they trust and resist those they don't.[64] Broken belonging impairs intelligence and achievement. Social exclusion reduces reasoning ability.[65]

> *Attachment and autonomy—Social exclusion impairs self-regulation.* Children with a secure base of attachment are able to develop autonomy.[66] Being excluded or rejected impairs self-regulation which impedes social acceptance.[67]

> *Attachment and altruism—Social exclusion decreases prosocial behavior.* Humans are socio-biologically designed to connect with and care for one another.[68] But the pain of rejection numbs emotions and suppresses empathy and concern for others.[69]

Connecting with kids in conflict is the focus of the following Action Research feature by resilience researcher John Seita of Michigan State University. John himself had a horrific childhood. He was removed from his substance-abusing mother at age eight and shuttled through fifteen foster care and residential placements. At age twelve, John was placed by the juvenile court at Starr Commonwealth where the authors had the opportunity to work with him. John has described his personal journey from trauma to resilience in two earlier books for which we were privileged to serve as coauthors: *In Whose Best Interest?* and *Kids Who Outwit Adults.*[70] Here, Dr. Seita describes the process of building positive connections with relationship-wary youth.

Reaching Disconnected Kids

John Seita

Consider these children to have fallen among thieves, the thieves of ignorance and sin and ill fate and loss. Their birthrights were stolen. They have no belongings.[71]

Karl Menninger

Stories of youth battling elders permeate literature. The Prodigal Son defies his father, Romeo and Juliet deceive their parents, and Huck Finn foils his foster mother and rafts away on the river. The account closest to my own experience is *Good Will Hunting* who employed clever tactics to outwit adults who had betrayed his trust.[72]

Secure bonds are essential for young people to grow, learn, and thrive.[73] But millions of modern youth are disconnected, struggling in overstressed families, depersonalized schools, and violent communities. Ironically, those who have experienced rejection and maltreatment display behavior that causes further alienation from caring adults.[74]

Challenges in Connecting

Youth at risk experience deep emotional pain and react with *pain-based behavior.*[75] They show a host of problems that hurt self and others, including anger, depression, substance abuse, gang involvement, bullying, and disengagement from school. Most troubled behavior is logical from the view of the actor.[76] The young person is trying to accomplish something—our challenge is to detect what that might be.[77]

Problem behavior is often a means of coping with a world filled with abuse, neglect, and abandonment. Kids who distrust adults seek to distance themselves from danger. Seen in that light, problems can be a sign of health, self-preservation, and self-determination. Michael Ungar notes that "defiant, delinquent, and disordered children are in a frantic search to find some way to feel good about themselves" and their troubled behavior is actually their way of trying to restore well-being.[78]

This idea that problems reflect strengths seems counterintuitive to those who have grown up in healthy environments. But being on guard is a protective response in a dangerous world. Yet, ultimately, such defensive resilience can be self-defeating. Connecting with adult-wary children and youth can be an endurance event. These young people present challenges in emotions, thinking, and behavior.

Amygdala Alert. Trauma, loss, and maltreatment can change brain activity.[79] For example, the emotional brain's danger detector, the amygdala, goes into overdrive to keep youth vigilant for possible attack or rejection. Our best efforts to connect can be thwarted by a healthy brain just doing its job of protection from perceived threats. Resisting relationships is actually an attempt to avoid further pain. Describing troubled emotions as "pain" is more than a metaphor as the phrase "hurt feelings" is literally true; physical and social pain share similar brain pathways.[80] Researchers scanned the brains of individuals excluded by peers from a computer simulated game. Even this contrived social rejection aroused precisely the same pain centers of the brain as those activated by physical pain.[81]

Distrustful Private Logic. Young people who have come to expect indifference or hostility from adults act accordingly. In his classic book, *The Problem Child*, Alfred Adler noted that when we fail to understand the *private logic* and goals of a young person, interventions may do more harm than good.[82] Youth who have been violated by adults see the world as a hostile place, which makes sense based on their experience. Each of us develops our private logic as we try to navigate our social world. This collection of thoughts and beliefs about self and others forms the basis for personal coping strategies. Perhaps the most deep-seated belief is trust versus mistrust.[83] A child who views adults as safe will seek them out in times of crisis. But those who mistrust draw away.

Adaptive Distancing. Kids who have been hurt may cope by keeping people at bay.[84] While this is a protective response, it starves the youngster of love. At age eight, the court removed me from my mother who was drowning in poverty, addiction, and abusive relationships. Whatever her problems, I lost my anchor of belonging. I sabotaged a series of fifteen foster homes to make sure nobody would get close to me and cause more pain and rejection. While many well-meaning adults tried to connect, they were rebuffed and spectacularly unsuccessful. My case file was filled with a menagerie of mental disorder labels. An accurate diagnosis would be *adult wary*. It would be years before I dared to trust again, first connecting with a novice youth worker who was fresh out of the university and too naïve to know I was hopeless. We found a common interest in baseball, and I slowly let others into my life.

Decoding Challenging Behavior

Science is clear: *youth at risk* are a product of *at-risk communities*. We recognize the role environment plays in the health of other creatures. No one blames a fish for dying in polluted water. While we do not excuse youth from taking responsibility for their behavior, the ecology of interpersonal relationships powerfully shapes coping strategies.

Behavior is a form of communication providing clues about what is missing in a young person's life. When a youth seems to be speaking a different language, we must decode messages buried in behavior. For example, persons desperate for belonging may act in what seem to be anti-belonging ways. They may reject adults, bond with other disconnected kids, and appear to be thoroughly *antisocial*. While the overt message is "stay away," the meaning behind the behavior is much different.

Young people who disengage from adults are usually reacting out of fear and wariness about the danger of getting close. All humans naturally use coping strategies to deal with perceived threats. As demonstrated in the true-to-life story of *Good Will Hunting,* adult-wary kids are skillful psychologists in dealing with the adult as adversary. Decoding these coping strategies is a prerequisite to building a helping alliance. This is the thrust of the Response Ability Pathways (RAP) training.[85] All who work with youth need the ability to respond to their needs instead of react to problems. This requires three skillsets: *connecting* to young people in conflict, *clarifying* challenges, and *restoring* respectful social bonds.

Since development starts with attachment, adults need specific strategies to deal with youth who are skillful at adaptive distancing. Our research has identified three categories of these protective behaviors: Fight, Flight, and Fool.[86] Success with challenging youth involves being able to decode these behaviors which block belonging.

Fight. This coping strategy can spring from multiple causes. Aggression in any species may be an automatic, reflexive reaction to frustration or threat. But human aggression has many other nuanced varieties that are products of our thinking brain.[87] Youth who have suffered violence may adopt the private logic of *hurt or get hurt* and present a tough front or threat display to keep others at a distance. A person who has been rejected may turn this pain on others with the private logic of *I will make them suffer.* Defiance may come from power struggles: *nobody tells me what to do.* Perhaps most challenging is the youth who operates in calculated ways to hurt or exploit others; the self-centered logic *I will get what I want* overrides empathy and conscience.[88] While aggression is never acceptable, the adult avoids being drawn into conflict and helps the youth develop more effective coping behaviors.

Flight. Strategies involving withdrawal are variations on the theme of hide or get hurt. Some wariness is a matter of shy temperament and personality traits. But since humans are inherently social beings, those who isolate are often operating on private logic that overrides their basic needs. The rejected child may avoid shows of friendliness such as physical closeness, smiling, and eye contact with the protective belief *I don't want to be hurt again.* Children who experience repeated failure avoid taking risks or investing in school, buttressed by beliefs like *I am stupid and will fail again.* The person who lacks self-confidence may internalize beliefs such as *I am helpless and powerless.* Others who think life has no purpose may use addictive behavior to replace human relationships.[89] The challenge is to build courage in these discouraged young people as we engage in a talent hunt to help them discover their strengths and greatness.

Fool. Instead of Fight or Flight, youth may use rational coping strategies believing *I can outsmart them.* Calling them *manipulative* is a backhanded compliment as this term means *to manage skillfully.* Not driven by fight or flight, they may appear callous and unemotional, which is usually far from the truth—most are reflecting lack of parental warmth.[90] Youth who have spent years dealing with untrusted adults can become virtual psychologists. One youth said, "I don't fight adults; I charm and disarm them." A girl living on the streets describes how she feeds invented problems to her counselor to gain support without real disclosure. They use mind games and clever insults to shred the adult's self-esteem. As peer leaders, they are masters at mobilizing group dynamics in an "us against them" battle with authority figures. The challenge is to tap the strengths of these youth without getting drawn into hostile encounters. Since manipulative youth are actually engaging instead of avoiding adults, their games can be seen as heavily camouflaged bids to connect. Once they trust, there is no need for contests to outwit adults.

Adults must join in the youth's private campaign to gain respect. We avoid taking challenging behavior personally lest we become trapped in our own maladaptive private logic, e.g., *This kid is jerk. I don't have to take that crap.* A healthy teen brain is just doing its job, protecting from potential threat. This defensive resilience will become adaptive if adults can show acceptance and set positive expectations. Challenging behavior provides unique opportunities for learning and growth.

1. Lay, 2000, pp. 68-69.
2. Barrett, 2015.
3. Deloria, 1943, p. 32.
4. Brown, 1991.
5. Baumeister & Leary, 1995.
6. Baumeister & Leary, 1995.
7. Seita, Mitchell, & Tobin, 1996.
8. Baumeister & Leary, 1995, p. 521.
9. Morgenthau, 1962.
10. Baumeister & Leary, 2007, p. 522.
11. Bowlby, 1969/1982.
12. Taussig & Culhane, 2010.
13. Ainsworth, 1989.
14. Taylor & Gonzaga, 2007.
15. Johnston, 1999, p. 41.
16. Way, 1993, p. 4.
17. Bowlby, 1969; Erikson, 1963; Maslow, 1943.
18. Carter, 2003; Taylor, 2002.
19. Ratey, 2002.
20. Nelson & Panksepp, 1998.
21. Hofer, 1987; Wexler, 2006.
22. Ratey, 2002.
23. Konner, 2002.
24. Carter, 2007.
25. Cozolino, 2006, p. 322.
26. Cozolino, 2006.
27. Porges, 2011.
28. Kok et al., 2013.
29. Aichhorn, 1951, p. 164.
30. Lewis, Amini, & Lannon, 2001, p. 69.
31. Bowlby, 1982.
32. Ainsworth, Blehar, Waters, & Wall, 1978.
33. Cicchetti, Rogosch, & Toth, 2006.
34. Panksepp & Bivin, 2012.
35. Cassullo & Capello, 2010.
36. Suttie, 1935.
37. Ferenczi, 1932.
38. Heinrich & Gullone, 2006.
39. Pedersen, 2004.
40. Sue, 2010.
41. Lieberman, 2013.
42. Izard & Ackerman, 2000.
43. Goleman, 2006.
44. Cozolino, 2006.
45. Hattie & Yates, 2014.
46. Hattie & Yates, 2014.
47. Bateson, Nettle, & Roberts, 2006.
48. Carter, 1998.
49. Provine, 2000.
50. Willner et al., 1970.
51. Digney, 2009.
52. Bower, 2007.
53. Restak, 2013.
54. Merker, 2007.
55. Foltz, 2008.
56. Cozolino, 2006.
57. Chambers & Henrickson, 2002.
58. Li & Julian, 2012.
59. Hanushek & Raymond, 2005; Levitt, Janta, & Wegrich, 2008; Newmann, King, & Rigdon, 1997.
60. Gambone, Klem, & Connell, 2002.
61. Gold, 1995; Hobbs, 1982; Morse, 2008.
62. Fulcher & Garfat, 2008; Wachtel, 2003.
63. Manso & Rautkis, 2011.
64. Morse, 2008.
65. Baumeister, Twenge, & Nuss, 2002.
66. Maier, 1982.
67. Baumeister, DeWall, Ciarocco, & Twenge, 2005.
68. Churchland, 2011.
69. Twenge et al., 2007.
70. Seita, Mitchell, & Tobin, 1986; Seita & Brendtro, 2005.
71. Menninger, 1982, p. 59.
72. Seita & Brendtro, 2005.
73. Baumeister, 2011; Shulevitz, 2013.
74. Brown & Seita, 2010; Seita, Mitchell, & Tobin, 1995.
75. Anglin, 2014.
76. Morse, 2008.
77. Anderson & Seita, 2005.
78. Ungar, 2007, p. 6.
79. Herrigna et al., 2011.
80. MacDonald & Jensen-Campbell, 2010.
81. Eisenberger, 2011.
82. Adler, 1930.
83. Erikson, 1963.
84. Whiting & Seita, 2008.
85. Brendtro & du Toit, 2005.
86. Seita & Brendtro, 2005.
87. Berkowitz, 1992.
88. Gibbs, 2014.
89. Chambers & Henrickson 2002.
90. Pasalich et al., 2012.

4

Achievement and Talent

The motive for mastery lies at the heart of man's love for challenge.
But when the goal is attained, boredom—or even apathy—replaces zeal
and a new prize is sought.[1]

Jerome Kagan

Mastery is the drive to strengthen one's knowledge, skill, or talent.[2] Researchers have long considered the desire to be competent as a biologically based human need.[3] While all children are born with motivation to achieve, faulty education and fear of failure can extinguish the love of learning. In his essay *To Teachers*, 1913 Nobel Prize-winning poet Rabindranath Tagore of India described his own gloomy school experience: "We are born with that God given gift of taking delight in the world, but such delightful activity is fettered and imprisoned. We sit inert, like dead specimens of some museum, whilst lessons are pelted at us from on high, like hail stones on flowers."[4]

Ironically, a Spanish youth who also hated school with a passion would one day win his Nobel Prize for discovering the neuron.[5] Santiago Ramon y Cajal was the wildly rebellious son of a Spanish physician and was expelled from several schools. At the age of 11, he used his genius to build a homemade cannon that he and his friends deployed to destroy a city gate. Although briefly locked in prison, Santiago was resilient and grew up to follow his father into medicine.[6]

Ramon y Cajal used his prodigious artistic talent to draw the central nervous system in great detail. This contradicted the prevailing theory that nerve circuits were continuous like blood vessels. His neuron theory has shaped all subsequent brain research. He proposed the radical notion that the brain has *adaptive talent*: it grows new pathways to repair damage or to meet environmental challenges.[7] He was describing what is now called neuroplasticity.

Intelligence as Resilience

Failure is simply the opportunity to begin again, this time more intelligently.[8]

Henry Ford

A recent book on brain science describes intelligence as a person's ability to respond successfully to challenges and to learn from such experience.[9] A review of many definitions of intelligence identified this common thread: the "ability to achieve goals in a wide range of environments."[10]

The IQ Debates

Alfred Binet originated the IQ test as an aid in teaching children intelligence. He was furious when others perverted his invention by using IQ to justify inequalities in race and social class.[11] Yet for a century, many argued that intelligence was "inherited, not due to teaching or training."[12] One researcher opined with precision that 75 percent of intelligence was due to genes and only 25 percent to environment.[13] Herrnstein and Wilson's *The Bell Curve* further spun pseudoscience to declare that IQ is largely inherited, there are strong racial differences, and interventions are unlikely to make an impact.[14]

With greater understanding of the brain, outmoded notions of intelligence are being disproven. Research shows that large variations in IQ are due to enriched or impoverished environments. Differences in scores between racial groups mainly result from lower socio-economic status. And, learning opportunities can have a powerful effect on success in school and life.[15]

To search for variations in intelligence, we must look to the physical and social environment. Many biological factors influence brain development, most having to do with poor nutrition or the presence of toxins. As will be seen in Chapter 7, the new science of epigenetics is revealing the many ways unhealthy ecologies can interfere with cognitive development.

The brain only develops its innate potential with rich stimulation, and socio-economic status (SES) strongly affects intelligence and learning.[16] Hart and Risely intensely studied language between parents and children in three settings: professional, working class, and welfare families.[17] During the first three years of life, a child in a professional family heard 30 million more words than a child in a welfare family.[18]

Both the quantity and quality of communication differ by SES groups. Children with professional parents received six encouragements for every reprimand. Those from working-class backgrounds got two encouragements per reprimand. But children of unemployed mothers in welfare families received twice as many reprimands as encouragements.[19] Young children given daily doses of rebuke instead of respect are living amidst stress and perhaps trauma. The services that would be needed to compensate for limited language and parenting practices far exceed available resources. A much more workable strategy is to train caregivers. Research shows that a curriculum of child development, parenting skills, and emotional support raises the intelligence of young children.[20]

When children grow up in highly stressful or impoverished environments, their IQ scores are significantly reduced. Those raised in stable and enriching environments have tested intelligence that more closely reflects their natural potential. For example, working class children adopted by middle class families show a 12-18 point boost in intelligence.[21] Thus the gaps in tested ability and achievement among children from poverty are largely due to environment and opportunities for learning.

Unique factors in the background and beliefs of Asian Americans often lead to higher levels of performance. This may be explained by deep differences in cultural beliefs—dating to Confucius, who was a teacher—that intelligence is a matter of hard work.[22] For thousands of years in China, the poorest villager could become the most revered leader in the land through study. Asian families from this background expect excellence from their children, and differences in achievement reflect cultural influences rather than genetics.

Intelligence, like race, is largely a social construction. With cultural enrichment, IQ scores soar. This is known as the Flynn effect, named for New Zealand political scientist James Flynn.[23] He found that average IQ scores of groups all around the world have been rising about three points a decade for a century. Thus, children in 1900 with an IQ of 100 would only score 60 by current test norms—leading to the bizarre conclusion that most of our ancestors were "retarded"—to use a discredited term. Of course, earlier generations were coping with completely different challenges requiring capacities not measured by modern tests. For example, traditional aboriginal Australians learned 500 kinship terms but were oblivious to the nuances of Western science. If the aboriginal vocabulary were on a test, the most highly educated would fail.

Robert Sternberg[24] identifies three types of intelligence: *analytic intelligence* is used to solve problems and to make judgments; *creative intelligence* involves new ways of doing things; and *practical intelligence* is an intuitive ability to confront and solve problems in our everyday life and relationships. When researchers asked people to define intelligence in their own words, three strong themes emerged: the ability to communicate, the ability to solve practical problems, and the ability to get along with other people. This emphasis on social intelligence reflects modern brain research but not modern schools.

Neuroplasticity

While the ability of the brain to redesign itself was discovered by Ramon y Cajal, his revolutionary concept of neuroplasticity was largely overlooked. It would be a half century until Canadian researcher Donald Hebb popularized the principle that neurons that fire together wire together.[25] Neuroplasticity refers to the brain's ability to form new connections in response to experience. Of course, plasticity is not all good news for it renders our brain not only resilient but vulnerable to outside influences. "Love, sex, grief, relationships, learning, addiction, culture, technology, and psychotherapies change our brains."[26]

Thinking, learning, and life events can change the brain's structure at any age although young brains are most malleable.[27] Even if damage has occurred, the adaptive brain can design a work-around, using new neural pathways to build adaptive capacity.[28] Contrary to theories that only young brains can build new neurons, humans have a lifelong capacity for neuroplasticity in areas involving new learning such as the hippocampus, amygdala, and cerebral cortex.[29]

Myelin is the insulation wrapping nerve fibers. Long-term learning changes neurons from *gray matter* by coating them with myelin which gives them the appearance of *white matter*. The more we fire a particular circuit, the more layers of myelin are built so our thoughts and actions become faster and more fluent.[30] Well-practiced brain circuits operate hundreds of times more efficiently than before. "Greatness isn't born. It is grown," says Daniel Coyle in his book *The Talent Code*.[31] Life experiences redesign the brain.

> *Each wrap of myelin is a unique tracing of some past event. Perhaps that wrap was caused by a coach's pointer; perhaps that one by a parent's encouraging glance, perhaps that one by hearing a song they loved. In the whorls of myelin reside a person's secret history, the flow of interactions and influences that make up a life.*[32]

When you get 50 layers of myelin on a brain circuit, you are an expert and this typically takes 10,000 hours of practice over 10 years of time.[33]

In 2000, Eric Kandel won the Nobel Prize for discovering how long-term memories are formed, performing experiments on a sea snail which has very large neurons.[34] Short-term memories are temporary traces in brain cells that quickly fade. Long-term memories require the construction of new brain pathways. Whether or not lasting memories are formed depends on two proteins which turn genes on or off. CREB-1 tells genes to store memories while CREB-2 says ignore this event. The brain is not like a computer that stores whatever is loaded into it. Instead, the brain is selective and is designed to retain two kinds of events in long-term memories—repetition and emotionally charged experiences.

Repetition involving multiple occurrences builds new brain circuits. An example is *rote learning* in school. However, the most profound repetitive learning comes from *cultural patterns* instilled over a lifetime. Therefore, when we seek to transform lives, such as helping traumatized children heal, it will take repeated experiences to inscribe new patterns. These youngsters will need multiple safe and nurturing experiences to override deeply imbedded fears of attachment.

Emotionally charged events need no repetition but can be instantly seared into memory. Emotions of *pleasure* tell the brain to repeat this activity, while *pain* signals a threat to be avoided. The brain is highly adept at conditioning fear memories. When a person is in crisis or dealing with painful events, a powerful teaching opportunity is presented as these memories are being recorded for better or worse. Young persons who have experienced trauma and pain in their lives desperately need positive memories as described by Jasmine, a homeless teen in Australia:

> *One of my doctors one day asked me to write out all the good things*
> *that happened to me as a child and all the bad things that happened...*
> *I started crying because I could not think of one good thing.*[35]

The Problem-Solving Brain

All problem solving starts with felt difficulty said John Dewey—we only think when we are confronted with problems.[36] Piaget described intelligence as "the capacity to resolve new problems by thought."[37] This involves attending to the challenge, searching for a solution, and coping with the problem. The brain is designed to become intelligent by learning to cope with challenges. René Descartes (1596-1650) observed, "Every problem I solved became a rule which served afterwards to solve other problems."[38]

Our brains are specifically designed to keep remembering uncompleted tasks and unsolved problems—this is called the Zeigarnik effect.[39] This mental tension motivates us to keep replaying unresolved conflicts in our mind or to seek to share this concern with a trusted person. The brain is not at peace until it does what it is designed for, finding answers to unsolved problems. Ironically, when youth are showing pain-based behavior, adults often disengage rather than use this as an opportunity for communication and learning.

Pioneering school psychologist John Morgan (1888-1945) proposed that "maladjustments in children should be considered merely as stages in the process of learning to be mature."[40] The brain-based protocol for problem solving is shown in the accompanying figure. CLEAR is an acronym for Challenge, Logic, Emotion, Action, and Result. Each problem-solving event begins with some *Challenge* which triggers the amygdala. This information is then passed to brain centers for *Logic* as well as for *Emotion*. The interplay of these higher and deeper brain systems leads to some *Action*. This action achieves some *Result,* i.e., consequences.[41] As these patterns are repeated, they form brain pathways for a particular style of coping with challenge.

To understand behavior, it is helpful to know what stressful event triggered the sequence, what feelings and thoughts were activated, and what was the behavioral outcome. When youth have difficulty coping, it is often a case of distorted *private logic* which interferes with making good decisions.[42] By talking with a person about some challenging event, we can get a window into how they cope in either adaptive or self-defeating ways. These conversations to clarify thinking can be used with individual students or in peer helping groups.[43] The goal is to correct thinking distortions and develop intelligent coping strategies.[44]

Figure 1. CLEAR Problem-Solving

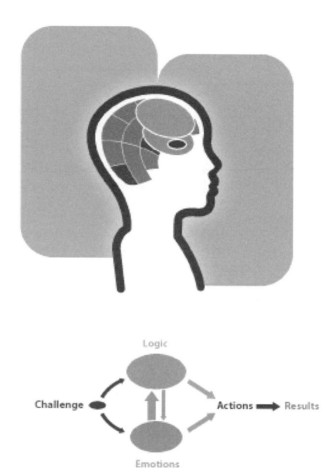

Growing Intelligence

Try again, fail again, fail better.

Samuel Becket (1906-1989)

When young children first enter school, most display a natural curiosity and motivation to learn. But for many students, this budding potential fades. Researchers studied the roots of success and failure with students. They hired teens to carry pagers which signaled them at random times, whereupon they completed quick questionnaires on precisely what they were doing, thinking, and feeling. When paged in school, most students were trying to concentrate, but this was due to concern about grades instead of intrinsic interest in learning. Even highly talented students showed this pattern since few were operating on internal motivation.[45] Youth were much more engaged when they were with peers, following their own interests without adult control.

Motivation to Learn

Researchers have identified two very different types of motivation for achievement. In *task motivation*, the reward comes from improving one's performance, which is a natural brain program. But, *egoistic motivation* involves comparing one's ability with others in the desire to be superior, as on an *ego trip*. The difference is very basic: Does one achieve in order to learn well or look good?[46]

Egoistic motivation results in defensive behaviors. Fearing failure, youth avoid difficult challenges and may show helplessness or resistance. Some build bravado fronts to mask failure and protect self-image. Egoistic motivation is exaggerated by high-stakes testing and point level behavior modification systems.[47]

Task motivation engages students in mastery learning. They are not discouraged by errors but use this feedback to design more adaptive responses. This intrinsic mastery drive is called *flow* since the brain is on a roll searching for solutions.[48]

Carol Dweck has shown that achievement is strongly related to one's belief about intelligence.[49] She taught middle school students how learning changes the brain to form new pathways of talent. Once students believe they can change their intelligence, learning spikes. A tough junior high boy who thought of himself as stupid was brought to tears upon hearing the life-altering news that intelligence was under his control. Dweck describes these two mindsets about intelligence:

A fixed mindset. These persons believe that talent is a trait you either have or don't: *Your intelligence is something about you that you cannot change very much.* They avoid risking failure and act helpless and give up in the face of difficulty. Failure is seen as a threat to self-worth.

A growth mindset. These individuals believe intelligence can be developed with hard work: *No matter who you are, you can change your intelligence a lot.* They have a *mastery* mentality and stick with difficult tasks until they succeed. They use failure as feedback in the belief that the more effort they exert, the more they will learn.

Ability is shaped by long-term goals. For example, students who believed they would be using music through high school and beyond greatly out-performed other students, regardless of how much they practiced. With a mastery orientation, they dove into difficult challenges, whereas children without long-term goals gave up when facing difficulty.[50] When we deliberately push ourselves beyond our comfort zone, we rewire our brains.

Research has shown that the best way to build a growth mindset is to teach this to young people. The fear of failure can be reduced when students learn that talent is something they develop, not something controlled by genes.[51] Of course, adults must also embrace this growth mindset if they are going to convey this to students.[52]

School success is a powerful predictor of positive life outcomes. But school failure damages self-esteem and motivates students to defy teachers and disengage from school. Ironically, the very policies that schools adopt to increase achievement are fostering failure and feeding the school to prison pipeline. Born of a fear of school violence, the zero tolerance mentality has stripped hundreds of thousands of students of educational opportunity.[53] There has been a massive increase in suspension and expulsion for violating policies about tobacco, drugs, dress code, and disruptive behavior. "Missing school contradicts the core goal of schools—achievement—and high-stakes testing further plunges students into failure, grade retention, and dropping out of school."[54]

Engaging Disconnected Students

University of Michigan researchers identified two essential qualities for success with students at risk.[55] *Teachers provide uncommonly warm emotional support.* The more students come to like teachers, the more interested they become in school and the higher their achievement. *Teachers prevent students from failing.* This involves frequent feedback and encouragement and individualizing the curriculum to their needs. Effective schools are also able to adapt curriculum and discipline procedures to meet the needs of students at risk. Such flexibility is absent when rules and consequences are doled out with unbending consistency.

Perhaps the most significant research finding on building positive learning communities is that youth culture is a mirror image of adult culture.[56] If staff believe in young people and work as a cohesive team, students thrive. But when staff are dispirited and morale is low, so it is with youth.

For decades, Starr Commonwealth has been a pioneer in building positive peer cultures and positive staff teams in schools for challenging students. In one study, researchers tracked achievement of 1,000 consecutive admissions throughout their enrollment in these alternative schools. These students entered with an achievement level averaging .65 years gain for each year in school. This gap increased each year, e.g., by tenth grade the typical student was achieving at a sixth or seventh grade level.

While one would predict the pattern of lagging achievement to continue, instead this trend was sharply altered by a new school environment which combined strong relational support with positive expectations for behavior and learning. Averaging across all students, the typical individual made approximately two years gain for each year in this setting. That is a three-fold increase in the prior rate of achievement growth. While the curriculum was the same as that in regular schools, a positive peer and staff climate made the difference. To translate research into simple terms, teachers know how to help failing students succeed and how to build relationships with students who do not like teachers.

Nicholas Hobbs observed that learners thrive when given the right level of challenge, which he called "Just Manageable Difficulties." This means selecting tasks or problems that are demanding but still surmountable. If tasks are too easy, life is boring; if too hard, life is defeating. Persons who achieve the right balance "will know zest and joy and deep fulfillment."[57]

The Joy of Learning

Across history, great educators were able to engage youth in the joy of learning. Jane Addams established youth programs to capture the adventuresome spirit of youth.[58] In the Ukraine, Anton Makarenko called for schools to teach the joy of learning and unleash the potentials of disengaged students. In New Zealand, Sylvia Ashton-Warner discarded the stilted government curriculum to unleash creativity in young Maori children. In modern terms, these pioneers were experts in brain-friendly learning, capturing the biosocial drive for curiosity, creativity, and problem solving. The challenge for today is to reclaim adventure in education.[59]

In his classic study of play, German psychologist Karl Groos described this as an inborn instinct enabling children to learn skills necessary to thrive as adults.[60] Beyond physical rough housing, they observe their elders and incorporate what they see into their play. They explore, construct, spin fantasies, and engage in constant social play. Play is tied to all biosocial needs—social bonds, competence, self-regulation, and empathy.[61] The lack of opportunity for play in modern schools and communities can intensify relationship problems, learning disorders, impulsiveness, and narcissism.[62]

Curiosity is driven by universal brain-based emotions which Jaak Panksepp labelled as *seeking* and *play*.[63] Curiosity fuels long-term learning. Young children are constantly testing hypotheses, experimenting, and figuring out how things work. Preschoolers are wildly curious and ask 100 *why* questions a day, but observational studies show this virtually vanishes in most schools.[64] Teachers who are under pressure to teach specific skills deflect curious questions by reminding pupils to stay on task.

Play constructs new neural pathways, so brains actually grow during recess![65] Play also fosters development of the frontal lobe, which involves planning and inhibiting action. This area develops more slowly in kids with ADHD. Their immature brains may need more rough and tumble play to develop behavioral control systems. Ironically, medications that reduce motor activity may inhibit the very brain structures necessary for developing self-control.[66] Throughout the lifespan, play activity enables the brain to continue constructing new neurons, even in nursing homes.

A dramatic new field of play has been created by the advent of computers and video games. Today's schools find it increasingly difficult to engage the video generation who may spend 10,000 hours gaming by age 21. Rather than decry youths' retreat into virtual reality, neuroscientist Jane McGonigal observes that video games fulfill four intrinsic human needs: human connection, hope of success, opportunities to exert power, and participation in something larger than self.[67] These mirror biosocial needs for attachment, achievement, autonomy, and altruism.

Like video games, computers can facilitate explorative play and intrinsic learning and are more engaging than the forced concentration of formalized instruction. Computers are widely used in schools but typically employ instructional methods of the last century to dispense standardized knowledge to all students. South African computer learning pioneer Seymour Papert sees the real power of computers as enabling students to construct their own learning and develop deep thinking skills.[68]

Perhaps the most dramatic demonstrations of Papert's vision are the "Hole in the Wall" experiments conducted by inventor Sugata Mitra of India.[69] He installed a computer connected to the Internet in a brick wall near a New Delhi slum, and hidden cameras recorded what happened next. Soon, small groups of curious children gathered to figure out what this strange TV could do.

Within days and without formal instruction, most of the children were using the computer to play games, create documents, and paint pictures. They discovered how to explore the Internet and began teaching these skills to one another. Mitra then established learning centers with computers in safe public places in remote Indian villages. Again, children quickly mastered the computer—even if they had to first learn English on the Internet. Their innate curiosity, along with peer interaction and support, motivated them to explore the environment and acquire skills.

Mitra is now working to create Self Organized Learning Environments worldwide. His Ted Talk on "Unstoppable Learning" describes how children who have never before seen a computer teach themselves everything from languages to DNA transcription. In Mitra's words: "My wish is to help design a future of learning by supporting children all over the world to tap into their wonder and their ability to work together. Help me build this school. It will be called the School in the Cloud."[70]

Trust and Talent

Trust is the glue that holds teaching and learning together.[71]

Nicholas Hobbs

The U.S. Centers for Disease Control has established school connectedness as a national health priority because it is closely related to both school success and positive life outcomes.[72] School connectedness has been defined to include *social belonging*—feeling close to fellow students and teachers and feeling *cared for and respected* by teachers.[73] These are prerequisites to school engagement and achievement.

Back to Basics

The great blind spot in grand attempts at school reform is the failure to focus like a laser on basics—and the most basic need of children is to trust. Decades of research show that effective teachers with disengaged students are able to develop both trust and talent.[74] A major study of school reform in Chicago found that a single factor—trust—separated failing schools from successful ones.[75] This included teacher-parent trust, teacher-principal trust, and teacher-teacher trust. While these are important relationships, the most influential bonds are teacher-student trust and student-student trust. While there were great differences in the effectiveness of individual teachers, traditional measures such as experience or education did not predict success.

Attempts to raise academic performance are futile if students are not connected to school. Research on junior high students from a dozen countries shows those in the U.S. feel most strongly that they do not belong.[76] They report being less socially connected to teachers and peers and rated their school climate worse than in any other country.

The most efficient learning usually occurs in relationship with others rather than as a solo performance. When guided by a more competent adult or peer, learners increasingly master more complex tasks than by working independently. These mentors provide models, challenge, and support so learners keep pushing the limits of their ability which Vygotsky called *zone of proximal development.*[77]

An overly individualized approach to education fails to tap into the power of the social brain. Cooperative learning optimizes achievement, and groups perform better than individuals on a wide range of tasks.[78] In fact, small groups come up with better solutions to problems than bright individuals working alone. Three persons working together is usually enough to activate this superior group problem-solving ability.

While research documents the power of the social brain, schools have been slow to tap this science. Decades of studies show that cooperative learning creates greater effort to achieve than competitive or individualistic efforts.[79] Students also need to be able to constructively resolve conflict.[80] However, such skills are acquired in groups and cannot be taught with posters, worksheets, and superficial character curriculums. Few schools have been able to fully integrate social, emotional, and academic learning.[81] Instead of a holistic approach, they either narrowly focus on raising academic achievement, thus failing in the social emotional domain, or, in a few cases, pursue social and emotional learning while neglecting high expectations for achievement.

Many social and emotional learning programs fall flat because attempts to foster a caring environment are seen at odds with expectations for academic excellence.[82] This is particularly true when the goal is to close achievement gaps among low income, urban students. When teachers are expected to meet both socio-emotional and academic goals, this can reduce the efficiency of each.[83] One solution is to provide extra staff resources dedicated to developmental needs such as youth workers in schools as widely used in Canada. Ultimately, given the intense pressures on schools to meet multiple goals, the most potent impact comes from changing the school culture.

Essentials for Success

Attending to social and emotional needs has been shown to advance both better behavior and academic achievement.[84] But traditional short-term interventions seldom are powerful enough to change either individual students or the school culture.[85] Instead, effective programs create a synergy of seemingly disparate goals. This means a dual emphasis on setting high expectations and meeting emotional needs.[86] Each is indispensable. A singular focus on accountability fails to tap the power of trusting bonds. But nurturing needs without setting expectations turns the indulgent adult into what Fritz Redl called *a friend without influence.*[87]

Herman McCall followed students transitioning from alternative school into regular education.[88] His research studied those who succeeded in alternative settings but later dropped out of mainstream schools. When these students failed, there were discrepant theories of blame. School officials typically attributed the cause to *poor parenting.* The main reason given by students themselves was *poor treatment.* Most did not believe any school staff really cared about them.

The prevailing practice of trying to return all alternative students to regular settings needs to be questioned if the regular school is unable to provide the academic and interpersonal support needed for success. McCall concluded that school personnel will need positive training if they are to be equipped to meet the needs of struggling and disruptive students. Such training would address key components such as these:

Turning problems into opportunities. Research shows that 90 percent of teachers do not feel competent to handle crisis or talk with children in times of conflict.[89] Staff need specific skills to disengage from conflict and connect with reluctant students.

Creating cultural safety. The fact that minority youth are over-represented in school discipline and disengagement provides a clue to action. This will require more than superficial tolerance training but transformational experiences to embrace the oneness of humankind.[90]

Creating respectful school climates. All kids benefit from positive cultures, but this is absolutely essential for vulnerable students. Without supportive peer and staff relationships, problems are exacerbated. Depressed kids become more desperate and the oppositional become more defiant.[91] The solution is to create climates of belonging where all students and staff join together in the pursuit of mastery.

When we are able to create a positive trusting environment, young people are free to develop their inherent greatness. We should assume that every young person has a hidden kernel of genius, even those who seem to be struggling. Resilience scientist Robert Brooks contends, "If there are oceans of inadequacy, there must be islands of competence—areas that have been or have potential to be sources of pride and accomplishment."[92] Perhaps this is best conveyed in the words of one student:

> *I was always afraid of messing up. When you make mistakes in school, they come down on you which is why I didn't participate. Here, teachers and peers help me if I make mistakes and teach me how to do it right. Nobody makes bad comments or calls me dumb. If I don't understand, the teacher will pull me aside and say, alright, if you try this, it will produce the right answer, instead of just telling me what I did wrong. My parents can see a difference in me. I think I carry myself in a successful "yes I'm worth it" way.*

Roots of Psychoeducation

Frank A. Fecser

We reject the notion that intelligence is a fixed attribute and maintain that intelligence can be taught. We see the human organism as far more flexible, far more responsive to opportunities to enhance capacity.[93]

Nicholas Hobbs

This is an exciting time in our field. Modern science is explaining the biology behind the education and treatment models developed by the founders of psychoeducation whose theories acknowledge the existence of the complex "inner child." Bruce Perry describes the crucial role of relationship in healing trauma and his Neurosequential Model measures treatment effectiveness through brain imaging.[94] Daniel Siegel, in his book *Mindsight,* says that the mind, brain, and relationships are not separate elements of life—they are aspects of one interconnected triangle of well-being.[95]

Contemporary research is affirming essential "truths" known for decades about emotional healing, learning, and growth. The constructs that underlie Life Space Crisis Intervention and Re-Education of Emotionally Disturbed Children (Re-ED) were developed by Fritz Redl and colleagues in the 1950s and 1960s. I would like to share some of Redl's observations regarding our approach to challenging children. We begin with his thoughts about the state of the profession penned in 1951:

> *All questions pertaining to techniques like punishment and rewards, praise or criticism, permission or verbot, indulgence or authority, encouragement or scolding, and the whole gamut of problems around the setting of limits, and what to do if they are trespassed, are still a "no-man's land" in which everybody can believe what he wants to, quite similar to the state of affairs in which our concept of body health, eating habits, etc. were about 100 years ago.*[96]

Despite a wealth of research on learning and behavior, walk into any two classrooms and you will find conflicting opinions and strategies about discipline, limit setting, rewards, and punishment.

We have benefited from the focus on evidence-based practices, but interventions are useful only if fully understood and properly implemented. While the screwdriver is designed to effectively remove screws, even this simple tool requires the user to hold it at the proper end. We can screw up the best of strategies if we do not know what we are doing. Further, as Bruce Perry tells us, it is not the approach that makes the big difference but the quality of the relationship.[97]

So what can guide us in choosing the new methods that are continually being proposed? We can draw on time-tested "truths" that have endured from the writings of the pioneers, such as Nicholas Hobbs and Fritz Redl, and are now being validated by current science.[98] Their practice wisdom is consistent with research on universal biosocial needs for attachment, achievement, autonomy, and altruism.

The most basic truth is that children absolutely require love and affection to learn and grow. Yet, in our daily encounters with youth who say and do hurtful things, we can become caught up in conflicts at a very personal level. At such times we suspend empathy and react by punishing the child's behavior. Again we turn to Redl's wisdom:

> The children must get plenty of love and affection whether they deserve
> it or not: they must be assured of the basic quota of happy, recreation-
> al experiences whether they seem to have it coming or not. In short,
> love and affection, as well as the granting of gratifying life situations,
> cannot be made the bargaining tools of educational or even therapeutic
> motivation, but must be kept tax-free as minimal parts of the young-
> sters' diet, irrespective of the problems of deservedness.[99]

If we opened the floor to debate on that statement, we might have a lively discussion, but that is not the point. Redl sets the standard against which we must measure any intervention. By way of analogy, consider a seed which contains all the necessary genetic blueprints to develop into the plant it is designed to become. Placed in decent soil, given adequate sunlight and water, the seed does what it is supposed to do—become a flourishing plant.

Sunlight and water are to the plant as love and affection are to the child. If our goal is to grow a strong and healthy plant, we would certainly not withhold sunlight and water. And if by chance the plant has been placed in poor soil, deprived of sunlight and water, and is now damaged as a result, we would not try to correct this by further depriving it of sunlight and water. Yet, this is exactly what happens in many schools and even supposedly "therapeutic" settings.

Emotionally hurt children re-enact their trauma and pull staff into their crises and conflict cycles. They are experts on how to suck us in. They may insult our body, hygiene, race, religion, or family—until they find that chink in our emotional armor. Even accomplished workers can be ensnared into shame or anger by adult-baiting youth! We have to consciously shift from our primitive, survival brain to our rational, executive brain to respond to the young person's need.

Perhaps Redl's most significant contribution to psychoeducation was to use crisis situations in the child's life space as teaching and learning opportunities. Life Space Crisis Intervention (LSCI) provides strategies to reclaim students displaying six common self-defeating behaviors.[100] Nicholas Long and Martin Brokenleg summarize how these reclaiming strategies are linked to Circle of Courage needs.[101]

1. **Limited skills:** Many youngsters want to do well but lack the tools for success. The goal is to teach specific coping abilities. These new tools can strengthen *belonging* and *mastery*.

2. **Imported problems:** Students carry in stress from outside school. The goal is to manage problems and provide relational support which fosters *mastery* and *belonging*.

3. **Errors in perception:** Distortions in thinking or perception can lead to maladaptive behavior. The goal is to help a youth clarify and understand reality. Clear thinking fosters *mastery*.

4. **Delinquent pride:** Some students purposely bully or exploit others without feeling remorse. The goal is to strengthen empathy and concern for others which fosters *generosity*.

5. **Impulsivity and guilt:** These youth feel appropriate guilt about problem behavior but may lack self-restraint and self-worth. Strengthening self-control fosters *independence*.

6. **Vulnerability to peer influence:** Some students are easily misled and manipulated by peers. Developing responsibility and decision making ability fosters *independence*.

We are challenged to work with and teach children who live in conditions of chronic toxic stress. Their constant state of hyper-arousal hijacks their intelligent brains as threat lurks around every corner. Imagine if you saw a person leaving a lecture and returning a few minutes later—you might notice this but it would not alter your state of arousal. But if the person returned with an assault weapon, your experience would be very different and you certainly would not be attending to the speaker! Instead, your amygdala would set off an alarm, flooding your body with adrenaline and cortisol to prepare you to escape danger. Only when you saw the "weapon" was really a toy would your parasympathetic nervous system begin to calm you down.

Children living in a world of continuous threat keep on guard, ready to react at the slightest perception of threat. In this state, their brains are not available for learning, and they misinterpret benign events as threats. As Daniel Siegel observes, we distort what we hear to fit what we fear.[102] Redl noted decades ago that troubled and traumatized children do not respond to simplistic behavior management methods. "On the contrary, administering constructive discipline is a more laborious task than is taking refuge in a few simple punitive tricks."[103] Fixating on surface behavior does nothing to help the young person examine inner struggles and form a new world view.

Advances in neuroscience have shed light on just how the brain retains traumatic memories. When a person experiences trauma, the memory of that event is stored in the limbic area—the seat of emotion—and in the right hemisphere. These are impressions, images, and sensory information. They have no access to language but are sensory, feelings-based memories. Without language to attach to memories, there is no way to "time stamp" them. Since the past cannot be separated from the present, the victim engages in re-enactments in self-defeating cycles.

Feelings of fear, distress, or anxiety are difficult to manage without language. This is a goal of Life Space Crisis Intervention—to help the child connect words to feelings and to gain insight into how events of the past continue to bring trouble. Our focus shifts from *What is wrong with you?* to understanding *What has happened to you?*[104] As we meet growth needs, we unleash their intelligence and talent. And this can occur only in a safe, trusting environment.

1. Condensed from Kagan, 1971, p. 54.
2. Kagan, 1971.
3. Maslow, 1943; White, 1959; McClelland & Atkinson, 2012.
4. Tagore, 1924, p. 703.
5. Ramon y Cajal, 1906.
6. Ramon y Cajal, 1901.
7. Ramon y Cajal, 1906.
8. Ford, cited in Andersen, 2013.
9. Sylwester, 2005, p. 87.
10. Legg & Hutter, 2007, p. 9.
11. Binet, 1909.
12. Burt, Jones, Miller, & Moodie, 1934, p. 28.
13. Jensen, 1969.
14. Herrnstein & Murray, 1994.
15. Nisbett et al., 2012.
16. Strenze, 2007.
17. Hart & Risley, 1995.
18. Adapted from Hart & Risley, 1995.
19. Hart & Risley research cited in Nisbett et al., 2012.
20. Turkheimer et al., 2012.
21. Nisbett et al., 2012.
22. Nisbett, 2004.
23. Flynn, 2012.
24. Sternberg, 1996.
25. Hebb, 1949.
26. Doidge, 2007, p. xvi.
27. Doidge, 2007.
28. Acharya, Shukla, Mahajan, & Diwan, 2010.
29. Gross, 2000.
30. Fields, 2011.
31. Coyle, 2009.
32. Coyle, 2009, p. 221.
33. Shenk, 2011.
34. Kandel, 2007.
35. Glasson-Walls, 2004.
36. Dewey, 1910.
37. Piaget, 1952, p. 395.
38. Descartes, 1637.
39. Zeigarnik, 1927.
40. Morgan, 1924, p. 10.
41. Gazzaniga, 2008.
42. Adler, 1930.
43. Brendtro & du Toit, 2005.
44. Crick & Dodge, 1994.
45. Csikszentmihalyi, Rathunde, & Whalen, 1993; Csikszentmihalyi & Larson, 1987.
46. Nichols, 1990.
47. VanderVen, 2009.
48. Csikszentmihalyi, 1990, 1996.
49. Dweck, 2006.
50. McPherson, Davidson, & Faulkner, 2012.
51. Nisbett, 2009.
52. Marzano & Pickering, 2011.
53. Wilson, 2014.
54. Wilson, 2014, p. 50.
55. Gold & Mann, 1984.
56. Gold & Osgood, 1992,
57. Hobbs cited in Newman, 2011, p. 28.
58. Addams, 1909.
59. Strother, 2007.
60. Groos, 1901.
61. Grey, 2013.
62. Louv, 2009.
63. Panksepp & Bivin, 2012.
64. Engel, 2009.
65. Bergen, 2006.
66. Panksepp & Bivin, 2012.
67. McGonigal, 2011.
68. Papert, 1980/1993.
69. Mitra et al., 2005.
70. Mitra, 2013.
71. Hobbs, cited in Newman, 2011, p. 26.
72. CDC, 2010.
73. McNeely, 2005.
74. Gold & Mann, 1984; Hobbs, 1982; Morse, 2009.
75. Bryk et al., 2010.
76. Juvonen, 2004.
77. Vygotsky, 1978.
78. Laughlin, Hatch, Silver, & Boh, 2006.
79. Johnson & Johnson, 2004.
80. Brown, Roderick, Lantieri, & Aber (2004).
81. Greenberg et al., 2003.
82. Schaps, Battistich, & Solomon, 2004.
83. Giles, 1975; Skogen, 2011.
84. Hawkins, Smith, & Catalano, 2004.
85. Wilson, Gottfredson, & Najaka, 2001.
86. Gold & Osgood, 1992.
87. Redl & Wineman, 1951.
88. McCall, 2003.
89. Dawson, 2002.
90. Longhurst & Brown, 2013.
91. Hyman & Snook, 2001.
92. Brooks, 2007, p. 11.
93. Hobbs, 1994, p. 267.
94. Perry, 2006.
95. Siegel, 2010.
96. Redl, cited in Garfat, 1987.
97. Perry & Szalavitz, 2011.
98. Hobbs, 1982; Redl & Wineman, 1957.
99. Redl & Wineman, 1957, p. 303.
100. Long, Fecser, & Brendtro, 1998.
101. Brokenleg & Long, 2013.
102. Siegel, 2010.
103. Redl, 1966, p. 254.
104. Bloom, 1997.

5

Autonomy and Power

*Ultimately, the only power to which man should aspire
is that which he exercises over himself.*[1]

Elie Wiesel

In every culture, people seek to control their own lives and influence others.[2] All major theories of personality attest to the importance of autonomy, which is defined as the natural need to exert personal power and resist unwanted influence or coercion.[3] Alfred Adler considered the will to power on a par with social interest as key motivators of human behavior.[4]

At a deep brain level, autonomy requires *self-regulation*, namely controls from within, which enable individuals to manage their own emotions and behavior.[5] As the higher thinking brain develops, children form beliefs about their *self-efficacy*, the ability to exert personal power and control over their environment. The need for autonomy is balanced by the need for belonging. When motives for power are not properly socialized, the result is unbridled aggression or a sense of helplessness.

From earliest childhood, children exert their fledgling power. Even as they struggle to manage their own motor behavior and emotions, they set out to control adults in their world. This is first seen in the negativism of the toddler who is resisting authority. Among peers, play becomes a proving ground for autonomy. Rough and tumble mock fighting is seldom violent as the young are just practicing their newly minted power.[6] Jaak Panksepp found that play is universal among young mammals and provides an avenue for building impulse control necessary for self-regulation.[7]

The quest for autonomy surges with the onset of adolescence as teens show a robust desire to do their own thing. Adolescence is by its very nature a prep course for independence. The Search Institute found that autonomy as measured by items like "I make my own decisions" increases more than any other value in early adolescence. Another goal that gains prominence during this period is "to do something important with my life." Young people want to make a difference in the world.[8]

Humans have an inbuilt motivation to exert power. The lower brain offers a quick and simple answer—dominate or submit. Whenever animals encounter a stressful social situation, primitive power programs kick in. The amygdala instantly reads nonverbal cues to determine whether dominance or submission is the best option. As they mature, children use social cues to provide more information about their status in the group, such as pride, shame, and friendliness.[9] The most harmonious groups and societies are those that respect the right to autonomy for all members.

The Will to Power

For a boy with bullying tendencies, the potential whipping boy is an ideal target. His anxiousness, defenselessness, and crying give the bully a marked feeling of superiority and supremacy, also a sort of satisfaction of vague revengeful impulses.[10]

Dan Olweus

In his book *Somebodies and Nobodies*, former college president Robert Fuller described his experience tutoring school dropouts in math. These young people believed they were nobodies in schools that devalued their importance. He found he could teach them math only when he engaged them as somebodies. All of us have had experiences of being treated as nobodies, and we resent it. Fuller coined the term *rankism* to describe this generic misuse of power.[11]

Rankism is at the core of all *isms*. Racism, sexism, ageism, and all such pseudo superiority mindsets are rankism. Whenever we treat another as less than our social equal, we show rankism. There is nothing wrong with high rank based on merit. We want our doctors and teachers, sports teams, and orchestras to possess high talent. The problem is when rank is used to hurt rather than to help and serve.

Rankism among peers is prominent in the form of bullying. The world's most renowned researcher on this problem is Dan Olweus of Norway, who has spent a career trying to change the bullying culture of schools. This proves particularly difficult when schools are run on hierarchical instead of democratic values.[12] Classic research by Kurt Lewin showed that when adults operated with authoritarian leadership, bullying increased among children.[13] Being the victim of chronic bullying fosters feelings of helplessness and actually lowers IQ scores.[14]

Researchers distinguish between reactive and proactive aggression. The first is an emotionally charged defense against perceived threat. The second includes unprovoked, pre-meditated aggression to achieve personal gain or status.[15] Reactive aggression results when amygdala alarm triggers the defensive right brain. Proactive aggression entails calculated actions using the logic and approach circuits of the left brain. It has long been known that reactive aggression in children is the result of rejection and relational trauma.[16]

Another strain of reactive aggression is fueled by cultures or communities where a real or imagined sense of danger is met with a "don't tread on me" mentality. Fighting to defend one's reputation against any sign of disrespect is a norm in some "cultures of honor."[17] Many of our students from the streets of Detroit have hair-trigger reactions to being dissed. In contrast, the forgiveness shown by an Amish community when an outsider massacred their children demonstrates the ability of moral values to reign in violence.[18]

Neuroscientist Shelley Taylor has shown that males when threatened are more primed to react with fight reactions while women are inclined to seek safety in attachments.[19] Yet the default program of the human brain is to seek out trusting relationships which she calls the "tend and befriend" instincts. This has been the basis of human survival.

Researchers argue whether social bonding or self-control is foremost in the prevention of antisocial behavior. In fact, social bonding is the primary brain program for developing self-control. Restorative interventions provide a direct means to rebuild social bonds and thus strengthen self-control. However, many punitive practices in schools and the justice system further disrupt social bonds and render these as weak interventions.[20]

Terms like aggression or violence lack precision but lump together a wide range of fight behaviors. Acts of aggression can range from self-defense to predatory behavior, from hate-filled revenge to impulsive rage, from protecting my homeland to invading yours. Fritz Redl described four key reasons youth learn to show defiance, all related to failures to meet developmental needs.[21]

> *Unloved.* The child who has been rejected or violated fights adults and has no reason to identify with authority.
>
> *Impulsive.* The child who lacks self-regulation cannot cope with challenges but gets stuck in self-defeating behavior.
>
> *Rebellious.* The youth frustrated in meeting needs for independence asserts power by fighting external controls.
>
> *Self-centered.* The young person showing little empathy silences the voice of conscience with distortions in thinking.

Self-centered youth present the most serious problems because they evoke hostility rather than empathy, thus rupturing relationships they desperately need.

Self-Regulation

Most powerful is he who has himself in his own power.

Marcus Annaeus Seneca (54 BC-34 AD)

Shortfalls in self-regulation underlie personal and societal ills including violence, health problems, school failure, and self-defeating behavior. "In contrast, effective self-regulation allows individuals and cultures to thrive by promoting moral, disciplined, and virtuous behaviors."[22] However, it takes over twenty years of cultural immersion and brain maturation to create responsible and autonomous adults.

At birth, children are largely ruled by their emotional impulses, and will-power requires developing higher brain processes. Decades ago, Walter Mischel and colleagues devised the simple marshmallow test to measure children's ability for self-control.[23] Basically, preschoolers were given the choice of having one treat now or waiting to have two treats some minutes later. Follow-up studies showed that kids who delayed gratification were better able to manage stress as teens and scored higher on SAT college entrance examinations. Thus, self-control came to be described as a *trait* more potent than IQ.

Mischel and colleagues explained the marshmallow difference in simple metaphor called the *hot* and *cool* brain systems. The hot system is an impulsive *go* action program while the cool system is a *know* thinking program.[24] The hot system enables quick, instant, simple emotional reactions useful for survival including fight and flight as well as pleasurable approach behaviors. This system rules early in life and is automatic and reflexive unless interrupted by the cool system for effortful control. The cool system is slow, thoughtful, and more emotionally neutral. With learning, brain maturation, and manageable levels of stress, the cool system enables rational decision making.

Certainly, children have difficulty delaying gratification, and there are inborn differences in impulsivity. However, more recent research suggests that children who decide "I want it now" may be making a rational decision.[25] Experimenters exposed small children to two kinds of adults—those who were reliable and followed through on promises and those who were unpredictable and broke promises. Then they replicated the marshmallow test where children had to wait fifteen minutes for an extra treat. Most of the children who had been with a reliable adult waited the full fifteen minutes. But only one of fourteen children with an unreliable adult held out for that long. This dramatic difference suggests that children who cannot delay gratification may in their own way be coping with a world which has taught them to grab what you can when you can get it. It takes trustworthy adults to enable children to learn self-control.

In group settings, self-regulation may be highjacked by the power of the crowd.[26] College students playing the role of guards in the Stanford Prison experiment began blindly acting with brutal violence toward their subservient "prisoners."[27] When adolescents are being observed by peers, they are more likely to engage in risky behavior; whether gambling or driving a car, they compromise their self-control to impress their companions.[28] In violent schools, neighborhoods, and correctional settings, many youth view belligerent behavior as a badge of honor.[29] In such environments, both adults and youth present a front of toughness for fear they will be seen as vulnerable. Changing these group climates requires bursting the myth of badness to draw out internal strengths in all youth.

Brain science debunks the notion that adolescence is a hormone-swirling tempest. Instead, the adolescent brain is actively charting a course to maturity. Teens are preparing for independence by connecting deeply with others beyond their family. And, by experimenting and taking risks, they are learning to exert power and deal with new challenges.[30] Risk taking is pervasive in adolescence, but not because youth are incapable of rational decisions. Rather, in emotionally-charged situations, their novelty-seeking brain overpowers logical controls.[31] Most youth prefer to be prosocial, but the desire to please peers and the absence of a mature executive brain to rein in emotions make them vulnerable to risky behavior.[32]

Teens may act in reckless ways, but contrary to popular belief, this is not because they believe they are invulnerable.[33] In fact, they over-estimate the odds of bad outcomes like contracting venereal disease or dying in an auto accident—but this calculation does not lead to safe sex or safe driving. Researchers scanned teen brains while asking such questions as: *Would you drink a bottle of Drano? How about setting your hair on fire?* Adolescents take twice as long as adults to come up with the answer! They get sidetracked weighing options in their newly-minted rational brain while completely losing the big picture.[34]

Teens are *smart* but not yet *wise*. Logical reasoning is not the best way to make quick moral decisions which is why fact dispensing, risk prevention programs often fail.[35] Until the executive brain is fully myelinated, teens find it difficult to manage emotional impulses. Mature adults draw on intuitive wisdom as their fully insulated brain circuits respond instantly.[36] It takes life experience and deeply internalized values to give young people an effective moral compass.[37]

The executive brain's job is "self-regulation to achieve goals,"[38] which includes managing emotions, maintaining attention, and planning ahead. A key executive brain task is *working memory*, which is the ability to temporarily juggle three kinds of information: visualization (inner eye), language (inner ear), and long-term memories already stored.[39] Short term working memory is crucial in self-regulation, learning, and problem solving. As children develop independence, their behavior is increasingly governed by:

future orientation more than immediate gratification,

self-regulation more than control by others,

cooperation more than solitary actions, and

prosocial values more than self-centered existence.

Self-Efficacy

> With the same set of skills, people may perform poorly, adequately,
> or extraordinarily depending upon their self-beliefs of efficacy.[40]

Albert Bandura

While animals can be conditioned into dominance or submission, the higher brain of humans develops a sense of self. This profoundly affects the appraisal of one's personal power. This is called self-efficacy and is grounded in decades of research by Albert Bandura and colleagues.[41] Self-efficacy is a person's sense of one's own capabilities, strength, or power to achieve desired goals. It is not just our actual ability but our beliefs about our ability that count.

Deeply embedded memories of success or failure prepare us to attack and surmount problems or to retreat in learned helplessness. "Those who believe they cannot manage potential threats experience high levels of stress. They judge themselves as highly vulnerable and view many aspects of their environment as fraught with danger."[42] This conditioned fear of failure overwhelms the ability to cope. In its most extreme form, helplessness in the face of a terrifying life event is the core of trauma.[43]

When children have little opportunity to exercise personal power, they show *learned helplessness* and experience deep feelings of inferiority and inadequacy.[44] They have little confidence that they can improve their lives or impact the world. Such persons have been falsely trained to believe that they have no power to control their environment. For example, they might resign themselves to accept abuse rather than take action to change their life circumstances. Over time, a temporary *state* of submission can turn into a pervasive *trait*.

Helplessness is often associated with pessimistic thinking, depression, and hopelessness. Children's private logic about the world is more powerful than reality. How one *interprets* events shapes self-concept, academic performance, and life goals.[45] In fact, holding somewhat inflated notions of one's abilities seems to contribute to healthy development and adjustment. Thus, an antidote to learned helplessness is learned optimism, a characteristic of resilience.[46]

Successful coping entails managing internal emotions, as well as physical and psychological arousal that signals some challenge or difficulty. *Danger* produces distress (negative stress), activating painful emotions like fear and shame.

Opportunity produces eustress (positive stress), activating pleasurable emotions like curiosity and excitement. The same stressful situation can be interpreted differently by various individuals. One person's threat is another person's thrill. Whether or not a challenging situation poses a threat depends on one's coping strengths, past experiences, and state of mind and emotion. Humans can handle extreme stress when supported by others.

Bandura describes various ways to build self-efficacy.[47] Children need mastery experiences. This does not mean quick success but the courage to fail and rebound from setbacks. They need models for resilience. Seeing persons similar to oneself succeed through effort raises beliefs about one's own efficacy. Young people also need encouragement and expectations that call forth their potentials for self-responsibility. Finally, they need opportunities for success—as well as protection from experiences likely to lead to repeated failures. Studies show that when teachers strengthen self-efficacy, students make gains equivalent of moving from the fiftieth to the seventieth percentile.[48]

With social support and brain maturation, most youth display considerable autonomy by about seventeen years of age.[49] They are confident and able to assert themselves and resist negative influence. They have perspective about the long-term effects of their actions on themselves and on others. With controls from within, they manage impulsivity and regulate their emotions. These young people are able to make responsible decisions to achieve important life goals.

Self-efficacy is a linchpin to responsibility. But this requires exercising power with concern for needs of others. We turn to examples of what happens when power has gone awry, and strategies to replace coercive discipline with self-discipline.

Self-Discipline

Responsibility is the first step in responsibility.[50]

W.E.B. DuBois

Prevailing philosophies of education and childrearing evolved across thousands of years of autocratic cultures. A vestige of this past is the belief that children learn mainly by external application of rewards and punishments. But research shows that discipline by obedience training blocks the development of self-responsibility. Imposed goals, high-stakes testing, evaluation, sanctions, and surveillance all undermine intrinsic motivation.[51] Of course, external controls are essential until children learn to regulate themselves.

The word punishment comes from the Latin *poena*, which means pain. Punishment literally administers pain as a consequence for pain-based behavior of kids in conflict. It works best with well-adjusted youngsters who need it least.

But it backfires wildly with defiant and traumatized children and youth, sparking explosive emotions and shattering fragile bonds with adults. Fortunately, a range of strength-based strategies are available to improve self-control.

Rethinking Discipline

There are three main types of discipline according to Martin Hoffman: power assertion, love withdrawal, and inductive discipline.[52] Excessive use of power assertion can impede the child's development of *autonomy and independence*, while love withdrawal is a direct assault on *attachment and belonging*. Inductive discipline relies on reasoning to control or change behavior, in particular recognizing how actions hurt oneself or others. This is the foundation for building individual responsibility and empathy for others.

Ramon Lewis of Melbourne, Australia, has studied behavior discipline practices in secondary schools worldwide.[53] While nearly all teachers want to avoid becoming punitive, they are easily drawn into conflict with their most difficult students. Attempts to quell behavior can lead to yelling at students, sarcasm, and even losing one's temper. Such strategies are counterproductive, causing students to behave in less responsible ways.

Although teachers have genuine regard for students and want to help them, their natural tendency is toward tit for tat, mirroring the antagonism of students. Afterwards, most regret their inability to respond in ways consistent with their values of concern. Lewis identified three theories of why well-intentioned authority figures are unwittingly drawn into punitive interactions. As adults gain new skills and mindsets, these conflicts can be eliminated.[54]

> *Attribution Theory.* Assigning negative qualities to the student justifies harsh methods: *He is just being a jerk.* When adults learn to see serious problems as pain-based behavior, they develop empathy and are better able to connect with these students.[55]
>
> *Efficacy Theory.* The adult feels stressed and reacts to a sense of helplessness in dealing with challenging behavior: *I am at my wit's end with her.* Rather than struggling for power with students, the adult needs training in disengaging from conflict cycles.[56]
>
> *Attachment Theory.* Without a positive bond, relationships become adversarial: *I just can't stand that kid.* In order to build a respectful alliance, adults need specific strategies to connect with angry, avoidant, or manipulative students.[57]

Instead of assuming there is some deficiency in the student, the focus is on building strengths and responsibility.

Self-discipline predicts positive outcomes in school and life.[58] However, there are natural variances in children's self-control. Jerome Kagan of Harvard has identified two types of temperament which impact self-regulation.[59] Children as young as four months were exposed to a novel experience such as a clown face. Low reactive children show little distress but seek out novelty. High reactive children are upset by strange stimuli. These are not pathologies but normal variations; humans would not have survived if everybody were either bold and reckless or timid and cautious. But these children require child-rearing methods attuned to their temperament.

Bold Temperament. Some youngsters are naturally fearless and impulsive. The amygdala is less reactive so they are not as easily controlled by punishment, shame, or guilt. Without positive guidance, they are vulnerable to developing problem behavior. However, with love and limits, they thrive and can become confident leaders.

Timid Temperament. Other children are by nature more cautious. The amygdala is very reactive, and they are more easily controlled by fear, shame, or power assertion. Without encouragement, they may be fearful and avoid challenges. Yet, with supportive parenting, they become confident and conscientious persons.

Children thrive when there is a "goodness of fit" between their temperament and the response of adults.[60] For example, a child with a reactive temperament has a good fit with a calm caregiver but will become highly reactive with over-stressed or easily irritated adults.[61] Attuned child rearing strengthens resilience.

From Coercion to Calm

Lags in self-regulation are at the core of many childhood behavior problems. This includes children with ADHD, autism, and relational trauma.[62] Underlying difficulties in self-regulation can be masked by a jumble of challenging behaviors, including anxiety, depression, irritability, impulsiveness, and difficulty managing aggression.[63] Medications may suppress symptoms but do not develop the brain-based self-regulation circuits needed for healing and growth. This will require relationships with adults who can connect with these children and help them calm turbulent emotions. Until youngsters develop self-control, they need to borrow the adult's calm brain.[64]

Infants and young children use adults to help them regulate their emotions. When upset, the tending instinct is activated and the adult soothes and speaks in a calm manner until the child's brain mirrors this tranquil state.[65] Thousands of such interactions create deep brain learning as children become able to calm themselves. But without secure attachment, problems with self-regulation can continue into later years. An oppositional teen is unlikely to trigger the tending instinct in adults who typically react by *coercion* to control behavior. In order to foster self-regulation, adults need skills at *co-regulation* as shown in the accompanying table.[66]

Table 1. Co-Regulation vs. Coercive Regulation

Co-Regulation	Coercive Regulation
Goal: Help the child to calm	Goal: Stop bad behavior
Soothing and assertive tone	Loud and aggressive tone
Deflect the child's outburst	Retaliate to the child's outburst
Attune to the child's needs	Ignore the child's needs
Focus on the child's feelings	Focus on the child's behavior
Adult is aware of own feelings	Adult is oblivious to own feelings

Co-regulation requires that adults manage this emotional intensity with self-control rather than mirroring the child's hostility and threats.

Throughout life, humans have two adaptive ways to respond to extreme stress and trauma. We can reach out to trusted persons for support. Or we can turn inward, calm ourselves, and reflect on how best to understand and direct our lives. In the aftermath of the twin tower disaster in New York City, Linda Lantieri and Daniel Goleman developed strategies for teaching children mindfulness to strengthen their inner resilience.[67] The value of quiet reflection is well known in many faith traditions; St. Augustine (354-430 AD) coined the word soliloquy, which means talking to yourself at a deep level.[68] Research indicates that mindfulness and meditation can help persons become agents in charge of their destiny rather than helpless victims.[69]

The Power of Peers

Superficial rituals of youth empowerment will be seen for what they are and will fail to enlist youth in a partnership with adults in authority.[70]

Beate Kreisle

Ironically, as children gain increasing independence from adults, they can become more vulnerable to peer influence. In *Confessions*, Saint Augustine tells of how he and his wild boyhood peers plunged headlong into delinquency and then bragged about who was more beastly.[71] How do we help youth develop self-discipline when groups wield such power to override individual self-will?

Sociologist Joan McCord described the process of "peer deviancy training" whereby some young people embolden one another's antisocial inclinations.[72] In group settings, youth receive nine times more reinforcement from peers than from adults.[73] But peer influence can be turned to prosocial goals. Positive Peer Culture (PPC) is an evidence-based approach for building respectful group climates in residential, school, and community settings.[74]

PPC is designed to enlist youth in problem solving to learn responsible thinking, values, and behavior.[75] For example, Gunther Opp and colleagues implemented PPC in German schools for students with behavioral and learning problems.[76] Young people are seen as genuine experts on their own lives and are enlisted in a peer helping process. As they resolve problems, they develop emotional regulation and prosocial behavior.

Extensive research on peer influence was conducted by Martin Gold and D. Wayne Osgood of the University of Michigan.[77] They studied court-referred youth in forty-five PPC groups in four Michigan residential facilities.[78] A particularly powerful finding was how crucial it is for young people to develop a sense of *autonomy*. This does not mean turning decision making over to youth but treating them with respect. Adults were not permissive but set high expectations for responsibility—in PPC terms, *demanding greatness instead of obedience*.[79]

The Michigan study showed that groups with greater autonomy became more prosocial than those with high staff control. Further, students in groups with greater autonomy developed closer attachment to adults. The most effective staff were those who could simultaneously set high standards for behavior and respond to students' needs.

The way staff handle their groups affects the young person's behavior more than the other way around. Young people were given more responsibility by staff teams with high morale. Staff morale was a composite of four variables: team cohesion, team involvement, belief in program, and beliefs about youth's potential for reform. A cohesive team of staff who believed in the potential for positive growth in youth conveyed these capacities to youth groups. There was almost a direct correlation (R=.89) between positive staff cultures and the autonomy they report giving to youth.[80]

Autonomy is best developed within a structure that sets high expectations for responsibility, defined by the core value that youth must care for one another. This is not a process of peer pressure but peer concern. Joan McCord's interest in peer deviancy training led to her participation in a focus group with students involved in a Positive Peer Culture program. This excerpt from that dialogue captures the goal of empowering youth for responsibility.[81]

> *Dr. McCord:* So many teenagers that I talk with say groups are harmful. They make me misbehave, I show off to them, that sort of thing. It is clear that you people are all saying being in a group is something that is helping you. Helping you figure out how to change your life, how to do something with it. I am trying to understand how that got started.

Youth: You were saying that groups are tough and that people are being hurtful. I see two things. If there is a lack of respect in group settings, that plays a part. I also think that if you have a good mindset, you will be more prone to respect somebody. If you don't have a very good mindset, you will be more apt to show disrespect.

Youth: There are a lot of challenges if people are disrespectful. But we are going to be faced with all of these things in the world; so if you can overcome them here, then when you go back into the community, it is a lot easier to overcome them there. I am thankful that this program is hard, because I feel it has made me a better person.

Pathways to Responsibility

Tom Tate, Randy Copas, & Beate Kreisle

Developing a climate of responsibility and self-discipline requires practical strategies to empower youth as partners with adults.

The early twentieth century was marked by widespread enthusiasm to replace coercive discipline with democratic approaches. By the 1920s, reformers like August Aichhorn in Austria and Clara Liepmann of Germany demonstrated that even "wayward youth" could become responsible citizens.[82] These pioneers noted that traditional punitive discipline had totally failed. Since antisocial behavior is a lack of inner will power, only self-discipline will make lasting change.

Pathways to Empowerment

The roots of reform in education and youth work can be traced to the nineteenth century.[83] Johann Jakob Wehrli (1790-1855) created schools for children living on the streets of Swiss cities. Learning and work were intertwined to teach them to live in a community. Initially, students brought the streets into the school, displaying bullying and rowdy behavior. Wehrli's solution was a council of self-governance with older students serving as positive role models. These youth mentors became deeply invested in guiding their younger peers.

The Boston House of Reformation was directed by Reverend E. M. P. Wells (1793-1878), who strongly believed no child was inherently bad, no matter how badly he or she behaved. A level system gave students feedback on their progress. Students would only lose a level if they failed to admit their wrongdoing. Every evening, students shared with peers on how to develop responsibility.

In Germany, Johann Hinrich Wichern (1808-1881) directed the Rauhe Haus where boys and girls up to the age of 14 lived together like families. Elected peer leaders called *Friedenskinder* (peace children) were given the task of instilling positive behavior within the group. Every four weeks, a new election was held so that many youngsters had the opportunity to practice positive leadership.

By the 1920s, Clara Liepmann was able to document a rich tapestry of self-governance systems across the United States and Europe. Each of these remarkable programs seemed to depend on the dynamic leadership of a committed and charismatic founder. However, when the founder departed, entropy soon set in and programs became routine, rigid, and coercive. Without a solid, value-based science of youth development and training models to give staff practical tools for success, the most magnificent efforts morph into the mundane.

Effective approaches require deep respect between adults and young people. This is surprisingly rare in societies tethered to longstanding traditions of *adultism*. This overlooked "ism" dates to an article by Jack Flasher in the journal *Adolescence*.[84] It is defined as abuse of the power that adults have over the young. Adultism is common not only among parents but also teachers, therapists, police, judges, and juries. The implicit assumption is that adults are superior and entitled to wield authority without regard to the voice of youth. Adultism impedes positive development by depriving youth of opportunities to develop responsibility and make meaningful contributions.

When young people defy the authority of adults, it is very difficult to see their positive potential. Here are three different ways that adults view challenging youth:

> *Victims.* A youth's behavior is seen as a symptom of underlying deficit, disturbance, or disorder. This justifies adult-imposed interventions or medications.

> *Villains.* The youth is seen as a threat to the community leading to interventions such as suspension and expulsion from school and incarceration in the justice system.

> *Contributors.* The youth is seen as a valuable resource possessing talents and capable of social responsibility. The goal is to develop strengths and self-discipline.

Partners in Empowerment

Genuine democracy is the antithesis of adultism since it calls for treating young people as *social equals*. This profoundly egalitarian concept was articulated by Austrian-American psychologist Rudolf Dreikurs (1897-1972), an early associate of Alfred Adler.

> *Youngsters looking for guidance and help find few adults who treat them as equals.... The more they need help and guidance, the more they are pushed around, punished, discriminated against, and made to feel worthless.*[85]

In spite of rhetoric about empowering youth, most adults lack specific methods for this purpose. While traditional authoritarian discipline keeps children subservient, permissive approaches lead to freedom without accountability. What is needed instead are new tools for building responsibility in young people. Here are some practical strategies which have been employed to enlist youth in positive peer leadership roles in schools and youth programs.[86]

Strengthening Social Interest

This principle is the cornerstone of Alfred Adler's classic book on positive discipline, *The Problem Child*.[87] Unfortunately, *social interest* is a neutered English translation of Adler's powerful German word, *Gemeinschaftgefühl*, which is more accurately interpreted as "the feeling of belonging to a community." Members of a community (*Gemeinschaft*) are bound together by trust and feel a shared responsibility and concern for one another.

Modern society provides few opportunities for young people to develop their natural potential for caring behavior. One cannot build a positive youth culture unless adults themselves model positive concern, *particularly in times when it is necessary to exercise authority*. Character is not constructed from a list of rules and consequences. Instead, core values of caring are continually reinforced. Youth internalize the ethos that no one has the right to hurt another, and all are responsible for helping.

Relabeling

Adult modeling alone is seldom powerful enough to instill prosocial values in the face of negative peer influence. Research shows that antisocial values are actively applauded in subcultures of disconnected youth. For example, some youth have invented the term *drama* as a euphemism for bullying. A strategy to reverse this thinking is the *relabeling* of behavior; the goal is to make caring fashionable and hurting highly unattractive.

At the onset, youth may cast their problem behavior as cool, sophisticated, and mature. Aggression, drug use, and the ability to manipulate and dominate others are misconstrued as measures of strength and maturity. On the other hand, showing concern and sensitivity are seen as signs of weakness among youth preoccupied with mutual displays of toughness. This can lead to *negative peer contagion* as youth reinforce one another in rule-breaking behavior.[88]

Specific techniques are available to transform peer deviance into peer helping.[89] Relabeling is an essential tool in this process. Simply, all hurtful behavior is reframed in pejorative terms while helping behavior is made admirable. For example, if youth are romanticizing violent acts (peer deviance training), then such behavior might be relabeled as "temper tantrums" or "acting like a hothead." In contrast, helping behavior (e.g., standing up for a bullied peer) can be described as strong, mature, and courageous. This relabeling produces a state of dissonance which motivates youth to cast hurting behavior in a negative light and embrace prosocial behavior.[90]

Reversing Responsibility

This is another important verbal strategy designed to build social concern and personal accountability. Youth (like their elders) often adopt thinking biases which allow them to avoid taking responsibility for their behavior. These rationalizations and distortions silence the conscience in order to justify behavior that hurts others.[91]

Like their elders, young people develop a raft of excuses to dodge responsibility for their actions. Attempts to *directly correct* these thinking errors are likely to be resisted. A more useful strategy is to *create dissonance* by posing a question to the person or group. For example, a teen may try to displace responsibility for drug abuse: "Well, what do you expect? My parents are alcoholics." The reversal of responsibility might be a simple rhetorical question: "Is Marie saying that all kids with alcoholic parents abuse drugs?" The goal is not to get into a tit-for-tat argument but simply to shift responsibility back to young people.

The Indirect Approach

Adultism presumes that the person in authority must exercise control over children and youth. For example, if there is bullying behavior, most adults would take a *direct approach* and confront the offender. This only reinforces the notion that positive behavior is the responsibility of the adult, not of young people. In peer helping programs, adults use an *indirect approach* to enlist youth in problem solving: "What does the group think about a stronger member picking on a weaker individual?" This builds a sense of group responsibility rather than just sanctioning the individual. However, this method only works if the group sees its role as helping rather than blaming members.

Addressing problems indirectly serves several purposes. First, the adult neither ignores nor overreacts to problems but conveys that these can be resolved without imposing punishment. Second, the indirect approach reinforces the principle that the group is responsible for helping one another. Third, the adult demonstrates faith in the ability of young people to solve problems and support one another.

Encouragement Replaces Praise

A staple of behavior modification is to praise children for their positive or compliant behavior. But praise may fuel adultism since it can be dispensed or withheld by the person in power. It also sends a message that the goal of behavior is to please the powerful adult. Rudolf Dreikurs proposed the alternative of encouragement, which by definition builds courage in youth.[92] Here is a comparison of each:

Praise: I was very pleased to see how well you did.

Encouragement: You must be proud of what you achieved.

Developmental psychologist Mary Wood notes that children until about age eight are largely oriented around pleasing adults who are the center of their social universe.[93] After that, kids realize that adults cannot really run the world, and they become ever more aware of their own growing power and the increasing influence of peers. Instead of fighting this transition toward maturity, adults should steer the development of growing independence.

Enlist Rather than Insist

Building positive peer cultures requires a partnership with youth instead of imposing adult authority. This mindset only makes sense to those who believe in the greatness of young people. This is the paradigm shift of democratic approaches to youth: Adults treat young people as social equals, not as inferiors. Problems present opportunities for growth, not punishment. Building responsibility makes imposing obedience unnecessary. Helping others creates community, hurting goes out of style.

Positive adult-to-youth relationships form the foundation of a culture of self-governance. But the lesson of history is that democratic ideals in education and youth work can easily default to adultism. Building positive youth cultures requires both inspired leadership and practical strategies to enlist youth partners in empowerment.[94] In the final analysis, only adults who believe in the greatness of youth can help them unleash their awesome potential.

1. Wiesel, cited in Johnson, 2006, p. 88.
2. Brown, 1991.
3. Murray, 1938
4. Adler, 1930.
5. Redl & Wineman, 1952.
6. Konner, 2002.
7. Panksepp & Bivin, 2012.
8. Benson, Williams, & Johnson 1987.
9. Givens, 2008.
10. Olweus, 1993, p. 142.
11. Fuller, 2003.
12. Juvonen & Graham, 2013.
13. Lewin, Lippitt, & White, 1939.
14. Kira et al., 2014.
15. Mullin & Hinshaw, 2007.
16. Jenkins, 1954.
17. Nisbett & Cohen, 1996.
18. Kraybill, Nolt, & Weaver-Zercher, 2007.
19. Taylor, 2003.
20. Mitchell & McKenzie, 2006.
21. Redl, 1966.
22. Bauer & Baumeister, 2011, p. 64.
23. Mischel, Ebbesen, & Raskoff-Zeiss, 1972.
24. Metcalfe & Mischel, 1999; Mischel & Ayduk, 2011.
25. Kidd, Palmeri, & Aslin, 2013.
26. Le Bon, 1896.
27. Zimbardo, 2007.
28. Smith, Chien, & Steinberg, 2014.
29. Athens, 1992.
30. Siegel, 2013.
31. Casey, Jones, & Sommerville, 2011.
32. Gardner & Steinberg, 2005.
33. Reyna & Farley, 2006.
34. Reyna & Farley, 2006.
35. Kahneman, 2011.
36. Coyle, 2009.
37. Gibbs, 2014.
38. Barkley, 2012, p. 60.
39. Baddeley, 2002.
40. Bandura, 1990, p. 315.
41. Bandura, 1994.
42. Bandura, 1990, p. 318.
43. van der Kolk, McFarlane, & Weisaeth, 2007.
44. Peterson, Maier, & Seligman, 1993.
45. Sternberg & Kolligan, 1990.
46. Seligman, 2006.
47. Bandura, 1990.
48. Tileston, 2006.
49. Steinberg & Cauffman, 1996.
50. DuBois, 1909, p. 235.
51. Kohn, 2006.
52. Hoffman, 2000.
53. Lewis, 2009.
54. Lewis, 2009.
55. Anglin, 2014.
56. Long, Fecser, Morse, Newman, & Long, 2014.
57. Brendtro & du Toit, 2005.
58. Duckworth & Seligman, 2005.
59. Kagan, 2010.
60. Chess & Thomas, 1999.
61. Kagan, 2010.
62. Schore, 2012.
63. Bloom & Farragher, 2011, p. 108.
64. Bath, 2015.
65. Taylor, 2002.
66. Bath, 2015.
67. Lantieri & Goleman, 2014.
68. Vandenberghe & Costa Prado, 2009.
69. Siegel, 2010.
70. Kreisle, 2010, p. 15.
71. Augustine, 397 A.D.
72. Dishion, McCord, & Poulin, 1999.
73. Buehler, Patterson, & Furness, 1966.
74. James, 2011.
75. Brendtro, Mitchell, McCall, 2007. Gibbs, 2013.
76. Opp & Unger, 2006; Opp, Unger, & Teichmann, 2007.
77. Gold & Osgood, 1992.
78. This included two state correctional schools and two private residential treatment centers, including Starr Commonwealth.
79. Vorrath & Brendtro, 1985.
80. Gold & Osgood, 1992.
81. Longhurst & McCord, 2007, p. 198.
82. Aichhorn, 1925; Liepmann, 1928.
83. Liepmann, 1928.
84. Flasher, 1978.
85. Dreikurs, 1971, pp. 100-101.
86. Tate, Copas, & Wasmund, 2012; Vorrath & Brendtro, 1985.
87. Adler, 1930.
88. Dodge, Dishion, & Lansford, 2007.
89. Brendtro, Mitchell, & McCall, 2007; Longhurst & McCord, 2007; Osgood & Briddell, 2006.
90. Vorrath & Brendtro, 1985.
91. Fiske, 2004.
92. Dreikurs, 1971.
93. Wood, Davis, Swindle, & Quirk, 1995.
94. Kreisle, 2008.

6

Altruism and Purpose

I do not ask whether my wounded brother suffers.
I will myself be this wounded brother.[1]

Walt Whitman

The term altruism was coined by French sociologist August Comte (1798-1857) from the Latin *alter* meaning other. He believed humans have a moral obligation to live for others by helping to relieve distress and to promote happiness.[2] Genuine altruism benefits another person without an expectation of reward, while pseudo altruism is self-serving.[3]

Empathy is the foundation of moral development and prosocial behavior.[4] The original word began in the German language as *Einfuhlung,* which is literally translated as *feeling into.* Empathy taps the ability of mirror neurons to display in our own brain the emotions, thoughts, and motives of another. Empathy allows us to share another's joy and pain and motivates care and concern.

Psychologists are now deeply invested in studying virtue, which has long been the domain of philosophers and poets.[5] "There is a vast empirical literature indicating that empathy facilitates altruistic, helping behavior; that it fosters warm close personal relationships; and that it inhibits personal aggression."[6] This most basic human quality ensures our well-being and survival.

Moral Minds

If I am not for myself, who will be?
But if I am only for myself, what good am I?[7]

Hillel the Elder (circa 30 BCE)

Humans have *moral minds*, say researchers in anthropology, psychology, and neuroscience. In 1873, Charles Darwin wrote that "groups with a greater number of courageous sympathetic and faithful members who were always ready to warn each other of danger, to aid and defend each other... would spread and be victorious over other tribes."[8] First, *Nature* builds a universal sense of right or wrong in the human genome. Then, *Nurture* develops—or warps—this natural capacity for virtue.[9]

Justice and Caring

The brain's primary moral scripts are *be fair* and *care for others*. Carol Gilligan[10] calls these principles *justice* and *caring*. Justice demands fairness, that all have equal access to liberties. Caring calls for sharing to help those in need.[11] At the core of both of these principles is empathy. Humans innately are disposed to treat others the way they want to be treated. This is the Golden Rule, which is universal:

> *Buddhism:* Hurt not others in ways that you yourself would find hurtful.

> *Christianity:* Do unto others as you would have them do unto you.

> *Confucianism:* What you do not wish for yourself, do not do to others.

> *Hinduism:* This is the sum of duty: do naught onto others what you would not have them do unto you.

> *Islam:* No one of you is a believer until he desires for his brother that which he desires for himself.

> *Judaism:* What is hateful to you, do not to your fellow men.

The ethic of care and be fair is designed into the human brain, and by school age, children have an inner voice of moral standards.[12] Unless something has gone awry, they reject aggression and show cooperation and kindness. Sadly, this early morality erodes in contemporary cultures. The Search Institute found that nearly three-quarters of sixth grade students embraced prosocial values for helping people. By grade 12, this had declined to less than half.[13] Young people immersed in a culture that glorifies materialism embrace opinions such as *I like to own things to impress others* and *It is important to make a lot of money when I grow up*.[14] Materialism is the antithesis to generosity as expressed in opinions like *I enjoy sharing things with others* and *I work to make the world a better place*. Ironically, materialism is actually associated with lower happiness and more risk behaviors.

Just as children have brain maps for learning language, they also have maps for an inborn *moral grammar*. Linguist Noam Chomsky proposed that the brain is designed to use natural social interactions to form both language and morality, without any formal instruction. Of course, the nature of our language and our morality varies depending upon our verbal and cultural environments.[15]

Giving is more rewarding than receiving—so say scriptures and neuroscience.[16] Subjects in a National Institute of Health study played a computer game while their brains were scanned. They received frequent cash rewards and could donate some to specific charities. Upon receiving money, the brain's pleasure center lit up with a rush of dopamine. But, giving money away lit up this and other reward circuits as well. According to researchers, the added warm glow of giving results from oxytocin released by generosity.

Altruism

Altruism is empathy in action, helping others in need. Neuroscientist Shelley Taylor shows how the instinct to *tend and befriend* is more central to human nature than selfishness and aggression.[17] Humans are unique in that both genders have the capacity for tending. We also have been caregivers throughout our existence. Ancient skeletal remains show that many people with severe crippling disorders lived long lives because someone was taking care of them.

The classic research on altruism is the Good Samaritan experiment.[18] That study involved a group of seminary students who believed they were late for a scheduled lecture on the parable of the Good Samaritan. When encountering a person in need (actually an actor), they hurried by. This demonstrated that when we are distracted or distressed, we fail to display altruism. If we do not see people's pain, empathy does not have a chance.

Many earlier researchers presumed that superior altruism was associated with lofty levels of cognitive moral development only possessed by a few moral giants. Now a remarkable series of studies show a very different picture. Altruistic behavior is strongly grounded in children from their earliest years.

Yale researchers found that six- to ten-month-old infants like helpful toys. Infants watched a toy figure struggle to climb an incline and another toy would help the climber up the hill. But then, a trouble-making toy would try to push the climber back down the incline. When encouraged to play with the toys, most infants chose the ones that acted nice.[19] Their young brains are designed to seek out those who help and shun those who hinder or hurt.

The little hands of toddlers reach out to help as early as 18 months of age. Scientists at the Max Planck Institute in Germany found that they readily display altruistic behavior when an adult is in need. When the experimenter pretended to accidentally drop a clothespin, the toddler tried to help by retrieving the object. Attempts to replicate this with mature chimpanzees were much less successful, apparently because they lacked the level of empathy shown by tiny children.[20]

Kurt Lewin found that by age eight, children were frequently "dominated by the ideology of generosity."[21] Children were given four good and four not-so-good toys and encouraged to share. Most gave all four of the best ones to peers, keeping the tattered ones themselves. When they were asked which toys they would really like to have, the eight year olds, of course, said they preferred the good toys. But in spite of these selfish wishes, their actions were dominated by their ideals.

In 1920, social psychologist William McDougal wrote that loyalty towards members of one's group was the principle moralizing force in society.[22] Modern research confirms this view. When we feel we belong to a group, our in-group empathy programs kick in and activate prosocial behavior without any need for external rewards. In contrast, those who feel socially excluded turn off empathy and may even react with aggression. This is the title of a classic study, "If You Can't Join Them, Beat Them."[23] Even well-adjusted university students can turn aggressive in response to a laboratory experience of social exclusion. But when rejection is real and when children grow up unloved, this impairs all areas of normal development.[24]

Social exclusion can evoke hostility toward others and prompt self-defeating behavior.[25] Both trust and empathy are compromised by social exclusion. Many such children protect themselves by shutting down their emotional system to avoid the terrible feelings of rejection. The most common response is to become wary about relationships, being reluctant to risk being hurt. People perform prosocial behaviors only if they trust and feel they will receive the benefits of belonging. They are highly sensitive to signs of antagonism, which causes them to suspend motivation to help others. "Prosocial behavior depends on believing that one is part of a community in which people mutually seek to aid, to support, and, occasionally, to love each other. Therefore, when people feel excluded, their inclination to perform such behaviors should be reduced or eliminated."[26]

Empathy versus Egoism

Although humans inherit a biological bias that permits them to feel anger, jealousy, selfishness, envy, and to be rude, aggressive, or violent, they inherit an even stronger biological bias for kindness, compassion, cooperation, love, and nurture—especially toward those in need.[27]

Jerome Kagan

The brain is endowed with programs for *virtue*, a word that comes from the Latin *virtus*, meaning strength. As social beings, humans need moral strengths to live successfully in groups.[28] While cultures define the specifics of virtue and vice, the brain already starts with inbuilt standards which are biased in favor of good over evil.

Morality is defined by our social emotions. We are inspired by some acts but find other behavior reprehensible. Polar reactions of inspiration and disgust send signals from brain to heart and gut on vagal nerve pathways. Positive emotions can cause a warm, tingly feeling in the chest. Disgust literally makes us sick to our stomach.[29]

The highest moral virtue is generosity, which is more than an ethical principle—it is mapped in our genes. William Damon describes how the human brain is programmed to provide a burst of *inspiration* when we act with empathy and benevolence to others. This is sometimes called helper's high. Only by being of value to others can humans derive full satisfaction for a truly meaningful life.[30]

Human brains blend social emotions with social reasoning to guide our decisions.[31] While cognitive psychologists emphasize how thinking shapes emotions, this is clearly a circular interaction. And when feelings are aroused, thinking can be easily distorted by emotions.

The high speed social brain makes snap judgments about problems involving others and triggers either blame or empathy. Blame is related to emotions like disgust or contempt while empathy is tied to sympathy and compassion. We are likely to blame those who cause us personal distress, particularly if we do not have a trusting relationship with them. Empathy is more probable when we have a positive connection with persons and are attuned to their pain or need.

We also make warp-speed judgments about behavior or personal traits we find attractive or repulsive. When we highlight a person's positive qualities, we are more motivated to tend and befriend. But focusing on negative qualities motivates fight or flight emotions. Our life experiences bias us to look for either the positive qualities or flaws in others. Just as youth who have been mistreated assume the worst about adults, their problem behavior may cause adults with pessimistic mindsets to demonize kids.[32] This makes a caustic combination.

Human empathy utilizes two separate brain systems. At the deepest level is *emotional empathy,* which is present from birth. This deep brain empathy is tied to mirror neurons which allow us to read emotions in others and experience them directly ourselves—*I feel what you feel.* As children mature, they develop cognitive empathy, which involves mindreading—*I understand what you feel and think.*[33] In a nurturing environment, moral reasoning develops in a predictable way to complement intuitive empathy.[34] Individuals become less egoistic and more attuned to the feelings and needs of others.

Figure 1. Levels of Moral Reasoning.

Researchers since Piaget have sought to identify levels of moral reasoning which are common across cultures. John Gibbs translates such research into simple terms as shown on the ladder illustrated here.[35] The lower two levels represent immature or delayed moral reasoning. Levels three and four represent mature or profound moral judgment. In order to advance beyond stage two, one needs opportunities to take the perspective of others. While level three represents a desire to cooperate with others, the limitation is that a person can be misled by peers or group influence. Thus the ultimate goal is to treat others with respect, even if that is not the prevailing norm.

Albert Bandura[36] has noted that all humans have the capacity for moral disengagement as individuals subvert their judgment to external forces or rationalize irresponsible behavior. Spanish researchers recently discovered that empathy circuits are in areas of the brain which overlap those used for aggression.[37] Presumably, the empathy circuits restrain violence while moral disengagement serves to override empathy. History abounds with horrendous examples of how good people turn evil.

> *We can assume that most people, most of the time, are moral creatures.*
> *But imagine that this reality is like a gearshift that at times gets pushed*
> *into neutral. When this happens, morality is disengaged.*[38]

Virtually all young people know what is right and wrong. When they continue to be involved in antisocial behavior in spite of negative consequences, this is often because thinking errors are disengaging the voice of conscience. Gibbs has developed training programs to help youth identify these cognitive distortions, which are summarized by the acronym BAMMS:[39]

Blaming: Shifting responsibility for one's own harmful actions to an outside source. *Others are always trying to start fights with me.* Of course, some young people blame themselves, which is not the same as taking responsibility. *I am worthless and don't deserve to live.*

Assuming the worst: Individuals attribute hostile intent to others or consider the worst case scenario. *You can't trust anybody; they lie to you.* Those who lack a sense of power or worth get caught in self-defeating ruminations. *Why try? I will probably fail.*

Minimizing and mislabeling: Problem behavior is depicted as causing no harm or even being cool. *Everybody does it so what's the big deal?* This also includes belittling and giving dehumanizing labels to others. *She's such a jerk; she had it coming.*

Self-centered: This is the overarching distortion that permeates all other thinking errors. People are only concerned about themselves but tune out the needs of others. *Why should I help anyone else? I take care of myself.*

Correcting these self-centered thinking errors requires higher level moral reasoning where individuals learn to show concern for the needs and rights of others. Lawrence Kohlberg pioneered the process of using discussions about moral dilemmas to help develop higher levels of moral reasoning. Yet building empathy and altruism is more than an intellectual process; direct experiences in helping relationships are a prerequisite.

Acts of generosity are reciprocated by feelings of gratitude. Norwegian special education pioneer Kris Juul contended that gratitude was a more powerful tool for behavioral change than social reinforcement. Social reinforcement conveys the message: *If I am good, I will be loved.* Gratitude taps into a much deeper motive for morality: *I am good because I am loved.*[40] Of course, each of these can be used as discipline strategies because they tap brain circuits that modify behavior. While positive reinforcement is by definition positive, withholding social reinforcement activates *pain circuits,* triggering fear of punishment, shame, and submission to authority. In contrast, gratitude activates *pleasure circuits,* fostering empathy, compassion, and prosocial values. While the sacred writings of all major religious traditions extol the benefits of gratitude, there is now scientific evidence that gratitude fosters prosocial behavior.[41] Gratitude in response to the generosity of others fosters social bonding and a sense of well-being.

The most courageous act of giving is forgiving. Both humans and animals have innate motivations towards reconciliation after periods of conflict. These positive moral emotions often do battle with hatred and vengeance. Children who have been deeply hurt by trauma need to find some way to leave it behind. Persons who have been victimized by crime also need to be able to heal. In Nelson Mandela's words, hatred is like drinking poison and hoping your enemy will die. Forgiveness frees persons from being prisoners of past pain. Such restorative practices offer a positive alternative to cultures of payback and retribution.[42]

Hooked on Helping

Great persons are able to do great kindnesses.[43]

Miguel de Cervantes

At a time when Freud thought sex and aggression were the most powerful drives, and when Abraham Maslow was still stuck on the idea that power was prime, Ian Suttie declared that children are born with a generous disposition. The need to give is just as vital as the need to receive. If a child senses that his or her gifts are being rejected, the child feels bad and unlovable.[44] Thus, from earliest childhood, adults can cultivate the spirit of generosity.

A fascinating study about the critical importance of generosity in children was led by neuroscientist Soo Hyun Rhee from the University of Colorado.[45] Researchers studied concern or disregard for others in children from ages 14 to 36 months. Participants were 476 pairs of same-sex twins. Each child was exposed to seeing an adult in distress—for example, the child's mother pretended to hurt herself and showed pain vocally and with facial expressions.

Most children this age show genuine concern by approaching, comforting, and helping their mother. However, some display the opposite reactions by running away from, laughing at, or showing hostility to the person in distress. Remarkably, disregard for others in distress assessed in early childhood predicted antisocial behavior into late adolescence. Because both identical and fraternal twins were included, researchers determined that disregard for others was not a result of genetics but environment—for example, negative parenting, maltreatment, and neighborhood influences.

Disregard for others was unrelated to the tendency of some children to be aggressive, which likely reflected immaturity rather than active hostility. And while there are natural variations in empathy among children, these are not necessarily associated with antisocial behavior. Thus, children with autism may have "passive" deficits in empathy but are not typically antisocial. Those with conduct disorders show "active" empathy deficits by responding aggressively to others in distress. Strengthening compassion may be the most direct way of countering antisocial behavior.

A caring school climate is a powerful contributor to both social and academic success. The best example comes from Japanese schools, known for their high levels of achievement. What is seldom recognized is that performance in high school is rooted in early school experiences and bind children to the school community.[46] From the time students enter primary school, the focus is not on individual excellence but the cooperative pursuit of learning. Japanese children learn to help one another master a challenging academic curriculum, outperforming American counterparts at every grade level. Japanese schools emphasize kindness, collaboration, and peer helping, not test scores. While class sizes are large, students operate in stable four- to eight-member groups which are like *families*, and the word for classmates is *friends*. While American teachers are cautioned not to get too close to students, Japanese teachers build relationships that touch the heart.

The critical connection between a prosocial school culture and academic achievement is demonstrated by the seminal research of Albert Bandura and colleagues in Italian schools.[47] Researchers sought to identify what factors in third grade children were most related to academic achievement by the time these students reached eighth grade. Aggression in third-grade children had little relation to their school success in eighth grade since most discontinued this behavior with maturation. While academic achievement in grade three obviously related to performance in grade eight, remarkably this was not the most powerful predictor of success. Instead, helping, sharing, and consoling (altruism) in third grade most strongly predicted engaged and achieving students in eighth grade. This knowledge should inform all efforts for school improvement.

Creating positive school cultures requires more than stomping out bullying and locking out violence.[48] The most powerful way to build prosocial behavior and values is to surround young persons with caring adults and peers. But in some settings, youth are afraid to abandon their tough façade lest they seem weak and vulnerable. Likewise, adults who are afraid of youth or do not believe in their potential will never inspire youth for change to positive purpose and greatness.

Generosity is not taught with a formal curriculum by breaking it into skills like we might teach an arithmetic lesson. Instead, we build a culture around this powerful norm: *Everyone has the responsibility to help, and no one has a right to hurt another person.* Students begin with helping one another and generalize this through broader service to the community. Such projects should seem challenging and appeal to their strengths, e.g., "This will be a tough job" rather than "This will be easy." Genuine helping projects should meet a real need and not just be an exercise in tallying up community service hours.

In thousands of service projects over recent decades, Starr students have made a direct positive impact on others in need. It may be as simple as serving in soup kitchens or as dramatic as helping residents of a town devastated by a tornado. Such experiences provide the ultimate proof of one's own worth, being of value to others. Youth who have been seen as society liabilities can be transformed into assets as they become hooked on helping. But the goal should always be on how one can improve the lives of those being served, not of those doing the service. Otherwise, concludes Martin Buber, those entering into helping to satisfy their own needs are condemned to a relationship that will never be complete.[49]

One cannot create positive environments for children and youth without a unifying theme of shared beliefs and values.[50] Philosopher Mortimer Adler[51] notes that most values are culturally relative, but absolute values are tied to universal human needs. Research has established that all humans have innate biosocial needs for attachment, achievement, autonomy, and altruism. Meeting these universal needs is the gold standard of effectiveness in education, treatment, and positive youth development.

Cultures of Respect

Erik K. Laursen

This is a roadmap for building positive climates in organizations and enlisting young people in pro-social values of care and concern.

Children are social beings who rely on interactions with others to survive and thrive. Since the human brain is wired to connect, cultures in schools and youth organizations must be designed so youth can bond to supportive peers and adults. Children learn through observation, modeling, and responding to people in their environments. Urie Bronfenbrenner described how a person's ecology shapes developmental pathways for children and youth.[52] Some organizations provide a nurturing ecology that respects children and treats them as individuals; others impose authoritarian structures with strictly enforced rules and hierarchical control. Relationships among teachers, counselors, youth workers, administrators, and students build the climate and culture of the organization.

The Centers for Disease Control identified four factors in schools that promote a culture of connectedness: adult support, belonging to a positive peer group, commitment to education, and a nurturing school environment.[53] Organizations working with children and youth should pay close attention to understanding, developing, and assessing their cultures. Positive climates promote development opportunities for youth to become self-sufficient contributing members in a democratic society.[54] These environments enhance the physical, emotional, and social health of youth and staff and ultimately contribute to creating an ecology where youth can thrive. Two approaches to designing positive cultures for organizations and youth are discussed:

Cultures of Respect in Organizations

Organizations are immersed in values conveyed not only with written policies but in relationships, rituals, stories, language, and the physical setting. Cultures of Respect (COR) integrates organizational theory with positive psychology, neuroscience, and strengths-based practice. Here are seven building blocks to construct environments where all children thrive.

Relationships. These involve trust, respect, and concern for others—both in our immediate life space and the broader community. Young people need adults who care deeply about them. In successful organizations, all are committed to support and encourage one another. Programs do not change people, people change people.

Engagement. Democratic values empower all to participate in decisions affecting their lives. When young people experience "voice and choice," barriers of mistrust begin to break down. As adults become fully engaged with fellow team members, they develop an *esprit de corps* that provides a model for the youth they serve.

Social Justice. Working with vulnerable children exposes deep social and economic inequities in society. This calls for honest dialogue about power and oppression. Values of social justice and mutual concern are cornerstones of effective organizations. As we advocate with children and families, they are equipped for self-advocacy.

Personal Mastery. This is a call to become the best that we can in all areas of life. Mastery involves a tension between current reality and our vision—hope and aspiration for the future.[55] Optimal learning occurs when we operate at the edge of our comfort zone. Failure becomes useful feedback as people develop grit and endurance. [56]

Empowerment. A key to building strengths is sharing power. Young people develop confidence in the ability to influence their lives. Autocratic systems are rooted in rankism as those in authority assume they have the right to control and colonize others through coercion.[57] Powerful cultures end the dance of dependency.

Diversity with Dignity. We share a common humanity but are diverse in nationality, ethnicity, culture, religion, sexual orientation, and financial status. Democratic organizations honor diversity and hold one another to the standard of dignity. This is a commitment to the oneness of humankind.[58]

Celebrating Strengths. All children, families, and communities have untapped talents and capacities. These may not always be visible but have to be identified and explored. Cultivating strengths provides hope and aspirations, transforming individuals and organizations.

Positive Peer Cultures with Youth

Positive Peer Culture (PPC) is a peer-helping model designed to improve social competence and cultivate strengths in troubled and troubling youth.[59] PPC is designed to convert otherwise negative peer influence into care and concern for others. Developing such social interest is the defining element of PPC, and this requires leadership and guidance from trained adults. Rather than enforcing obedience, PPC demands responsibility, empowering youth to discover their greatness. Caring is made fashionable, and any hurting behavior is challenged.

Positive caring norms are established when group members learn to trust, respect, and take responsibility for the actions of self and others. This not only counters antisocial conduct, but, more importantly, reinforces prosocial attitudes, beliefs, and behaviors. As group members become committed to caring for others, they abandon hurtful behaviors and gain increased self-worth.

Peer group programs have grown from ecological models of youth development.[60] Young people exert influence and are influenced by relationships in their immediate life space of family, school, peers, and community. Urie Bronfenbrenner notes that in contemporary culture, the "vacuum left by the withdrawal of parents and adults is filled with an undesired—and possibly undesirable—substitute of an age-segregated peer group."[61] PPC intentionally designs the living and learning environment to meet developmental needs.

While practitioners have long known that care and concern are essential to positive development, there was little research to document the power of empathy. But emerging neuroscience shows that self-centered behavior signals developmental lags in the social brain, particularly in empathy and affect regulation.[62] PPC intentionally designs a milieu to decenter and develop prosocial capacities.

The most comprehensive research on PPC was led by Martin Gold and Wayne Osgood of the University of Michigan.[63] Their quasi-experimental studies spanned 10 years and involved over 300 delinquent youth in four residential schools. Researchers defined the characteristics of effective peer helping programs and the staff climates essential to developing these positive cultures. Subsequent research has established the evidence base for these peer helping programs.[64]

Effective programs create a culture to meet developmental needs for Belonging, Mastery, Independence, and Generosity.

Belonging. All humans have an innate need to belong. Among teens, peer influence is omnipresent—whether positive or negative. Positive peer cultures intentionally build values based on peer concern, not peer coercion and confrontation. Caring peers and adults provided opportunities for youth to build attachments and change their lives. Youth who are most closely connected to positive peers and adults develop skills for success in school and community.

Mastery. Adults in effective programs believe in the potentials of all young people. Problems are not seen as weakness but as rich opportunities for learning and growth. The focus is on the "here and now" and solving real life difficulties. Daily challenges provide opportunity to explore one's behavior, thinking, and feelings. Youth who become aware of how their actions affect self and others build social and emotional intelligence. Research shows investment in school and learning predicts successful outcomes, even when youth still have stressors in other areas of their lives.

Independence. Youth develop responsibility only by involvement in decisions that impact their lives. They participate in developing personal goals and shaping their futures. Youth join with peers in solving problems and developing plans for learning and growth. Research shows that a sense of autonomy in youth reduces the attractiveness of counter-cultural values.[65] Further, positive interpersonal relationships develop executive functions that manage emotional regulation.[66]

Generosity. Gold and Osgood found the principle of care and concern for others to be the normative value in positive peer cultures. Youth are engaged in peer helping and become primary change agents. No other education or treatment approach more directly taps empathy for positive transformation and moral development.[67] While group or classroom meetings can provide the foundation for building a culture of caring, peer helping must be generalized to everyday events.[68]

The principles of Positive Peer Culture form the foundation of all successful peer helping programs. Examples of research-based application of this peer helping model include the EQUIP program[69] and Aggression Replacement Training.[70] Traditional theories of sociology presumed that children filled passive roles while adults in authority trained them to enter society. But the power of peers in modern culture makes young people active agents in their own socialization. This peer influence can be a force for good or evil. All youth-serving organizations develop either positive or negative adult and peer climates. Our challenge is to create Cultures of Respect which tap the awesome power of peers, enlisting them in transforming themselves and their world. As youth contribute to others, they can develop proof of their own worth—they are of value to others.

1. Whitman, cited in Key, 1909, p. 339.
2. Paul, Miller, & Paul, 1993.
3. Feigin, Owens, & Goodyear-Smith, 2014.
4. Gibbs, 1994.
5. Haidt, 2003.
6. Tangney, 2001, p. 133.
7. Hillel cited in Cory, Jr. 2000, p. 41.
8. Darwin, 1873, p. 156.
9. Hauser, 2006.
10. Gilligan, 1993.
11. Rawls, 2002; Barraza & Zac, 2009.
12. Tancredi, 2005.
13. Benson, 1990.
14. Kasser, 2005.
15. Hauser, 2006.
16. Moll et al., 2006.
17. Taylor, 2002.
18. Darley & Batson, 1973.
19. Hamlin, Wynn, & Bloom, 2008.
20. Warneken & Thomasello, 2006.
21. Lewin, 1943/1999, p. 335.
22. McDougal, 1920.
23. Twenge, Baumeister, Tice, & Stucke, 2001, p. 1058.
24. Nelson, Fox, & Zeanah, 2014.
25. Twenge, Catanese, & Baumeister, 2002; Twenge et al, 2007.
26. Twenge et al., 2007, p. 56.
27. Kagan, cited by Goleman, 2006, p. 62.
28. Tancredi, 2005.
29. Keyes & Haidt, 2003.
30. Damon, 2008, p. 40.
31. Hauser, 2006.
32. Seita & Brendtro, 2005.
33. Smoller, 2012.
34. Gibbs, 2014.
35. Gibbs, Potter, & Goldstein, 1995.
36. Bandura, 1999.
37. Moya-Alibio, Herrero, & Bernal, 2010.
38. Zimbardo, 2007, p. 17.
39. Gibbs, Potter, & Goldstein, 1995.
40. Juul, 1981.
41. Mikulincer & Shaver, 2010.
42. Wachtel, 2003; Kraybill, Nolt, & Weaver-Zercher, 2007.
43. Cervantes, 1615, Book 3, Chapter 32, p. 66.
44. Suttie, 1935.
45. Rhee et al., 2013.
46. Lewis, 1995.
47. Caprara et al., 2000.
48. Gibbs, Potter, Goldstein, & Brendtro, 1996.
49. Buber, 1970.
50. Wolins & Wosner, 1982.
51. Adler, 1985.
52. Bronfenbrenner, 2005.
53. CDC, 2010.
54. Laursen, 2009; Thapa, Cohen, Higgins-D'Alessandro, & Guffey, 2012.
55. Senge, 2006.
56. Duckworth, Peterson, Matthews, & Kelly, 2007.
57. McCashen, 2005.
58. Longhurst & Brown, 2013.
59. Vorrath & Brendtro, 1985.
60. Bronfenbrenner, 2005; Morse, 2008; Redl, 1966.
61. Bronfenbrenner, 2005, p. 231.
62. Siegel, 2012.
63. Gold & Osgood, 1992.
64. James, 2011; Laursen, 2010.
65. Osgood, Gruber, Archer, & Newcomb, 1985.
66. Perry & Szalavitz, 2007.
67. Gibbs, 2014.
68. Hoffman, 2000.
69. Gibbs, Potter, & Goldstein, 1995.
70. Amendola & Oliver, 2013.

7

The Vital Balance

Robert Foltz, Larry Brendtro, & Martin Mitchell[a]

*Hippocrates believed that nature, by her tendency toward maintaining
and reestablishing an equilibrium, restored health. This was the earliest statement,
perhaps, of the vital balance.*[1]

Karl Menninger

At 26 years of age, Harvard-trained psychiatrist Karl Menninger (1893-1990)
co-founded the Menninger Clinic, which became the world's largest psychiatric
training center. At age 74, he began a second career by establishing The Villages
and training professionals for work with troubled children. When we asked Doctor Karl which of his many books was most important, he responded, *"The Vital
Balance*—because it is 50 years ahead of its time."[2] Published in 1963, *The Vital
Balance* chronicled the history of psychiatric labels from Hippocrates to modern
times and called for an alternative, strength-based view.[3] Stated simply, *symptoms of mental distress are attempts by persons in crisis to restore health and balance.*

Menninger saw stress as the core of most psychiatric symptoms. He was
inspired by Hans Selye who discovered the stress reaction triggered by the HPA
axis.[4] Moderate stress is managed by normal coping devices like social support
or exercise, which serve to preserve *self-control*. When this fails to reduce tension,
persons experience *dyscontrol* and cope by internalizing anxiety or overt aggression. If still unable to manage stress, individuals retreat to *disorganization* including psychosis and extreme depression or self-harm. Thus, mental distress is part
of a continuum: adaptive and problem behavior differ only in degree; both are
attempts to restore balance.

---

a *Robert Foltz, PsyD, co-author of this chapter, is associate professor at The Chicago School of Professional Psychology.
His research and clinical interests include child and adolescent psychopathology, psychopharmacology, the psychological
and neurological impact of trauma, and critical evaluation of evidence-based treatments.*

Ironically, on the 50th anniversary of *The Vital Balance*, the American Psychiatric Association published its fifth edition of the *Diagnostic and Statistical Manual of Mental Disorders (DSM-5).*[5] Menninger's paradigm-shifting views are now being repeated in direct challenges to the core assumptions of the DSM medical model. Psychiatrist Allen Frances of Duke University, former chair of the *DSM-IV* task force, published a scathing critique called *Saving Normal*—the subtitle says it all: *An Insider's Revolt against Out-of-Control Psychiatric Diagnosis, DSM-5, Big Pharma, and the Medicalization of Ordinary Life.* In a capsule:

> *Anyone living a full, rich life experiences ups and downs, stresses, disappointments, sorrows, and setbacks. These challenges are a normal part of being human and should not be treated as a psychiatric disease.*[6]

The Safra Center for Ethics at Harvard reported that fully 70 percent of persons on the *DSM-5* task force have connections to the drug industry.[7] Big Pharma spends billions directly marketing to consumers. While television ads are required to list dangerous side effects, the viewer's amygdala is distracted by innocent images and soothing sounds. Not surprisingly most substance abuse now comes from legally-prescribed medications.

Seventy percent of persons with a DSM disorder have at least one other diagnosis, and drugs are available for each. Allen Frances describes these causes for the serious problem of polypharmacy:

Treatment creep. Add new medications without stopping the old.

Diagnostic creep. Prescribe medications for each diagnostic label.

Doctor creep. Patients secure drugs from multiple providers.

Pharma creep. Market a pill for every human unhappiness.

Frances sees polypharmacy as "unsupported by research, unmonitored, harmful, and even dangerous."[8] For example, medicating youth for bipolar disorder may shorten their life span 12 to 20 years.[9]

The National Institute of Mental Health (NIMH) no longer considers DSM as a *Diagnostic Bible* but rather as a *Diagnostic Dictionary* with definitions to clarify communication about problem behavior. DSM only describes clusters of surface symptoms but will no longer be central in federally-funded research which seeks to identify the underlying processes beneath these problems.[10]

In their definitive Minnesota study of risk and resilience, Alan Sroufe and colleagues show that the same processes of normal adaptation govern the development of disturbance.[11] Most childhood behavioral problems result from facing stressful life events without adequate support. Conditions such as autism are the exception and not the rule, but these children also have the same developmental needs and potential strengths. In contrast, the widespread use of medication may be seen as "an implicit endorsement of a deficit model."[12]

Menninger broke from traditional psychiatry, contending that most emotional and behavioral problems were not diseases but attempts to restore balance. He predicted the movement from deficits to strengths in the historic evolution of this field. Originally, the focus was on mental illness. Next came the study of mental health. Finally, the goal will be to help persons become weller than well.[13]

Sad, Mad, and Medicated

There are two kinds of medications: cosmetic drugs and curative drugs.... Every single drug on the shelf of the psychopharmacopoeia is cosmetic.[14]

Martin Seligman

Martin Seligman, director of the University of Pennsylvania Positive Psychology Center, observes that psychiatric drugs are unlike curative medications such as antibiotics that kill invading bacteria. Since insurance companies want only to reimburse cheaper treatments, "therapy and drugs are now entirely about short-term crisis management and about dispensing cosmetic treatments."[15] While symptom relief can be a precursor to cure, most of the effects of these quickie interventions are little more than placebo. In fact, in half the studies where the U.S. Food and Drug Administration approved antidepressants, there was no *clinically* significant difference between placebo and drug.[16]

Every morning and night, millions of young people begin and end their day by taking psychiatric medications. So, whether attempting to keep depression at bay, calm anxious nerves, tame angry rage, or even pay attention in school, chemicals are promoted as the solution. As a society, we are expecting drugs to alleviate any form of emotional or behavioral distress.

While emotional discomfort impacts all, people show their pain in different ways. Some *internalize* problems in the private experience of anxiety, depression, and a loss of self-worth. Others *externalize* problems with anger, defiance, and reckless behaviors. While pain is a natural part of being human, the routine use of medications is seldom the best solution. A disconcerting example is the doubling of the use of antipsychotic medications with children age two to five years, while at the same time psychotherapy services decreased.[17]

Massive advertising drums the message that the use of these medications is rooted in scientific study. This, however, is far from the truth. Psychotropic drugs supposedly achieve their effect through a "mechanism of action," meaning they alter brain chemistry. But just what they actually do is unknown as the brain is unimaginably complex. David Healy, who headed the British Association for Psychopharmacology, authored a book with the poignant title, *Pharmageddon*. He notes that "these drugs do not just have the action we are told about but often have much greater effects throughout the body than the one the company markets."[18]

The descriptor "side effects" is a euphemism that conceals the reality that these chemicals can produce toxic consequences.[19] As will be discussed later in this chapter, chemical exposure can alter gene expressions throughout brain and body by a process called epigenetics. For example, the highly promoted drug Abilify is widely administered to children well beyond the scope of research. Yet, the *Physicians' Desk Reference* lists dozens of iatrogenic effects, including permanent neurological damage such as tardive dyskinesia.[20]

While psychoactive drugs are promoted to restore "chemical balance" in the brain, in reality they can disrupt the equilibrium of the entire body. Billions of neurons communicate with each other through brain chemicals called neurotransmitters. Drugs may increase *or* reduce the availability of a neurotransmitter—simply, they activate or dampen down the system. Antidepressants like Paxil, Zoloft, and Prozac raise levels of available serotonin. Even if this modestly reduces symptoms of depression, the brain may become more susceptible to future episodes after the drug is discontinued. Further, since serotonin regulates life processes throughout the body, medication can produce a host of other problems.[21] Such complications are well established in the scientific literature but are widely ignored in practice. A prominent research study concludes that "the weight of current evidence suggests that, in general, antidepressants were neither safe nor effective; they appear to do more harm than good."[22]

For a century, psychiatry has debated the degree to which the brain is implicated in emotional and behavioral problems.[23] Certainly every variation of thought and action involves the mind, but this does not mean the brain is to blame.[24] Although the medical model casts emotional and behavioral problems as disorders or diseases with symptoms, only a few childhood problems are actually caused by known brain deficit. Most childhood difficulties are developmental or adjustment problems.[25]

Paul McHugh of Johns Hopkins University conceptualizes psychiatric problems from a top-down or bottom-up framework.[26] The vast majority of symptoms emerge from "top-down" traumatic experiences, frustrated aspirations, broken relationships, or personal conflicts. These problems are products of our lived experience and can best be remedied through meaningful relationships.

Other problems do not seem directly attributed to experience but are "bottom-up" and rooted in neurologically different brains. Autism is a prominent example. Such children keep a distance from others and may find social interaction almost painful. These brain-based problems result from organic differences, but even so, would medications be the solution?

Research indicates that drugs often reduce symptoms without eliminating them.[27] The rigorous CAMS study showed that combined use of drugs and therapy had some effect on anxiety; yet many who improved still experienced problems. Even if numerous persons in a study fail to benefit, the *average* results may be *statistically* significant. Psychiatrist John Werry describes a study on an insomnia medication that increased duration of sleep from seven hours to seven hours and ten minutes. That may have been *statistically significant,* but it was *clinically insignificant.*[28] Symptom reduction that fails to eliminate distress or produce fulfilling relationships falls short of Menninger's standard of becoming weller than well.

The profuse prescription of medications lacks credible scientific rationale. This includes antipsychotic drugs which generate billions of dollars in sales annually. These are dispensed to children and youth to suppress such symptoms as irritability, impulsivity, and temper tantrums which trigger DSM diagnoses of ADHD, Bipolar Disorder, Conduct Disorder, and the latest ominous-sounding label, Disruptive Mood Dysregulation Disorder.

Antipsychotic medications were designed decades ago to tranquilize the terror of adult psychosis. These are now used with youth—not to cure brain disorders but to suppress disruptive, angry, or erratic behavior. Such drugs fail to address conditions underlying these problems. Instead, medicating symptoms is like taking the batteries from a smoke detector. Since pain-based behavior is a warning sign of distress in a young person's life, chemical controls on the brain can block our ability to detect what is really hurting our kids.

One cannot become an athlete simply by eating protein nor a good student by taking Ritalin. Even if medication has some benefit, this does not lead to mental, emotional, and interpersonal health. Recovery from emotional pain requires positive social engagement through relationships involving family, friends, school, and community.

American children consume most of the world's ADHD medications, typically to reduce inattentiveness in school. Summarizing decades of research, the American Psychological Association stated succinctly, "Stimulants have no effect on academic achievement in the short-term. No long-term effects have been reliably reported on any outcome measure."[29] The most immediate effect of these medications is to improve "on-task behavior" which mainly means sitting in a desk. Jaak Panksepp found that any mammal ingesting ADHD medications stops play and exploration.[30] In fact, hyperactive children may actually need more play to develop their neural circuits for behavior regulation. While reducing disruptive behaviors has obvious benefits, this does not reliably translate into academic success. Moreover, early benefits of stimulants often disappear with ongoing use.

The Multimodal Treatment of ADHD research is a major longitudinal study which followed youth for over eight years. It compared four groups of children who either received Ritalin, behavior modification, a combination of both, or community treatment. In the first few months, the combination yielded the greatest improvement, but these benefits quickly dissipated. After three years, all youth were virtually identical across ADHD measures regardless of the treatment received.[31] Over the long-term, those maintained on medications were still impaired on 91 percent of the outcome measures.[32] Yet millions of children and teens take these medications every day. Balancing the benefits of medications requires that we also consider their drawbacks.

The Slippery Slope

There are many theories to explain the dramatic increases in medication prescribed for youth. On the surface, it is fair to assume that well-intentioned physicians are providing treatment that they or parents believe works. But exponential increases in medication are reaching into younger and younger ages without sufficient scientific support.

Almost all nations consider direct marketing of drugs to consumers as malpractice. In a recent year in the United States, a staggering $1,100 per second was spent on antidepressant, antipsychotic, and ADHD drugs.[33] A trade journal reported that each dollar of advertising antipsychotic drugs returns $27 in sales.[34]

The staggering rise in diagnosis and drugging for childhood behavior problems is the result of a multi-decade campaign of Big Pharma to promote pills to doctors, educators, and families.[35] Slick advertising terrifies parents that untreated ADHD will lead to job failure, fatal car wrecks, criminality, and venereal disease—threats that are total fabrications. Kids themselves are targeted with comic books claiming medications will stop failure and bring them friends. By age eighteen, one in seven young persons receives a diagnosis of ADHD. At adulthood, drug companies work to keep their clients' business for a lifetime.

Overuse of medications is also due to the practice guidelines issued by medical organizations such as the American Association of Child and Adolescent Psychiatry (AACAP). These are based on published research, much subsidized by the pharmaceutical industry which also underwrites the organization's journal. Most studies include adults, and there is a paucity of research on outcomes with children.

Since drugs are being marketed for virtually every DSM diagnosis, new labels means new business. In the mid-1990s, Pediatric Bipolar Disorder became the diagnosis du jour leading to a 4,000 percent increase in supposed incidence. Twenty years later, this proved to be an unreliable diagnosis based on weak science. In response, the fifth edition of the Diagnostic and Statistical Manual created a new category called Disruptive Mood Dysregulation Disorder, which targets irritable, oppositional children with temper tantrums. Ironically, dysregulation is the core symptom of relationship trauma.

Such troubling results are not unique to Bipolar Disorder and raises serious concerns about the viability of matching medications to clusters of symptoms. Further, young people are particularly susceptible to the side effects of these powerful drugs. Metabolic, cardiac, gastrointestinal, neurological, and reproductive complications are serious systemic concerns. Moreover, exploding neuron growth in childhood and adolescence makes it impossible to predict the long-term consequences of prescribing psychoactive drugs. Given their limited effectiveness across many disorders, it is reasonable to be concerned about unnecessarily exposing youth to these medications. Ironically, many psychoactive drugs have an unlisted side effect: they may reduce levels of oxytocin, the hormone necessary for trust and bonding and the foundation of the therapeutic alliance.[36]

Voices of Youth

Medication is only a way of hiding pain and not allowing you to be yourself.[37]

Teen describing drugs

The Adolescent Subjective Experience of Treatment (ASET) study is an effort to understand the perspective of youth placed in residential treatment. This survey looks at individual psychotherapy, milieu approaches, trauma exposure, resiliency, and psychotropic medication. The results from 74 youth are highlighted here.

All youth were asked, "Overall, how do you feel about being on medication?" As seen here, almost half had a negative response to this question while a third felt positive about being on medications. An interesting finding was that even when youth noted some benefit in symptom control, many still felt negative about being on medications.[38]

Table 1. ASETS Study of Youth Receiving Medications and Therapy

MEDICATIONS

Positive Comments

- They really help.
- I'm glad I'm taking them.
- I know I need them.

Neutral Comments

- Sometimes they help, sometimes not.
- Ok. I know some people have to take them.

Negative Comments

- I wish they were never invented.
- I know I don't need them.
- I hate them.
- I don't like people to know that I'm taking them.

THERAPY

Positive Comments

- Been in it for a long time, it's very helpful.
- Good—may be tough at times though.
- It helps me get through things. I think everyone should be in therapy.

Neutral Comments

- All right.
- It's fine—sometimes helpful.

Negative Comments

- I don't like it—they're too nosy.
- I don't think I need therapy.

Most youth in the ASET study were taking multiple medications, some as many as five. More than two-thirds were prescribed antipsychotic medications. Negative attitudes about being on medications increased for those on three or more medications.

Youth Reaction to Medications and Therapy

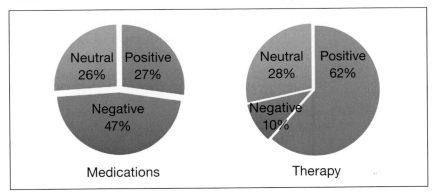

Youth described their experience with therapy in a dramatically different light. When asked if being in therapy helped them learn how to better manage anger, 80 percent agreed. Most (85 percent) agreed that having their family involved helped them deal with their difficulties. Notably, a great majority (82 percent) had confidence in the ability of their therapist to help them improve.

A remarkable finding from the ASET study is the extreme trauma exposure endured by these youth as measured by the Adverse Childhood Experiences questionnaire. This includes ten specific traumatic childhood events summarized below. This instrument is based on responses from over 17,000 adults; only a small percentage had four or more ACEs. However, in the ASET study, 68 percent of these youth in treatment had four or more. This level of trauma can have a staggering impact on a person's overall functioning emotionally, cognitively, and interpersonally.

Adverse Childhood Experiences[39]

Household Dysfunction
Substance abuse
Parental separation/divorce
Mental illness
Battered mother
Criminal behavior

Abuse
Psychological
Physical
Sexual

Neglect
Emotional
Physical

Because trauma can have such a damaging impact, conducting a thorough and interpersonally-focused evaluation is essential for the thoughtful application of any treatment, including medications.

Rethinking Assessment

Youth referred to mental health professionals are struggling with behaviors or emotions. Typically, they are seen briefly, diagnosed with a disorder, and prescribed treatment. Pressure to contain costs means that evaluation can take as little as 30 minutes. Trying to rush this process is a disservice to the person in distress. While a clinician may be able to quickly complete a diagnostic checklist, this does not identify the needs of the youth and family.

Every young person being evaluated should be screened for exposure to trauma. Symptoms of trauma commonly mimic conditions such as Disruptive Mood Dysregulation Disorder, ADHD, Bipolar Disorder, Depression, Conduct Disorder, and many others. Such labels tell us very little about what got the young person to that point in life.

A research study using ASET data compared treatment goals for youth diagnosed with Bipolar Disorder versus PTSD. Both had the same levels of trauma. However, treatment plans showed bipolar youth were given medication while PTSD had trauma-informed goals.[40] Blindly resorting to symptom management by medication for behavioral dysregulation will likely result in treatment failure. While the drugs may contain behavior, trauma goes untreated, thereby impeding positive growth.

Traditional assessment of childhood behavior focuses on deviance and deficit. While these may describe the typology of problem behavior, they are silent on the person's strengths, goals, or needs. The Developmental Audit, discussed in Chapter 9, is an alternative model of a strength-based assessment.[41] A unique feature is that the young person is fully engaged in this assessment process.

Reducing Medications

Entertaining the idea of reducing the use of medication challenges what many regard as a commonly-accepted practice. But, even the best evidence is worthy of scrutiny, and weighing the evidence on overuse of medications raises considerable concern. The reluctance to reduce or eliminate medication is rooted in the potential for a worsening of symptoms. Even when medications are "effective," in most cases, they only achieve a modest symptom reduction. Thus the notion that reducing medications will create problems presumes that major symptom relief was achieved through their use, which is usually not the case.

The potential benefits of reducing medication were shown in a study by child psychiatrist Chris Bellonci and colleagues.[42] They embarked on the process of reevaluating the use of medications with troubled youth in residential care. In reviewing the treatment of over 500 youth, 55 percent were able to reduce medications successfully while only 14 percent experienced medication increases. The remaining youth had no changes to medications or were not on medications at admission. In behavioral outcomes, the most dramatic reductions in assaults and restraints were seen in children whose medication was reduced.

In summary, we have become too comfortable using powerful medications that have not reliably proven themselves in the treatment of youth. Examination of this evidence should compel us to reevaluate our current practices on psychotropic medications and instead reinvest in a more strength-based application of care.

Designer Genes

Our environment affects the behavior of our genes.[43]

Richard Francis

Long-standing debates about nature versus nurture are rendered mute by the new science of *epigenetics*. Researchers mapping the human genome hoped to find genes causing mental disorders. Instead, it became clear that genes and environment are in constant interplay. Epigenetics—*epi* means on top of—shows that genes are not destiny. Instead, events in the environment actually turn genes on or off.

The Epigenetic Revolution

The first genome of a multi-cell organism was mapped in 1992 using a round-worm one millimeter long—less than the thickness of a dime. Although tiny, this nematode has 20,000 genes.[44] It was predicted that humans would have 100,000 genes. How humiliating that we also came in with only 20,000 genes. But what is distinct is our capacity to use environmental cues to turn various combinations of genes on or off to adapt better to our environment—a grand example of the vital balance. But, first a bit of Genetics 101.

Human genes are located on 46 chromosomes, half coming from each parent. Remarkably, all chromosomes with their genes are packed tightly into the nucleus of virtually every one of our trillions of bodily cells. Life begins with a clump of all-purpose fetal stem cells, the ancestors of every other type of cells in the body. If a stem cell could speak, it would proudly say, "I can become anything I want to be."

Cell Specialization. An early definition of epigenetics described how fetal stem cells produce other specialized bodily cells. They do this by turning on a specific set of genes needed to design any of 200 cell types such as skin, liver, or whatever. Fetal cells can also repair other damaged or diseased cells because they replicate the kind of cell surrounding them.

Gene Switches. The more recent definition of epigenetics describes how environmental experiences from chemicals to caregiving switch genes on or off. This is a lifelong process, and even identical twins become epigenetically different with each passing year. In 1952, James Watson and Francis Crick discovered the double helix structure of DNA, and all eyes were on the genes, which were the rungs of this curved ladder. Yet when DNA was mapped, genes occupied less than five percent of available space. Crick called the rest *junk DNA*. This was a colossal error since there were hidden treasures in this uncharted DNA.[45] A massive study called ENCODE[46] has identified four million *gene switches* that enable cells to adapt to their particular environment.

All organisms have evolved an amazing variety of epigenetic switches to adapt to events common in that species. Plants adjust their genes to variations in climate and chemicals. Humans redesign their brains to adapt to challenges throughout a lifetime. Many epigenetic changes occur *in utero*.[47] When pregnancy occurs during a famine, growth hormones are altered to produce a smaller child. A pregnant skink lizard who smells a predatory snake gives birth to a supersized baby that cannot be swallowed. Women moving to extremely high altitudes develop a larger artery to provide more oxygen to their fetus.

While so far these examples seem adaptive, some epigenetic changes are wild cards. Thus, toxic chemicals throw epigenetics out of balance. There are 80,000 substances in the environment not normally found in nature, and there is virtually no research on which are safe.[48] For example, many common chemicals like Bisphenol A in plastic water bottles wreak havoc when dosed in lab animals—producing obesity, diabetes, and hypertension. Ironically, toxic chemicals may include pharmaceuticals which have iatrogenic effects on mental and physical health, as documented by epigenetics researchers Antonei Csoka and Moshe Szyf.

> *Although it is now becoming well-established, one class of compounds that has been largely absent from most studies so far is pharmaceutical drugs. Based on our rapidly accumulating knowledge of gene environment interactions, it stands to reason that drugs in current therapeutic practice would affect the epigenomic state of genes.*[49]

They reviewed evidence that commonly used drugs may cause epigenetic changes, namely drug-induced adverse events. These may even persist after the drug is discontinued, as with the neurological disorder *tardive dyskinesia*. Informed scientists are calling for analysis of epigenetic effects in assessing the safety of all pharmaceutical drugs. Given the billions in profits at stake, one can predict that the drug industry will try to delay this for decades as was the case with tobacco and cancer, another epigenetic "side effect."[50] On a more positive note, besides detecting toxic effects, epigenomic screens might identify potential drugs that would be of use in treating disease.[51]

Caregiving Designs Genes

Michael Meaney and Moshe Szyf of McGill University in Montreal were attending a conference on epigenetics in Spain at the Cajal Institute—named after the originator of neuron theory. While it was well-known that chemicals can produce epigenetic change, they wondered whether child neglect, drug abuse, or stress might also have epigenetic effects.

The Canadian researchers arranged a study of the maternal behavior of Norway rats.[52] By nature, some mothers are highly responsive caregivers, grooming and calming their pups by frequent licking; others are detached and do not dish out much nurturance. This research showed that the mice with loving mothers became resilient and intelligent. But those neglected became distressed and afraid to explore their world. To test for whether this was due to nature or nurture, pups were fostered to other mothers; this showed that caregiving, not genes, determined the pups' resilience or reactivity.

What happened to both nurtured and neglected rats involved the stress system.[53] To simplify, licking, a measure of good mothering, diminished the stress response; these pups became more resilient, able to manage challenge and could calm themselves. But neglect affected neurons in the hippocampus that regulate stress reactions. As you might guess, this applies equally to humans. Notably, victims of relational trauma also have disrupted stress systems and emotional dysregulation.[54]

Stress is not pathology but an inbuilt coping system that serves to maintain the vital balance. Michael Meaney explains that quality of caregiving prepares offspring for the kind of environment to expect.[55] Thus, poor mothering or abuse forecasts a dangerous, unpredictable world, and hypervigilance is an evolved coping strategy. Also, since lack of nurturing lowers oxytocin levels in offspring, poorly parented pups—like children—are more likely to neglect their own offspring.

Meaney explains that females deprived of nurturing have epigenetic programs to offset their lack of oxytocin for nurturing: they enter puberty at a very early age and have higher levels of sexual activity, substituting reproductive quantity for quality.[56]

Temperament is intertwined with epigenetics.[57] Since we are born with natural variations in behavior and personality, it was long assumed that temperament was simply genetic. But temperament is an epigenetic dance—even the prenatal environment may impact personality traits. With a *goodness of fit* between child temperament and caregiving, children thrive.[58] A classic study by Stella Chess classified temperament in children as *easy*, *difficult*, and *slow to warm up*. But the label *difficult* was changed to *feisty* when research showed that in conditions of famine, these children got attention by their loud protests while their calmer siblings did not survive.[59] Temperament differences are not disorders but have some adaptive purpose.

Jerome Kagan found that some children at four months of age were *high reactive* (timid and cautious) while others were *low reactive* (bold and fearless).[60] Maltreatment affects these children differently. Abuse and bullying can seriously disrupt the stress management system in highly-reactive youngsters who have certain variations in genes affecting serotonin levels (5HTT).[61] Other children with a less reactive temperament can weather adverse experiences more easily—they are more insulated from effects of the environment. Emotionally-reactive children may actually have advantages since they respond more positively to warmth and acceptance. They have high neuroplasticity and mirror their world—for better or for worse.[62]

Epigenetic changes are caused by experience and thus are potentially reversible. The resilient human brain has remarkable ability to redesign itself throughout the lifespan. Most epigenetic markers are erased during the production of sperm or egg cells, giving offspring a clean slate. But a remarkable discovery is that some epigenetic changes can be passed on for up to three or four generations.[63] This is one cause of cross-generational effects of trauma. Thus, violent oppression of a great-grandparent may cause a great-grandchild to inherit epigenetic ill effects although never directly experiencing abuse.[64] These include heightened stress reactivity and chronic health problems seen in dominated groups worldwide: obesity, diabetes, immune problems, heart disease, cancer, and shortened life span.

Scientists are discovering that the social system impacts humans through epigenetics.[65] Epigenetics sheds new light on historic trauma which results when the vital balance of entire cultures is disrupted. As with personal trauma, effects of cultural trauma can be long lasting and permeate a whole group of people. In war, slavery, and cultural conquest, an entire community is traumatized. Cultural trauma is profound among indigenous populations whose civilizations were devastated by colonial domination, leaving few human anchors to reset resilience.[66] Research on intergenerational trauma is providing a powerful new lens to understand how dominated groups might restore vital balance in culture and individuals.

A Maori colleague in New Zealand was moved to tears when he first made the connection between epigenetics and historical cultural trauma. He was acutely aware of how discrimination affected his people but never could quite understand why it was so hard for Maori families to break out of the intergenerational culture of poverty and despair. To him the exciting news was that, while genetics is fixed, epigenetics is a result of experience, and new experiences can create resilient pathways.

Research is showing the powerful effects of epigenetics on health, child care, learning, and culture. It is also clear that many common childhood problems have some epigenetic component. But epigenetics is not genetics, so we have the capacity to prevent and perhaps ameliorate these conditions and create environments where young people become in Menninger's terms, *weller than well*.

Kids in Pain

James P. Anglin

Young people in distress show pain-based behavior. This often causes others to react to their problem behavior rather than respond to their needs.

Many actions of troubled children and adolescents disguise and conceal their ever-present and deep-seated psycho-emotional pain. Adults living and working with these youth may overlook this pain in a strategy of avoidance. Labeling troubling behavior as *outbursts, explosions,* or *acting out* ignores the inner world of the child. Instead, adults in authority react with superficial demands, such as, "Get a grip on yourself!" or "Don't speak to me like that!" This can quickly escalate into conflict cycles with consequences such as time-out, grounding, withdrawal of privileges, or exclusion.[67]

The concept of *pain-based behavior* emerged from my earlier research interviewing staff and young people in ten Canadian residential group care settings.[68] This term is a succinct way of saying that problem behavior is an expression of psycho-emotional pain. The residue of unresolved past trauma can make interactions with youth in such pain unpredictable and volatile. Further, staff themselves can have unaddressed pain triggered by unresolved problems in their own backgrounds. When youth act out, similar behavior can be exhibited by staff. Pain-based behavior is a common human experience.

Much literature in education and child and youth care is overly focused on behavior management. One experienced supervisor articulated his preoccupation with the issue of control:

> *Make no mistake about it…these children are from a very different social group. And the bottom line is large competent people who can control…. If there is no control, there is no listening…. The place has to be controlled.*[69]

These thoughts were expressed in an interview only a few weeks after that agency had been subjected to a riot by the residents. In this incident, young people broke windows, emptied cupboards, and generally trashed the place until police were called to restore order. While other programs in the study experienced individual residents losing control, this was apparently the only occasion where an entire program went wildly out of control. In such situations, the staff fear of loss of control tends to breed aggressive reactions. Acknowledging the pain youth are experiencing and encouraging them to make good choices decreases the incidence of explosive behavior.

Children and adolescents in alternative and group settings have often experienced abuse, neglect, or other traumatic life events. They come with deep-seated and often long-standing pain. Young people in this study describe experiencing the following:

Grief at abandonment and loss, often the death of a loved one

Persistent anxiety about themselves and their situation

Fear or terror of a chaotic present and a hopeless future

Depression with a lack of meaning or purpose

Psycho-emotional paralysis in numbness or withdrawal

Carrying chronic pain within, these young people become veritable time bombs. Invisible triggers attached to internalized traumas can set off an explosion without a moment's notice. Or, slow-burning fuses can be lit unknowingly and detonate some time later if the tell-tale smoldering signs are not detected and addressed. Effective workers interpret this behavior and respond sensitively rather than immediately trying to impose external controls.

Even well-functioning homes in this research study sometimes showed evidence of pain-based outbursts with holes in the walls, broken windows, and damaged furniture and appliances.[70] On one visit, the manager of a group home greeted the researcher with fresh wallboard filler on his hands and in his hair, in the midst of doing some major repair work after a difficult weekend. The young "offender" had been helping him repair the damage. Responding with understanding and respect does not necessarily prevent such outbursts but can turn problems into learning opportunities.

A number of labels other than pain have been used to describe these internal experiences, including *stress, distress,* and *troubled*. Yet, some of the most powerful writing in this field is authored by former youth in care and explicitly uses the word *pain*.[71] Thus, it seems most appropriate and accurate to highlight this term rather than gloss over the stark and deeply painful reality of their lives.

According to the testimony of youth in the ten residential group homes studied, *every young person without exception* had experienced deep and pervasive psycho-emotional pain upon entering the program and throughout their time in residence. Most of these settings were in the child protection domain, although one served young male offenders. It would be reasonable to assume that the reality of separation from one's family of origin was itself an added source of pain.

The manner in which adults respond to pain is a key indicator of the quality of care experienced by youth. In order to make successful transitions toward independence, young people need self-awareness and self-management skills to deal with underlying trauma and the potential for re-emergence of pain-based behavior. The literature on adult survivors of childhood trauma suggests that the pain may never fully disappear. However, being able to cope with a sense of normality requires that the pain be named, owned, and placed within a personal story that can lead to a positive future. Effective programs assist in launching this process by fostering investment in education, meaningful employment, sustainable relations with family members, and successful independent living. Positive outcomes are closely linked to an acceptance of the past, the development of self-management skills, and a sense of hope for the future.

Many staff choose this work with the motivation of "making things better" for youth who have endured the kind of pain and trauma *that the staff themselves have experienced*. Approximately half of the workers interviewed indicated a personally painful childhood background. Lingering effects of abuse, rejection, or neglect can be re-awakened in the intense interaction with these youth in pain. Developing self-awareness in staff entails ongoing supervision, especially in relation to worker "anxiety" which is pain-based fear. Even as a researcher visiting group homes, I experienced considerable distress from the often overwhelming pain-based behavior exhibited by these youth. On several occasions, I awakened in the night, troubled by what I had experienced the day or evening before.

Given the depth and pervasiveness of psycho-emotional pain experienced by traumatized children and youth, it is essential to prepare educators and caregivers to meet these demanding and complex challenges. Effective intervention requires a deeper understanding on the origins and management of this pain-based behavior so that responsive human relationships can help these young people heal and live in harmony.

1. Menninger, 1963, p. 367.
2. Personal communication, April 18, 1983.
3. Menninger, 1963.
4. Selye, 1956.
5. APA, 2013.
6. Frances, 2013, jacket copy.
7. Cosgrove & Krimsky, 2012.
8. Frances, 2013, p. 107.
9. Moreno et al., 2007.
10. Insel, 2013.
11. Sroufe, Egeland, Carlson, & Collins, 2005.
12. Sroufe, Egeland, Carlson, & Collins, 2005, p. 242.
13. Menninger, 1963.
14. Seligman, 2011, p. 46.
15. Seligman, 2011, p. 46.
16. Seligman, 2011; Moncrieff & Kirsch, 2005.
17. Olfson, Crystal, Huang, & Gerhard, 2010.
18. Healy, 2012, p. 236.
19. Csoka & Szyf, 2009.
20. PDR, 2015.
21. Andrews, Thompson, Amstadter, & Neale, 2012.
22. Andrews, Thompson, Amstadter, & Neale, 2012, p. 13.
23. Southard, 1914.
24. Suttie, 1935.
25. McClellan & Werry, 2000.
26. McHugh, 2006.
27. Ginsburg, 2011.
28. Werry, 2013.
29. APA, 2006, p. 43.
30. Panksepp & Bivin, 2012.
31. Jensen et al., 2007.
32. Molina et al., 2009.
33. Smith, 2012.
34. Leonhauser, 2012.
35. Schwarz, 2013.
36. Foltz, 2008.
37. California Council on Youth Relations, 2007, p. 18.
38. Foltz & Huefner, 2013.
39. www.ACEstudy.org.
40. Fitzsimmons, 2015.
41. Brendtro, Mitchell, Freado, & du Toit, 2012.
42. Bellonci et al., 2013.
43. Francis, 2011, p. 157.
44. The C. elegans Sequencing Consortium, 1998.
45. Hall, 2012.
46. The ENCODE Project Consortium, 2012.
47. Meaney, 2012.
48. Gupta, 2010.
49. Csoka & Szyf, 2009, p. 771.
50. Risch & Plass, 2008.
51. Csoka & Szyf, 2009.
52. Meaney, 2001.
53. Rettew, 2013.
54. van der Kolk, 2014.
55. Meaney, 2012.
56. Meaney, 2012.
57. Rettew, 2013.
58. Chess & Thomas, 1999.
59. Thomann & Carter, 2009.
60. Kagan, 2010.
61. Sugden et al., 2010.
62. Belsky & Pluess, 2009.
63. Francis, 2011.
64. Kuzawa & Sweet, 2009.
65. Szyf, McGowan, Tureicki, & Meaney, 2010.
66. Bombay, A., Matheson, K., & Anisman, 2009.
67. Long et al., 2014.
68. Anglin, 2002; 2011.
69. Anglin, 2002, pp. 108-109.
70. Holden, 2009.
71. Brown & Seita, 2009; Raychaba, 1993.

8

Conflict, Trauma, and Resilience

Howard Bath, Larry Brendtro, and Martin Mitchell[a]

Called by various names, conflict and trauma are central to the human experience. Most current publications ignore the rich century-long history of research and clinical practice in this field. The earliest in-depth clinical study of trauma was suppressed by Freud and followers who thought that accounts of sexuality between adults and children were merely fantasies. The person who tried to get this child abuse out of the psychoanalytic closet was Freud's once heir-apparent, Hungarian psychiatrist Sandor Ferenczi. In 1933, he published over Freud's furious objections "Confusion of Tongues between Adults and Children," which described how children crave tenderness but are victimized by aggressive and sexual passions of caregivers.[1]

> Even children of very respectable, sincerely puritanical families, fall victim to real violence or rape much more often than one had dared to suppose.[2]

Ferenczi described how childhood trauma leads to guilt, shame, and ambivalent emotions of love and hate.[3] This trauma was not limited to sexual abuse, but includes neglect, physical, verbal, and emotional abuse, and failure of empathy in caregivers.[4]

Ferenczi decried the "professional hypocrisy" of detached therapists who only pretend to listen to, but fail to recognize that, patients are the best experts on their trauma. Tenderness is foremost in healing since trauma and love deprivation are two sides of the same coin. "After the naughty defiant child has fired off all the shots in his locker in vain, his concealed demands for love and tenderness come naively into the open."[5] Healing involves more than talking. The child's need for tenderness requires trusting relationships where it is safe to relive trauma and find new ways of coping.

---

a **Howard Bath, PhD,** who co-authored this chapter, has served as the first Commissioner for Children in the Northern Territory of Australia. He has a rich career in work with children and adolescents and consults worldwide.

Ferenczi's philosophy of tenderness was embraced by Ian Suttie of Scotland and impacted John Bowlby's research on attachment and loss. Rather than focusing on pathology, Ferenczi championed empathy as the core of treatment, contending that warmth builds the trust needed for disclosure. His humanistic psychology influenced Otto Rank, Carl Rogers, and Abraham Maslow.[6] These relationship-based philosophies also became central in the psychoeducational traditions established by Fritz Redl and colleagues.

The most notable qualitative study of childhood trauma was conducted by Fritz Redl and David Wineman in the 1950s in Detroit, Michigan.[7] At the apt-named "Pioneer House," graduate students documented in rich detail what it was like to care for and teach these youth. Here is an excerpt from their book with the forever-timely title, *Children Who Hate: The Disorganization and Breakdown of Behavioral Controls.*

Traumatic Life Events

"All children encounter experiences which have some degree of traumatic impact. Ordinary experience cannot be so protected that the human organism is spared, in its development from infancy, from encounters with various circumstances that have some shock effect. The child who is severely hurt in an automobile accident and has to spend long weeks or perhaps months in a hospital away from parents has been traumatized. Similarly, children who lose a parent through death are certainly exposed to trauma, even if their future experience is most carefully protected through the most loving adult handling from parent surrogates. Even these, however, are traumata whose basic impact can somehow be coped with by the child if his total environment is friendly and devoted to his needs. Seldom do we see children who have been so grossly and continuously exposed to traumatization on so many different levels as the 'children who hate.' With them benign experience is the exception, trauma is the rule."[8]

Kids in Conflict

Sometimes I say I hate you because I am afraid you don't love me.[9]

Theta Burke

Fritz Redl worked with Nicholas Long at the National Institute for Mental Health, where they piloted interventions for traumatized aggressive children. Long developed the Conflict Cycle model to explain how two persons can become caught in a reciprocal escalation of aversive behavior. The pattern is distressingly common as an angry child and adult become locked in emotional combat. The Conflict Cycle is also central in the origin and perpetuation of relational trauma. Caregivers either fuel stress with coercive interactions or calm children caught in reenactment of trauma.

The Conflict Cycle is an essential foundation of Life Space Crisis Intervention (LSCI) widely used in work with challenging children and youth. Carol Dawson compared two middle schools for high-needs students in an urban setting. One school trained all staff in LSCI while the comparison school used a point and level system for behavior management.[10] Frequency of crises decreased significantly in the LSCI school while increasing in the control school. Positive outcomes also were seen in better attendance, fewer suspensions, and more students mainstreamed to less restrictive settings.

The Conflict Cycle is a toxic example of the innate capacity of the human brain to mirror the emotional state of others; in fact, caring behavior can set up a cycle of mutual kindness. Understanding the Conflict Cycle has profound implications for parenting, education, and treatment. Here we briefly summarize some of Long's seminal work.[11]

Tit for Tat

Decades ago, psychologists had a competition to create a computer program that would simulate human conflict. The winner was Canadian psychologist Anatol Rapoport.[12] His "Tit-for-Tat" principle was very simple: *On the first encounter with another person, be cooperative. Then reciprocate their friendly or hostile reaction.* Because Tit for Tat operates across all cultures, it is probably embedded in our DNA. But the Tit for Tat rule is too limiting in today's high stress world where tense encounters can quickly escalate into rage. It is also morally suspect. Whereas *The Golden Rule* requires empathy, *The Tit for Tat Rule* can be a payback scheme.

Tit for Tat is also a profoundly maladaptive strategy for raising children. Strong emotional reactions are inevitable, but the challenge is to prevent a vicious cycle in which hate is answered with hate.[13] The Conflict Cycle model was developed for dealing with challenging behavior in families, schools, and treatment programs.[14] It describes how stress can escalate into crisis, drawing individuals into hostile confrontations. By understanding this Tit for Tat process, adults and youth are able to disengage from Conflict Cycles.

A Conflict Cycle follows a four-stage circular track: 1) A stressful event is perceived as a threat; 2) which activates feelings and thoughts; 3) leading to a behavioral response; 4) and others react to this behavior. This can create ever more stress as the cycle spirals into crisis.

Once embroiled in a Conflict Cycle, it is very difficult to extricate oneself. A feeling of righteous rage pushes one to control or punish the adversary. Hostile payback can actually be rewarding, as captured in the German word *Schadenfreude*, and we get pleasure from our adversary's pain. To respond with anger mirrors problem behavior but backing down might enable the youth's coercive tactics.[15]

Figure 1. The Conflict Cycle

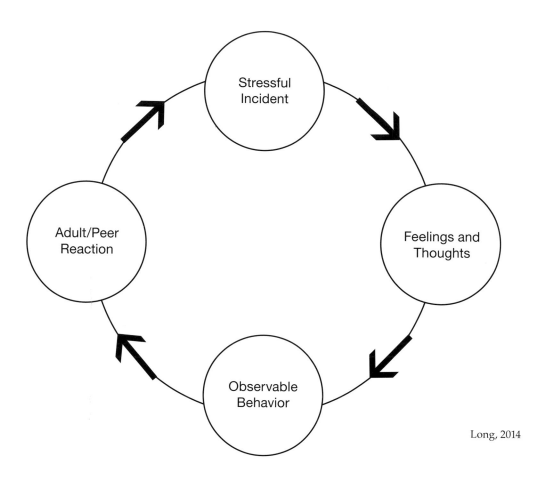

Long, 2014

A typical conflict starts with a trivial disagreement, and before anger dissipates, hostile barbs fuel an ever-higher surge of intense feelings. A study of 100 violent incidents in New York City schools showed that most begin as minor disagreements but escalate to dangerous levels as participants could not back away from conflict.[16] Since Tit for Tat can have positive outcomes, the goal is to convert Conflict Cycles into cycles of respect. Here is how to understand what happens in a Conflict Cycle:

Stress is triggered. This state of heightened physical and psychological arousal results when a person perceives some situation as posing a potential threat.[17] This triggers negative emotions like fear, anger, and shame. The inability to regulate stress underlies most emotional and behavioral disorders.[18] Many medications are used to reduce symptoms of distress. Therapy may better serve this purpose by redesigning connections of the brain that control shame, fear, and aggression.

Stress arouses emotions and thinking. Both feelings and thoughts interact to determine the intensity of stress. Emotions trigger bodily changes that motivate specific coping behaviors. Anger preps the body for a burst of aggression, fear motivates escape, and shame leads to social withdrawal. Emotions register on our faces, giving others some idea of how we are feeling so they know how to act. Reading emotional cues in self and others provides an opportunity to disengage from conflict. Calm demeanor and respectful communication tamp down angry feelings and logic. Otherwise, conflict can escalate into crisis.

Behavior is goal directed. All behavior functions to create change within the person or the environment. Whether adaptive or not, it serves some purpose or goal. Both conscious reasoning and emotional conditioning influence the course of behavior. Young children and those lacking emotional regulation are likely to act impulsively. As the executive brain develops, children have better emotional regulation and can use reasoning to solve problems.

Behavior triggers reactions. Behavior has consequences. These include reactions from others as well as internal thoughts and feelings. When adults or peers react in Tit for Tat fashion to the child's emotions and behavior, the Conflict Cycle has been engaged. While either party can exit, the primary responsibility lies with the adult who is responsible for modeling prosocial behavior. Those who understand the dynamics of the Conflict Cycle can teach this to others, providing them with essential skills for coping with life challenges.

Relational Trauma

Every trauma survivor I've met is resilient in his or her own way,
and every one of their stories inspires awe at how people cope.[19]

Bessel van der Kolk

Researchers distinguish between simple or Type I trauma in which a person is exposed to a single traumatic event, and complex, or Type II trauma, which involves exposure to multiple such events over a period of time.[20] Bessel van der Kolk defined complex trauma as "the experience of multiple, chronic and prolonged, developmentally adverse events, most often of an interpersonal nature... and early life onset."[21] There are many proposed variations of complex trauma. While beyond the scope of this chapter, two variants require mention:

Identity trauma involves exposure to prejudice, exclusion, and chronic micro or macro aggressive acts due to one's identification in a stigmatized population, including racial, ethnic, religious, gender, sexual orientation, or other identities that create chronic minority stress.[22] Such stigmatization is a medium for inflicting pain and is global in its reach.[23] Ken Hardy describes the hidden wounds of racial trauma on young people of color:

Racial oppression is a traumatic form of interpersonal violence which can lacerate the spirit, scar the soul, and puncture the psyche. Without a clear and descriptive language to describe this experience, those who suffer cannot coherently convey their pain, let alone heal.[24]

Bottom-up Trauma refers to attachment difficulties not caused by any maltreatment by adults, but by variations in brain function—such as autism, which may make human contact aversive. Unless children can use caregivers to calm, otherwise mild stressors trigger fear and even terror. This is unlike Bruno Bettelheim's disproved thesis that refrigerator mothers were causing autism. Instead, the emerging theory is that autism is a type of brain based "bottom-up" trauma described by psychiatrist Paul McHugh.[25] Instead of trauma from overwhelming events, in autism, an overwhelmed brain is unable to be calmed by connecting to a caregiver.

The terms complex trauma, relational trauma, and developmental trauma disorders are often used interchangeably. While trauma can have widespread repercussions across the life span, there is clear research and clinical evidence about elements that influence healing and growth.[26] Since interpersonal factors are key in both trauma and healing, the term relationship trauma will be used in this chapter to refer to complex or developmental trauma.

The Three Pillars of TraumaWise Care

While trauma treatment models are widely available for therapists, there are few research-grounded approaches for those who work with children in what is called *the other 23 hours.*[27] This is a crucial need because there are never enough therapists to provide the ongoing, caring relationships needed by traumatized children. Most of the healing takes place outside of the 50-minute therapeutic hour, and many can recover from trauma through support from family, friends, and other supporters.[28]

Parents, counselors, teachers, coaches, direct-care workers, case managers, and others are all in a position to help a child heal.[29]

To synthesize the vast literature on trauma, Bath and colleagues focus on what they call The Three Pillars of TraumaWise Care.[30] This is designed to provide key knowledge and skills for those who live or work directly with these children, including parents, teachers, foster families, residential care workers, community youth workers, and mentors. On a daily basis, they must deal with behavior that is frequently baffling and challenging. The Three Pillars framework informs and empowers those who deal directly in care or education with children of trauma. This chapter identifies three critical factors for creating environments of healing and resilience.

There is a growing synergy of the sciences of trauma and resilience. As van der Kolk notes, many supposed "symptoms" of psychiatric disorders might better be seen as strategies for self-protection.[31] Adults who know how to provide secure relational support and guidance enable these young people not only to survive but thrive.[32]

The literature on trauma and resilience has produced long lists of risks and protective factors, but these can be distilled into a few fundamental principles.[33] These are closely related to the core growth needs of the Circle of Courage.[34] Here are The Three Pillars for creating an environment that fosters healing and resilience:

> 1. *Safety* entails an environment where one can feel secure and attend to normal developmental tasks. Safety is not only physical but is closely related to attachment bonds.

> 2. *Connections* involve trusting relationships with caring adults and peers. Building connections meets growth needs for *belonging* and *generosity*.

> 3. *Coping* enables the individual to meet external challenges as well as to manage emotions and impulses. Successful coping strengthens *mastery* and *independence*.

Pillar I: Safety

Major developmental theorists such as Abraham Maslow, Erik Erikson, John Bowlby, and Mary Ainsworth saw safety as a core developmental need of children. Unfortunately, the defining experience of relationship trauma is that of feeling unsafe. Healing starts with creating an atmosphere of safety; formal therapy is unlikely to be successful unless this critical element is in place.[35]

The overwhelming stress of recurrent trauma leads to changes in the brain. Trauma can impact reactions to threat, emotional control, and cognitive abilities.[36] Bruce Perry observes that such children "reset their baseline state of arousal, such that—where no external threats or demands are present—they will be in a physiological state of persisting alarm."[37] A person who lacks the ability to discriminate between safe and dangerous environments will respond inappropriately to many perceived threats.

A traumatized child learns to be alert to danger when in an abusive environment; unfortunately, that survival strategy is carried into other settings where it is not appropriate. Many behavioral problems of abused and neglected children are linked to concern about security and expectations that adults will be unresponsive or rejecting.[38]

Beyond physical safety, young people need to be secure in their interpersonal relationships. Emotional safety includes acceptance, empathy, and compassion. Cultural safety is jeopardized in a world where diversity can be marked by discrimination. While we cannot protect children from every risk, care givers and teachers should not be a source of threat. Rather, these should have a calming effect so that youth can move from reactive defense to proactive engagement.

James Anglin notes that those who work with traumatized children have to be able to manage pain-based behavior without piling on more pain through punitive or coercive reactions.[39] A similar concern is expressed by van der Kolk: "Faced with a range of challenging behaviors, caregivers have a tendency to deal with their frustration by retaliating in ways that uncannily repeat the children's early trauma."[40]

While the focus on safety will vary with different situations, the goal is always the same—that the child is safe and feels safe and is thus able to join in the journey to healing and growth. Safety is closely related to the quality of interpersonal connections because it is only in relationship with others that a child can begin to feel genuinely safe.

Pillar II: Connections

The second pillar is building or rebuilding social bonds. Children carefully study how adults present themselves, their mannerisms, tone of voice, and body language, and it is the child who "ultimately determines who is a safe person."[41] Connections include emotionally satisfying relationships with caring adults and peers, but also normative connections such as with schools, sporting teams, churches, and community. These social supports help children to surmount adversity and develop resilient life outcomes. However, by definition, relationship trauma is a disruption of supportive connections. When the child faced terror and helplessness, adults were unable or unwilling to protect or were themselves the source of the trauma.

Relationships in early development "indelibly shape us in basic ways, and, for the rest of the life span attachment processes lie at the center of all human emotional and social functions."[42] People carry scripts of early attachment which serve as blueprints for later relationships, behavior, and communication.[43] Unfortunately, many children and young people have not had the benefit of a sound, secure relationship, so a profound insecurity colors interactions. It is our job to create the conditions that help children alter these maladaptive scripts and learn to connect with positive, caring adults and peers.

The Quest for Normality

Children have a strong drive to be normal, to feel normal, and to be treated as normal. James Anglin identified this quest for normality as an unexpected but a strong theme among youth in care.[44] For children of trauma, even therapeutic interventions can signal that they are anything but normal. Children are assigned to special classes or schools, referred to therapists, sent to live in placements away from their family—constant reminders that set them apart from their peers. They express a sense of shame, a deep feeling of not being good enough, of being unworthy, different, and defective. Brene Brown defines shame as "the intensely painful feeling or experience of believing that we are flawed and therefore unworthy of love and belonging."[45]

Research on resilience reaches similar conclusions: caring relationships between children and caregivers, teachers, or mentors are foremost. Some young people embrace or even flaunt their differentness, which may be a healthy sign of independence and defiance. However, most retreat into a deep sense of exclusion and shame. Thus, we need to help young people engage in normal activities and settings such as regular schools, sporting teams, scouts, and sleepovers with friends. Normalized activities create opportunities for forming new connections. The more healthy relationships children have, the more likely they will be to recover from trauma and thrive. Relationships are the agents of change.[46]

Building Connections

There is solid scientific evidence about the therapeutic value of trusting relationships.[47] Decades of research on psychotherapy shows that it is not specific treatment models or techniques, but positive relationships (i.e., a therapeutic alliance and empathy) that drive change. Research on resilience reaches similar conclusions: caring relationships between children and caregivers, teachers, or mentors are foremost.[48]

The primary goal for all who care about children and young people is to be responsive to their needs. Vera Fahlberg describes the arousal-relaxation cycle that comes naturally in parenting infants: caregivers respond to needs instead of reacting adversely to the child's distress.[49] During times of high emotional arousal (e.g., when children are angry, fearful, or disappointed), the adult helps to restore calm. This fosters secure attachment in infancy and also can be applied with older children with insecure attachment.

Children are particularly vulnerable in times of crisis, and these situations can provide an opportunity to build relationship beachheads.[50] When hurt, frightened, lonely, or sick, a previously guarded young person may abandon well-entrenched defenses against adults. Decades of research on the significance of crisis suggests that humans are more susceptible to helping relationships and more responsive to therapeutic attempts at these times of stress. The valence of a relationship can undergo a marked change after some crucial incident which draws the adult and child closer together.

Another everyday connection-building skill is the engaging of children in activities characterized by reciprocity. The late professor Henry Maier observed that when two parties are involved in reciprocal interactions—such as playing table tennis, throwing a ball, dancing, or playing music together—a positive connection is created. "It is almost impossible," he observes, "to dislike someone while you are rhythmically in synch with them."[51] The use of such everyday skills promotes positive connections and helps to ensure a safe environment. Respectful connections are necessary as we help children cope with their challenging circumstances and unruly emotions.

Pillar III: Coping

Classic research by Lois Murphy showed that coping involves mastery of the environment (Coping I) and managing one's internal balance (Coping II), the ability to manage external problems as well as internal emotions and impulses.[52] The primary impact of traumatic stress is a breakdown in the capacity to regulate internal states like fear, anger, and sexual impulses.[53] Young people need to develop effective coping strategies to survive and thrive. Children of trauma develop their own coping strategies to deal with the fallout from relationship trauma, particularly when adults have so often let them down. Some such strategies are helpful and adaptive; for example, self-reliance and development of radar for danger. Other coping strategies are counterproductive in the long term.

Many of the most intractable public health problems are the result of compensatory behaviors such as smoking, overeating, and alcohol and drug use, which provide immediate partial relief from the emotional problems caused by traumatic childhoods.[54] Without trusting relationships, many chronically distressed individuals rely on addictions, criminal activity, or risk taking behavior to relieve their pain.[55] Our role is to understand empathically the coping strategies children employ; provide safety and support so that they have less need for maladaptive strategies; and guide them toward safe, healthy, socially wise ways of coping.

Alan Schore considers struggles with emotional self-regulation to be the defining characteristic of early relationship trauma.[56] Such children "may be chronically irritable, angry, unable to manage aggression, impulsive, anxious or depressed."[57] Thus, the third pillar focuses on helping survivors of relationship trauma safely manage strong emotions and impulses and maintain their emotional equilibrium.

Verbal Skills

Many of the adjectives that we use to describe traumatic experiences suggest that the intensity of these experiences defies verbal description. For example, we hear about unspeakable horror, mute terror, and indescribable fear. Trauma is not experienced in the higher brain where reason prevails, but in deep brain areas where there is no language.[58] Thus, cognitive therapy may be ineffective until trust calms the sensory brain.

Even if traumatized children are not yet ready for verbal therapy, caregivers can help young people develop verbal competencies and the capacity for self-reflection. Just as parents would do with small children, we can help children verbally process their day-to-day experiences. Research shows that the mere act of consciously naming feelings can calm the brain's amygdala and reduce emotional intensity.[59]

Active Listening, a foundational human relations skill, assists children in identifying and naming emotions, skills that are often lacking in traumatized children.[60] Attuning to nonverbal cues, asking questions, and reflecting content feelings are part of the Active Listening toolkit. Setting aside our adult as expert role, we become witnesses to the child who shares stories on the journey from trauma and loss to healing.[61]

Co-regulation

Infants and young children cannot regulate their own emotions but need adults to loan them this control. By being soothed, stroked, rocked, and spoken to in a calm, soft manner when they are upset, they experience calming through the adult's presence and support. In time, they learn to self-soothe by mirroring their carer's responses. Most importantly, they learn that there is a responsive, committed caregiver to offer support. Developmental psychologists call this interactive process between carer and infant co-regulation.

With older children and young people who have not yet learned the skills of self-regulation, adults either respond to problem behavior by co-regulating with the child or attempting coercive regulation on the child.[62] Without soothing by caregivers, the traumatized child is unable to restore emotional equilibrium.[63] Adults manage this intensity with self-control rather than mirroring the child's hostility and threats. Not all problems are dysregulated behavior; one must be able to distinguish between problematic behaviors that are goal-directed and those which result from emotional flooding.

At its root, the ability to learn self-regulation requires trustworthy, empathic caregivers. There are now many publications and training programs that promote the development of self-regulation. These include life space techniques that encourage children to reflect on crisis events as a way of promoting insight and change.[64] The process of reflecting on thoughts, emotions, and actions fosters the development of mindfulness. Such everyday interventions are powerful strategies for healing and growth with children affected by relationship trauma.

Each of The Three Pillars is closely inter-related. There can be no felt safety in the absence of positive connections. Adaptive coping and self-regulation only develop in the context of sound connections with adult carers. Safety, connections, and coping are not the only important elements in a healing environment but are essential to positive growth. In sum, connections strengthen belonging and generosity. Coping develops mastery and independence. These essentials provide a roadmap for success with children and young people who have been exposed to chronic adversity and trauma.

The Road to Resilience

Resilience rests fundamentally on relationships.[65]

Suniya Luthar

Resilience is from the Latin word *resilire,* meaning to leap back. Resilience means bouncing back from difficult experiences. The American Psychological Association defines resilience as the process of adapting well in the face of adversity, trauma, tragedy, threats, or significant sources of stress.[66] Noted resilience researcher Ann Masten of the University of Minnesota identified four waves of resilience research.[67]

What are the risks and protective factors? This resulted in long lists of negative and positive qualities. Many presumed that resilience was a personality trait of invulnerable children.[68] But it soon became clear that no child was invulnerable. Both risk and resilience are human universals. Ernest Hemingway said it best: "The world breaks everyone and, afterward, many are strong at the broken places."[69]

How does resilience develop? Masten has summarized a mass of information into a short list of resilience factors. Some relate to the social ecology, such as caring parents and other supportive adults, prosocial peers, protective teachers, and safe communities. Others are internal strengths, including problem-solving skills, self-regulation, positive beliefs about self, spirituality, and a sense of purpose.

How can resilience be promoted? Resilience is not some rare and special quality possessed by a few but rather ordinary magic, says Masten. Resilience is built into the adaptive brains, bodies, and minds of children. Emmy Werner found that the common thread in successful outcomes was that the youngsters had at least one person who accepted them unconditionally, regardless of their temperament, attractiveness, intelligence, or behavioral idiosyncrasies.[70]

What can we learn about the brain, epigenetics, and resilience? The science of epigenetics creates a hopeful outlook that young people will be able to thrive with supportive relationships. Key systems in the brain and ecology play a crucial role in positive development.[71] The brain-based systems parallel the biosocial needs: attachment systems, mastery motivation, self-efficacy processes, and systems for spirituality and purpose.[72]

The epic studies of resilience by Werner and Smith followed high-risk children from the island of Kauai from birth into adulthood.[73] They found the developmental outcome of virtually every risk condition depended on the quality of the rearing environment. Although these children from high-risk backgrounds had many difficulties while growing up, early adulthood brought new possibilities. By middle adulthood, about 60 percent made positive adjustments, regardless of childhood risk situations.

There is a growing interest in studying post-traumatic growth.[74] If children are given social support in an environment where they can express feelings and discuss problems, this will lead to a sense of competency and a belief in the ability to handle future problems. Positive growth and change following trauma and adversity is an example of resilience. It is not distinctly different from normal human development.[75]

Adversity may have either a sensitizing effect or a strengthening *steeling* effect.[76] A certain manageable amount of stress builds resilience. Without exposure to some adversity, individuals are not challenged to manage stress so their potential for coping with challenge has been under-developed. This process has been called steeling, thriving, and immunization.[77] The person develops resilient brain pathways with a greater capacity to manage future threat.

Resilience Research and the Circle of Courage

In 1955, the first longitudinal study of resilience began on the island of Kauai and would continue for over half a century.[78] We asked Emmy Werner, the principal investigator, to share her perspectives on the process by which many children overcome adversity and thrive.[79]

Question: The Circle of Courage resilience model focuses on belonging, mastery, independence, and generosity. Could you summarize the importance of these factors in your Hawaiian research? Let us begin with belonging and attachment.

Werner: I would say that is the key element. Even though children came from poor homes, if they had one adult who cared, this was consistently treasured by them. I saw it again in middle school, when they elicited relationships with special teachers, but also with one good friend who kept them going. I saw it again much later in middle age, when after maybe a dysfunctional first marriage, a second partner really accepted them, and they changed for the better. So I think that is really the most basic thing on which you need to build everything else.

Question: Years ago, Robert White[80] said that competency motivation was one of the core human motives. What did your research say about the importance of mastery and achievement?

Werner: Keep in mind that we are dealing with a population where more than half of the parents have not graduated from high school, where people generally are not—as wonderful as they are—as communicative as, say, middle-aged professors. But within that framework, I would say that mastery became a very important motivator. It was not just narrowly academic. This could be learning to help out at home when someone else needed to work part time to provide food. Many would take care of younger siblings. It could be just showing that you were good at hula. Competence, broadly based rather than just academic, was an important motivator. That continued in adulthood. Those who recovered from previous problems were often the ones who looked for higher education, adult education, or vocational education. Often they joined the armed forces in order to get those skills. So mastery was a very important motivator.

Question: Research shows the importance of self-efficacy and self-regulation.[81] So when you look at this dimension of independence and autonomy, what did your study say about that?

Werner: It was there and developed more strongly as they reached adolescence and young adulthood. It was linked together with a sense of required helpfulness. They were using that autonomy not in selfish competition—"I'm going to get to Harvard if I have to trample on many toes"—but rather "I am going to take care of myself because in this way I can help my sister who may be struggling with my parents' alcoholism." It was that sort of combination. Belonging is really the most basic thing on which you need to build everything else.

Question: So it was not "I am free to be my own person" but a sense of responsibility in partnership with others. This brings us to generosity and altruism. What do you see are the significant links to resilient outcomes?

Werner: Some sort of shared sense of faith was very predominant. The specific religion did not matter. There were Catholics and Buddhists (Buddhism is a major religion in Kauai). There were Mormons and Seventh-day Adventists. It was their knowing that whatever they were doing they were not alone, they were in a community. And it did not matter how often they went to church, but that somehow what they were doing had some meaning.

Werner: We called our 1982 book *Vulnerable but Invincible: A Longitudinal Study of Resilient Children and Youth*.[82] But in my opinion, the term resilience has been grossly misused. We have to keep clarifying that we cannot label a person as resilient; it is a process. Over time, young folks raised in adversity can adapt successfully to whatever demands are made of them. It is not that being resilient in the teen years means someone will be resilient at age 100, because there are changes. Most of the changes are in a positive direction.[83]

Cultivating Resilience

Resilience is not a trait of the individual but a quality of the interpersonal ecology in which young people grow and develop. We accent this point by highlighting four examples of resilience-building programs developed on opposite sides of the globe. The Circle of Courage Trust New Zealand has piloted programs to build resilience in *families* and *schools*. Starr Commonwealth in Michigan has developed programs for building strengths in *peer groups* and in *communities*.

Strengthening Families: Rolling with Resilience

Families need practical strategies to replace conflict with harmony and cultivate strengths in young people.[84] Rolling with Resilience (RwR) provides experiential learning to apply the Circle of Courage in solving problems and building assets—unlike parenting courses that focus on problems and consequence-based discipline. Developed by New Zealand educators Diane Guild and Deborah Espiner, participants explore practical ways to strengthen belonging, mastery, independence, and generosity in their own families and communities.[85] The course culminates with a resilience survey which becomes a visual presentation of a young person's strengths and highlights areas where more support can be given. One parent observed, "In our family, we were in constant tension and conflict with our daughter Amelia. We were at our wit's end about what we should do. Now we have a more positive outlook, focusing on her strengths instead of always looking at her faults. We are now her coaches instead of controllers as Amelia moves towards maturity. Rolling with Resilience gave our family the courage to try new things."[86]

A Circle of Courage School

Mount Richmond Special School in Auckland, New Zealand, serves 130 students with a wide range of intellectual, social, and behavioral needs, and diverse backgrounds, with Maori and Samoan being the largest groups. As the Ministry of Education embraced a strengths perspective, Mount Richmond adopted the Circle of Courage model. Every employee completed extensive training on the Circle of Courage, including the Response Abilities Pathways (RAP)[87] course focusing on three essential abilities: 1. *Connect* to provide support to children in need; 2. *Clarify* challenges and problems; 3. *Restore* harmony and respect. Staff gained new competence to succeed with challenging students using communication stead of coercion. Outcomes included closure of time-out rooms and major reduction in physical control and restraint. One teacher noted: *Staff are more compassionate and aware—students are valued and respected.* Another remarked: *This life-changing course has made me more aware and more understanding of both adults and students and why they behave and react as they do.*[88] In sum, the school environment moved from a reactive to a responsive culture.

Positive Peer Influence

The most extensive study of peer group influence among youth presenting behavioral challenges was conducted by Gold and Osgood at the University of Michigan, in collaboration with Starr Commonwealth and funded by the National Institute of Mental Health.[89] Researchers tracked over 300 youth in 45 separate groups designed to create prosocial helping behavior. Decades of studies had suggested that placing problem youth together can lead to negative peer influence.[90] Earlier confrontative peer group approaches were found to be ineffective or destructive. The Positive Peer Culture model is focused on developmental needs. Summarizing this research:

Attachment—Youth who bond with staff and peers engage in more prosocial behavior;

Achievement—Relational support and interest in school led to achievement gains and better community adjustment;

Autonomy—Staff teams who respect youth fostered the turn-around to prosocial behavior;

Altruism—Caring is demonstrated by peer helping, directly countering climates of victimization.[91]

Program youth uniformly saw their environments as safe, and effective staff teams were able to engage them in adaptive prosocial roles.

The Art of Resilience: A Community Festival

Sylvia Ashton-Warner, who taught Maori children in New Zealand, described their minds as "a volcano with two vents: destructiveness and creativeness."[92] With leadership by John Hollingsworth and Jeff Cornhill of Starr Commonwealth, the Art of Resilience summer youth festival in Detroit brings together thousands of people to celebrate creative expression of youth in one of America's most challenged urban communities. This is a showcase for the strengths and resilience of young people who participate in music, dance, acting, creative writing, and visual arts. Participants are inspired by stories of resilience that counter the stigma so many face. The arts are particularly important as many schools neglect this essential element of education and growth. Young people join with renowned musicians in restoring buoyancy and vibrancy to the city. Aspiring young entrepreneurs sell colorful handmade creations and donate proceeds to youth organizations. This event mobilizes the entire community—non-profits, churches, schools, business, and the media—in a celebration of strengths. Luther Keith, executive director of ARISE Detroit, summed up the goal of the Art of Resilience: "These kids doing these incredible performances are the norm, and they are our future."[93]

Healing Trauma, Building Resilience

William Steele & Caelan Kuban

*Traumatized children who are involved in their own healing feel safe
and empowered—transformed from victims to survivors and thrivers.*

While trauma is widely viewed through a deficit lens, The National Institute for Trauma and Loss in Children (TLC) has pioneered strength-based, resilience-focused interventions with young people. Trauma and loss are not seen as diagnostic disorders but as painful experiences with which the child is struggling to cope. Instead of being a detached diagnostician, the helping adult becomes a witness seeking to understand the deeply painful experiences of traumatized children. The collective voices of traumatized youth have repeatedly said:

> *If you don't think what I think…feel what I feel…experience what I
> experience…see what I see when I look at myself, others, and the world
> around me…how can you possibly know what is best for me?*

The Pains of Trauma

Childhood trauma is marked by an overwhelming sense of terror and powerlessness. Loss of loving relationships is yet another type of trauma that produces the pain of sadness and grief. The resulting *symptoms* only reflect the neurological, biological, and emotional coping systems mobilized in the struggle to survive. These young people need new strategies for moving beyond past trauma, regulating emotions, and coping with future challenges.

Trauma is experienced in the deep affective and survival areas of the brain where there are only sensations, emotionally-conditioned memories, and visual images. These define how traumatized youth view themselves and the terrifying world around them. Reason, language, and logic needed to make sense of past experiences are upper brain cognitive functions that are difficult to access in trauma.[94] This explains the limitation of traditional talk therapy or narrowly cognitive interventions. Therefore, TLC's Structured Sensory Interventions for Traumatized Children, Adolescents, and Parents (SITCAP) starts with the youth's subjective experience that drives their behavior.

Young people need the opportunity to safely revisit and rework past trauma, beginning with sensory memories of experiences. SITCAP is designed to support safety, emotional regulation, and empowerment.[95] Sessions begin and end with calm activities such as guided imagery or breathing techniques that engage youth in practicing self-regulation. Trauma-focused questions are open ended and tied to non-language, sensory-based activities such as drawing. The therapist is a curious witness rather than an all-knowing expert.

Curiosity by the adult empowers the young person to take the lead and set the pace of intervention. They are given permission to say "yes" or "no" to whatever is asked and discover that saying "no" is honored. Safety is the primary process and the adult's genuine interest fosters a sense of trust. Youth identify the ways their body responds to stress. When traumatic memories are activated by present events, they learn to "resource" their body to regulate reactions.

SITCAP in Action

Drawing is a primary therapeutic activity in SITCAP and yields far more information than initially asking youth to talk about their experiences. More than words, drawing allows children to access and externalize the sensations, memories, and iconic images shaped by trauma. Drawing activities can focus on the primary themes of trauma—terror, worry, hurt, anger, revenge, guilt, shame, and powerlessness. Artistic expression also enables young people to create new images of self that are strength-based and resilience-focused as illustrated in the following case example.

Erica, a 16 year old, was exposed to multiple sexual assaults in her home. She was asked to draw a picture that would tell a story about what happened to her. She created a drawing of her abuser and the room where the abuse took place several times a week. At the bottom of her paper, she drew a box and identified this as the "Dance Area." This was not only the room where she was repeatedly abused, but also where she would come and dance for hours. She turned her place of terror into an island of safety. There she could engage in a self-regulating activity to buffer the fear she felt each night when it was time to go to bed. This significant information had not been discussed previously but was only revealed through her drawing. Music and dance became resources for resilience and self-regulation and were integrated into her treatment plan. Erica's story demonstrates how we can help youth trapped by traumatic memories to create a safe refuge where they can begin to regulate the constant worry of being traumatized.[96]

The healing value of SITCAP is supported by research and practice in varied settings with youth who have experienced a wide range of trauma.[97] Young people move from trauma to resilience as they reframe their thinking from the role of victim to survivor. The youth's own experiences guide treatment. Trusting bonds and repetitive safe and structured activities provide new opportunities for youth to view themselves and their world with hope and resolve. Being empowered to participate in their own healing gives young people a renewed sense of safety, self-control, and purpose.

The essential biosocial needs that underpin positive youth development mirror those that foster healing. A strength-based approach to trauma and loss taps the inner resilience of youth to turn adversity into an opportunity for growth:

> The Circle of Courage pillars of belonging, mastery, independence, and generosity form the framework within which missing developmental needs can be met to create the resiliencies that promote healthy behavior...the goal in any setting where children live, work, or go to school is to meet developmental growth needs, and, if the circle is broken, to provide restorative interventions.[98]

1. Ferenczi, 1933.
2. Ferenczi, 1933, p. 226.
3. Ferenczi, 1934.
4. Stanton, 1993.
5. Rentoul, 2011, p. 69.
6. Rentoul, 2011.
7. Smith, 2004.
8. Redl & Wineman, 1951, p. 66.
9. Burke, 1976, cited in Brendtro & Ness, 1983, p. 49.
10. Dawson, 2003.
11. Long, 2014.
12. Rapoport, 1960.
13. Winnicott, 1965.
14. Long et al., 2014.
15. Reid, Patterson, & Snyder, 2002.
16. Long, Fecser, & Brendtro, 1998.
17. Lazarus & Folkman, 1984.
18. Bradley, 2000.
19. van der Kolk, 2014, p. 278.
20. Terr, 1991.
21. van der Kolk, 2005, p. 402.
22. Meyer, 2003; Pascoe & Richman, 2009.
23. Alexander, 2012.
24. Hardy, 2013, p. 25.
25. McHugh, 2014.
26. van der Kolk, 2014.
27. Trieschman, Whittaker, & Brendtro, 1969.
28. Briere & Scott, 2006.
29. Greenwald, 2005, p. 37.
30. Bath, 2015.
31. van der Kolk, 2014.
32. Perry & Szalavitz, 2010.
33. Masten, 2014.
34. Jackson, 2014a; 2014b.
35. Greenwald, 2005.
36. Enlow et al., 2012; Teicher et al., 2003; van der Kolk, 2005.
37. Perry, 2006, p. 32.
38. Seita, 2010.
39. Anglin, 2002.
40. van der Kolk, 2003, p.310.
41. Steele & Malchiodi, 2012, p. 91.
42. Schore, 2012, p. 27.
43. Siegel, 2012.
44. Anglin, 2002.
45. Brown, 2012, p. 69.
46. Perry & Szalavitz, 2006.
47. Assay & Lambert, 1999; Wampold & Imel, 2015.
48. Benard, 2004; Werner, 2012.
49. Fahlberg, 1991.
50. Trieschman, Whittaker, & Brendtro, 1969.
51. Maier, 1992; Maier personal communication, 1992.
52. Murphy & Moriarty, 1976.
53. van der Kolk, 2005.
54. Felitti & Anda, 2010.
55. Bloom & Farragher, 2011.
56. Schore, 2012.
57. Bloom & Farragher, 2011, p. 108.
58. Steele & Kuban, 2013.
59. Lieberman et al., 2007.
60. van der Kolk, 2005.
61. Steele & Kuban, 2014.
62. Bath, 2008.
63. Schore, 2003.
64. Brendtro & du Toit, 2005; Long, Wood, & Fecser, 2001; Nunno, 2001.
65. Luthar, 2006, p. 760.
66. American Psychological Association, n.d.
67. Wright, Masten, & Narayan, 2013.
68. Anthony & Cohler, 1987.
69. Hemingway, 1929, p. 216.
70. Werner & Smith, 1992.
71. Masten & Obradović, 2006.
72. Masten & Obradović, 2006.
73. Werner & Smith, 1992.
74. Cryder et al., 2006.
75. Joseph & Linley, 2008.
76. Rutter, 2012.
77. Seery, Holman, & Silver, 2010.
78. Werner & Smith, 1992.
79. Werner, 2012, p. 21.
80. White, 1959.
81. Bandura, 1997.
82. Werner & Smith, 1982.
83. Werner, 2012, p. 20.
84. Calame & Parker, 2013.
85. Guild & Espiner, 2015.
86. Guild & Espiner, 2014, p. 41.
87. Brendtro & du Toit, 2005.
88. Espiner & Guild, 2010, p. 26.
89. Gold & Osgood, 1992.
90. Dodge, Dishion, & Lansford, 2006; Polsky, 1962.
91. Giacobbe, Traynelis-Yurek, & Laursen, 1994.
92. Ashton-Warner, 1986, p. 33.
93. Hollingsworth, 2014.
94. Levine & Kline, 2008; Perry, 2009.
95. Steele & Kuban, 2013.
96. Steele & Kuban, 2013.
97. Further information on research supporting SITCAP programs is listed on the California Evidence-Based Clearinghouse and the Substance Abuse Mental Health Services Agency (SAMHSA) National Registry of Evidence-Based Programs and Practices (NREPP).
98. Steele & Kuban, 2013, p. 181.

9

Ecologies for Growth

The concept of strengths is that children, youth, and families have assets
that can help them through challenging times. Focusing on identifying,
developing, and using these assets is the heart of strength-based planning.[1]

John Lyons

Strength and resilience cannot develop in isolation but only through relationships in the immediate world of family, school, peer group, and community.[2] Each of these areas of the social ecology form the foundation of positive youth development by meeting universal growth needs. In this chapter, prominent leaders explore innovative ideas for developing assets in young people. Raquel Hatter highlights principles and strategies for building family strengths. Steve Van Bockern and Tim McDonald outline the essential components of Circle of Courage schools. Richard Quigley draws on forty years of experience in building democratic group cultures that empower children for success. In the words of positive psychology guru, Christopher Peterson, our goal is nothing less than *growing greatness.*[3]

The Action Research feature by Mark Freado describes the Developmental Audit, a unique format for strength-based, ecological assessment. The Audit reflects the new wave in measurement in human service enterprises, which John Lyons calls *communimetrics.*[4] Each significant person in the child's ecology is a stakeholder in assessment, and a premium is placed on the communication value of the plans we formulate. While focusing on strengths, symptoms are smoke signals alerting us that lives are not in balance. Young people are seen as the primary experts on their lives, counter to the common cynical notion that they will not be honest in trying to express their needs. Useful assessments seek to measure what matters most rather than using simplistic schemes to label kids. Growth planning is complex, but we will not settle for incremental "fixes" in broken kids; rather, the goal is transformational change that will unleash their hidden potential.

Building Family Strengths

Raquel Hatter

*Family is perhaps the most powerful experience in shaping one's life course—
regardless of the experience.*[5]

In the decades since John Bowlby pioneered research on the lifelong impact of the parenting bond, family research and practice has flourished.[6] Families give us our first messages about self and shape our sense of value and worth. Families can be a source of pride and shame, support and stress, joy and pain. Families provide conditional or unconditional love, rejection or trust. Modern neuroscience documents the toll taken when family bonds are broken, but also the human ability to bounce back from adversity.

Much of the early literature on families focused on problems but overlooked strengths. Some of the strongest challenges to this pessimistic bias came from parents of children with emotional and behavioral problems. Barbara Huff, an early leader in the Federation of Families for Children's Mental Health, called for a moratorium on use of the adjective *dysfunctional* when describing families. If labels are needed, better terms might be *overstressed* or *undersupported*.[7]

A pioneer in studying families is child psychiatrist and noted family therapist Salvador Minuchin.[8] He directed attention away from dysfunction toward finding positive solutions to the challenges families face. This philosophy has also been embraced in the field of residential group care.[9] Nevertheless, as Terry Cross, founder of the National Indian Child Welfare Association, asserts, the practice of removing children from their families into foster care may deprive them of both their parents and their culture.[10] This is a long standing concern among indigenous populations worldwide, something Aboriginal Australians refer to as the Stolen Generation.[11]

The focus on family strengths lays the foundation for cultivating resilience, the capacity to adapt and recover from challenging adverse circumstances. Resilience is not a rare quality but an innate human capacity to thrive with support.[12] Highlighting strengths does not mean ignoring challenges that are very real. Instead, we recognize the opportunities that lie even amidst problems, and we maximize factors that lead to resilience. Here we highlight three emerging family initiatives drawn from our publication, *Building Family Strengths*.[13]

Family Citizenship

The Search Institute conducted a study including 15,000 families from diverse cultural and economic backgrounds reflecting the U.S. census.[14] In each family, they surveyed one parent and one young adolescent aged 10-15, reflecting a critical period of transition in family relationships. Researchers focused on 21 strengths that are relevant to family resilience. Eugene Roehlkepartian and Amy Syvertson summarized these strengths in five categories:[15]

Nurturing Relationships—Healthy relationships begin and grow as we show each other care about what each has to say, how we feel, and our interests.

Establishing Routines—Shared routines, traditions, and activities give a dependable rhythm to family life and help to imbue it with meaning.

Maintaining Expectations—Each person participates in and contributes to family life. Shared expectations require talking about tough topics.

Adapting to Challenge—Every family faces difficulties, large and small. The ways families together adapt to those changes helps them through adversity.

Connecting to Community—Community connections, relationships, and participation sustain, shape, and enrich how families live their lives together.

What is surprising is that overall level of family strengths does not differ significantly by parent education, single versus two-parent families, household income, and other factors. There were slight differences by race, ethnicity and different types of communities, but there were more similarities than differences. All types of families have strengths to tap and challenges to overcome. "Young people and families with more strengths are more engaged in school, take better care of their health, express positive values, and develop the social competencies needed to thrive."[16]

This research points to the importance of interventions which strengthen developmental relationships—"the active ingredient upon which the effectiveness of other program elements depend."[17] Past studies of families have often focused on risk and vulnerability. Shifting attention to strengths can increase resilience in the face of adversity. But engaging families can be exasperating, particularly beyond childhood. Current strategies do not seem to work—families just do not show up, and our efforts become trivialized. It may be time to shift from doling out *family support* to celebrating *family citizenship*.

Engaging Families in their Homes

Ronald Thompson and Sarah Koley describe Boys Town In-Home Family Services.[18] These were developed to help families at risk for a wide range of problems, including domestic conflict, child behavior and school problems, abuse, and neglect. Such families present multiple stressors and sometimes are not able to benefit from formalized office interventions.

A critical feature of successful interventions is to be able to engage family members. This can be a challenge since families may see referral for services in their home as a failure subjecting them to judgment and scrutiny. Not surprisingly, high-risk families often enter the program reluctant to trust professionals. Therefore, the program has developed specific formal and informal engagement strategies that can be tailored to the needs of each family. These are summarized below:

First Steps—Before help begins, it is important to find out as much as possible about the family's history and culture, including information on those currently living in the home as well as extended family relationships and other social networks. These details are seldom available in the limited information found in referral documents. Exploring these topics with family members allows the worker to understand needs of the family without judgment or scrutiny.

Cultural Competency—Two homes in the same neighborhood will have distinct cultures, values, and beliefs. The responsibility of the worker is to understand and empathize with each family culture. Families have the right to be who they are in their own domicile, speaking their own language, rough as it may be. Workers should quickly memorize names and ages of children, even those who have been removed from the home. Whatever their problems, they value their children, and the worker conveys this as well.

The First Meeting—The worker expresses appreciation for being able to be a guest in their home. It is helpful to get the family's perspective before proceeding with prior assumptions. For example, one might say "I received some information about your family but would like to hear your story as my job is to support you." It is important to explain in clear and simple terms the purpose of family services and relate this to the family's agenda, including expected benefits of services.

Quick Engagement Intervention—The worker tries to identify a problem that can have a quick solution. A mother stated she did not have transportation to go to the immigration office, and the worker offered to drive and interpret. Another worker provided a pack of toilet paper for a family who could not afford any at the time. Workers must be ready to help families do dishes, change diapers, or whatever it takes to build trust and engage families.

Individualized Interventions—Identifying needs involves ongoing assessment, both through communication and by using formal instruments such as the Strengths and Stressors tool.[19] These ratings are completed in a conversation format so families are actively involved in planning for growth. In all interactions, the worker solicits and graciously accepts feedback. Sessions are not just sedentary discussion but may include some shared task or activity such as taking a walk.

Accountability—Many families have histories with previous providers who did not follow through. Workers must prove they are different. To show respect for families, they strive to be on time and call if they are running late. Modeling accountability encourages families to reciprocate. Workers who are willing to meet at a variety of times display dedication to family progress. Accountability is paramount in engaging families: mean what you say and say what you mean.

Genuine Humor—Finally, successful workers share the unique ability to join in appropriate, genuine humor. Particularly when families are facing stressful events, comic relief can be a positive way to cope with chaos. When we are secure enough to make fun of ourselves, we are humbled in the presence of families.

Family Privilege

A very different perspective comes from persons who themselves had troubled family backgrounds. Social work professor John Seita of Michigan State University was removed from his family as a child and lived in 15 placements. He coined the term *Family Privilege* to describe the benefits most take for granted if they never had to struggle without a family.[20] He has described his own childhood experiences growing up in high-risk families and foster care.[21]

A generation ago, the typical family included two parents and a bevy of kids living under one roof. Now, every variation of blended caregiving qualifies as family. Whatever the configuration, in an increasingly fractured society, all children need a supportive family. When primary caregivers cannot deliver Family Privilege, others in the broader community must step forward.

In every culture that has ever existed, there were always some parents who were too young, immature, or troubled to parent their offspring properly. The solution was a network of *virtual* parents in the extended family who shared child rearing and backed up overly stressed parents. Seita proposes creating family privilege by focusing on these four growth needs:

Belonging—Building Trust. In their book *Growing Up in the Care of Strangers*, Waln Brown and John Seita document the gripping reflections of human service professionals who as children were removed from their homes and placed in foster care, residential treatment, or juvenile corrections. A common thread is their powerful, raw desire to belong in a loving family. Even as adults, that longing remains. A psychologist who grew up without parents tells how clueless she was about what a normal family provided children. As a teen, when she saw a neighbor hugging her child, she thought he must be sick and was surprised to learn that parents hug their children just because they love them. Children who lack family privilege need substitute sources of belonging.

Mastery—Cultivating Talent. In kinship cultures, children were reared by the village which guaranteed abundant opportunities for mastery. The young were taught to observe carefully and listen to elders and more experienced peers. Russian psychologist Lev Vygotsky considered the mentoring process as the foundation for competence, since a person can learn much more from models and skillful instruction than when learning in isolation.[23] In the quest for mastery, families provide modeling, practice, shared history of lessons learned, wisdom, and competence. In short, a well-functioning family is a pathway for success.

Independence—Fostering Responsibility. Competence is not enough without confidence in the power to control one's destiny. Authentic independence is rooted in secure belonging. Seita describes his own pathway to responsibility. While he lived in a group home, he was able to attend public school in the community. He had brief glimpses of what a real family might be on occasions when he visited in homes of fellow students. But when the time came to enroll in college, he was set adrift. "I lost my most important connections. While the 'sink or swim' approach to independence eventually worked for me, in the short term, the pain, loss of belonging, and confusion was almost unbearable."[24] We know enough about the science of youth development not to rely on luck and pluck. Instead, all young people need supports on the challenging pathway to independence.

Generosity—Finding a Purpose. Most indigenous cultures are more rooted in spiritual than materialistic values; children are reared to be generous and treat others with respect. Now modern research is validating the importance of generosity. Note the title of brain scientist Bruce Perry's book, *Born for Love: Why Empathy is Essential—and Endangered.*[25] Showing concern for others gives meaning to life. But without first experiencing love, one has little reason to care for others. It is no accident that many who had painful childhoods are committing themselves to careers in service to children with similar backgrounds. By helping others, we create our own proof of worthiness.

A prerequisite in building strengths is belief in the capacity to grow and flourish. Families want to know we actually care about them and that how they fare makes a difference.[26] They want us to listen and treat them with respect—regardless of their history. But most of all they need to know that we believe they can surmount adversity and begin the climb toward transformation and growth. We refuse to accept problems as a fixed state but search for the hidden strengths in every family.

Circle of Courage Schools

Steve Van Bockern & Tim McDonald

Nothing happens unless first a dream.

Carl Sandburg

Dream what a school would be like if the purpose were to meet the needs of children and the larger community so that all could lead a good life. The Circle of Courage model identifies four essential human needs that transcend time and place: belonging, mastery, independence, and generosity. These needs are validated by contemporary research and reflect the values of cultures that deeply cherish children. From a neuroscience perspective, our basic hard wiring requires that these "need circuits" are repeatedly fired in order to foster well-being.

Adults who seek to meet the growth needs of children must themselves be aware of the importance of these same needs in their own lives. Of course we all are in the process of growth and face difficulties. Relationships go sour, we experience failure, control is not always in our hands, and we can lose sight of our purpose. Even so, our ability to bounce back and recover is a powerful human characteristic and is part of the fabric of well-being.

Schools that fail to provide opportunities for growth are toxic to children. Though they may raise math and reading scores, unless they help children grow in all ways—to flourish—they are missing their mission.[27] A school that embraces the vision of meeting the needs of children must address four overarching goals: emotional intelligence, instructional competence, democratic values, and a shared vision.

Emotional Intelligence.

A positive emotional climate is prerequisite to academic learning. Thus, the first goal is for adults to work at becoming emotionally intelligent themselves if they are to foster this with students. Emotional intelligence entails the ability to manage one's own emotions and be attuned to feelings of others; such persons can self-motivate and build healthy relationships.[28] Beyond spending time with emotionally intelligent people, professional development can enhance this capacity. For example, opportunities to learn about power struggles and resolve conflicts develop emotional intelligence.

Instructional Competence.

This goal ties to the crucial cognitive domain of the Circle of Courage. Thousands of studies have shown how effective schools can promote learning, even with students from high-risk backgrounds. A rich body of evidence identifies characteristics of successful schools. This research is summarized below.[29]

School Level Factors

1. Schools provide safety and order through teaching self-discipline and responsibility.

2. Schools set academic goals that are challenging with high expectations for all students.

3. Schools manage how much content is taught in order to give adequate instruction time.

4. Schools foster student achievement through a climate of staff collegiality and professionalism.

5. Schools build parent and community support to enhance student success.

Teacher Level Factors

1. Teachers balance assertiveness and cooperation in positive relationships where students respect teacher authority.

2. Teachers engage learners and provide multiple exposure to complex knowledge.

3. Teachers have with-it-ness to quickly identify and deal with problems.

4. Teachers are empowered since their individual decisions have primary impact on classroom environment.

5. Teachers are emotionally objective and responsive in managing rules and discipline.

Student Level Factors

1. Students are engaged in learning and construct long-term projects of their own design.

2. Student problems are addressed through individualized positive interventions.

3. The student's home atmosphere influences achievement so schools and families communicate and set positive expectations.

4. Students enrich their life experiences, and wide reading strengthens language and knowledge.

5. Students receive feedback on their learning and discover how expectations and motivation lead to school success.

In any setting, without effective discipline, learning cannot occur. Tim McDonald developed a practical text on classroom management built on the Circle of Courage model.[30] Positive learning environments meet growth needs of students. Instructional competence involves developing safe and accountable learning environments where all students are actively engaged. This requires enriched curriculum where students learn meaningful content in nonthreatening ways.[31]

Democratic Principles.

The third goal is for adults to share developmentally appropriate power with students. In spite of lip service to democracy, schools have traditionally been slow to abandon hierarchical systems. Rudolf Dreikurs notes that few adults treat young people as social equals, particularly students presenting problems. Methods of reward and punishment that worked in an autocratic era are now obsolete, making youth feel rebellious or worthless.[32] Certainly, adults with their maturity, education, and responsibilities outrank children; but they are not better than children. Democratic schools find ways for students to experience their personal power in appropriate ways. Beginning in the earliest grades, shared power is practiced in such ways as classroom meetings, choices in learning, classroom responsibilities, and respecting diverse opinions.

A Unifying Theme.

Without a shared vision, confusion and conflict reign. But when staff, students, and families share a positive, unifying theme, schools are transformed.[33] As belonging becomes preeminent, traditional policies on suspension and exclusion are replaced by restorative discipline.[34] Genuine mastery trumps the practice of turning schools into test prep centers. Student engagement and intrinsic motivation build independence. Finally, generosity and mutual respect create a powerful environment for learning and growth.

Courage in Action

At first glance, the Circle of Courage is a simple model that identifies four basic human needs necessary for individuals to thrive. Upon closer examination, these universal needs are complex and interrelated and can spark divergent definitions and perspectives. The following list provides a summary of specific indicators for putting Circle of Courage principles into practice:[35]

Circle of Courage School Indicators

Belonging: *Meeting attachment needs of all students*

1. The school is a warm, friendly, and welcoming place.
2. The school is a safe and secure place.
3. The school provides positive connections with adults and peers.
4. The school has input from all constituents.

Mastery: *Meeting achievement needs of all students*

1. The school meets academic standards so all learn at high levels.
2. The school teaches appropriate social and emotional skills.
3. The school honors multiple ways of knowing and learning.
4. The school makes sure students experience success.

Independence: *Meeting autonomy needs of all students*

1. The school ensures support and encouragement with the family.
2. The school provides developmentally-staged responsibility.
3. The school promotes self-regulation by teaching rather than punishing.
4. The school emphasizes "strength-discovering" assessments.

Generosity: *Meeting altruism needs of all students*

1. The school provides opportunities for students to serve in satisfying ways.
2. The school promotes hope and optimism through rituals and ceremony.
3. The school is a place of caring, compassion, empathy, and kindness.
4. The school promotes wellness of body, mind, and spirit.

Creating a Circle of Courage school requires the right combination of heart and mind. Thoughtful, intelligent, and discriminating persons who know the research literature translate this knowledge into practiced skills. Participants are committed to developing emotional intelligence in self and others. Adults see children as their social equals and share power in developmentally-appropriate ways. A Circle of Courage school requires a vision or a dream that is continuously shared.

In the final analysis, a Circle of Courage school is a place where the need for belonging is met through relationships of trust so that each child can say, *I am loved.* The inborn thirst for mastery is nurtured as the students learn to cope with the world and believe *I can succeed.* The need for independence is met by increased responsibility so that the young person can acclaim, *I have power to make decisions.* And, generosity of character is shown by concern for others in order to look to the future in hope with the belief, *I have a purpose for my life.*

Empowering Our Children

Richard Quigley

When our conversations frame groups of young people as a threat,
we will keep them at a distance, contain them, and demand to be protected from them.
This very process of creating distance from adults is what caused
disengaged young people to be criminalized.[36]

Lloyd Martin & Anthea Martin

The polar opposite of coercion—empowerment—is essential to reclaim the hearts and minds of struggling young people. Without a sense of personal power, a young person literally feels worthless and lacks the confidence to engage in meaningful relationships with positive peers and adults. Many further alienate themselves by how they dress, act, and battle mainstream society. The typical adult response is complete disdain as communities reject, rebuke, and disrespect them. Our challenge is to engage these young people with empowerment strategies that unleash their untapped potential.

Respect for the Disrespected

Alienated young people are not hard to identify. They are known by parents, teachers, neighbors, and especially their peers and classmates. These vulnerable teens live on the blurred edges of society, gravitating to others who also feel like outcasts. As communities build bridges of engagement, youth can develop their assets and become constructive members of society. Empowerment is the art of finding the greatness in every person.

Disenfranchised young people do not naturally engage with adults, prosocial peers, or traditional youth groups. Most are not ready to believe that they have undiscovered talents. Just being told one has worth does not break the logjam and open a young person to self-exploration. Instead of reacting to their negative behavior, we maintain the focus on their untapped assets, talents, and strengths.

Young people must experience some real accomplishments in order to sense they have substance and can be of value to others. Successful youth programs enlist youth in community helping activities that call forth pro-social behaviors. When a youth who has long felt worthless begins to feel respected for genuine accomplishments, this is a first step on the pathway to empowerment.

Every young person has a need to feel a sense of personal power in order to move toward responsible independence. Being of help to someone of need is a potent elixir for youth with shaky self-esteem. Through service to others, they slowly build pride, a positive self-image, and sense of purpose. Involvement in some honorable cause fosters prosocial growth and fuels feelings of self-worth.

Engaging the Disengaged

Beth had a long history of abuse and neglect when admitted to Woodland Hills, a residential treatment center in Duluth, Minnesota. This 15-year-old girl was extremely angry and would not allow anyone to get close to her. Beth screamed foul insults, physically attacked peers and staff, and regularly cut on her scarred wrists. Concern for her safety and that of others was a major issue. No therapeutic techniques were working, and patience was wearing thin. We began seeking a locked facility where this very challenging girl could be contained. Beth appeared doomed for more failure, and her future seemed bleak.

One day Beth made comments to another student about playing the piano. Seizing on this sliver of strength, we arranged for regular piano time. This seemed to give Beth short periods of relief, and she occasionally smiled. Soon others were making positive comments to Beth about her musical skills. Her daily violent behavior diminished, so she was given the opportunity to participate in a student-created musical play. Her character in the drama was based on her own painful life, and she worked hard to memorize the lines.

As Beth's interest in music took center stage, we discovered that she was also a good singer. She seemed to enjoy having something to feel proud about, and the frequency of her explosions continued to decrease. The play took on greater importance when she learned that the event would be open to the public and performed in a downtown theatre. Her central role and obvious talent was garnering genuine respect and admiration.

The play gave Beth a level of self-respect she had never known. This was a dramatic change from her past of anger, chaos, and sadness. She was discovering her talents and beginning to view herself in a more positive light. Beth was even invited to sing before the Board of Directors annual Christmas party. She began participating in individual, group, and family therapy. Now engaged with activities and people, she was less self-absorbed with her painful past.

Beth's debut as the star in the community play was a smashing success, and she received a standing ovation. These opportunities gave her the opening to rethink who she was and to disengage from volatile behavior. Her new and emerging self-image was built on her talent and creativity, not past trauma and failure. Concerned adults and peers found a way to empower her with the hope she desperately needed. Her new sense of self-worth also may well have saved Beth's life.

Creating Visions of Success

Beth's story shows the importance of meeting developmental needs if youth are to grow and thrive. Beth was initially alienating herself from belonging, failing to display mastery in spite of talent, using her power to fight others, and living with the emptiness of knowing her life was of no value to others. Such youth cause adults to give up—which was what Beth was doing herself. Even sophisticated professionals often see only pathology instead of promise. Building assets and strengths with a young person is much more productive than pouring hours into analysis of problematic behaviors and traits.[37]

Empowerment applies in any setting serving young people. Schools and community centers are splendid practice grounds where we can help youth gain personal autonomy and a sense of worth. We also must think outside of the box when addressing community mental health issues, moving from fixing flaws to empowering strengths. Our communities can envision a future where all young people have the opportunity to develop and display their skills.

It is time to change the definition of what it means to be a successful adolescent. What if schools would empower all youngsters toward responsibility with the same passion we place on academic and athletic achievement? Schools can become motivational forces to build hope and inspire young people in their new roles as contributing citizens. Learning to respect and care for family and community should hold the same prominence as academic valedictorian awards.

Across more than four decades in education and youth work, I have personally felt the tragic loss of beautiful and capable children. Gun shots, suicides, chemical overdoses, and prison needlessly claim an appalling number of our young people. Yet I have felt the exuberance of seeing children empowered to succeed and find a way out of their once painful life. I have watched thousands of young people blossom into successful college students, athletes, nurses, police officers, counselors, parents, and stalwart citizens. This success was not some stroke of luck but the result of hard work as teams of adults focused on creating environments that empower. Children were cared for, taught, and mentored to find their innate talents and strengths.

We can no longer allow our disenfranchised children to be ignored and fail. Adults bear the responsibility of providing opportunity and hope to every child. Self-respect and dignity is the foundation of citizenship. We build a healthy society by empowering our children to find the pathway to personal pride and respect.

Don't Let Me Give Up

Mary Steiner with students from Woodland Hills

How do you know if an adult respects you?

Arthur: They expect me to be my own person.

Cassandra: By the way they act towards me.

Ella: The honesty they give you. The quality of time they spend with you. If they look you in the eyes as they talk.

Joe: They are kind and don't place judgment.

Marshun: If they listen to what I have to say without cutting me off.

Tessa: When they listen to me actively and use eye contact. When they don't interrupt me and don't give me all the answers.

If you are struggling or experiencing a crisis, what could an adult do to help you?

Arthur: Be their own selves. If they want to help—great, if not—don't.

Cassandra: Be there for me even though I don't want them to be there.

Ella: Be forgiving for the things that I may have said or done.

Joe: Remove me from the situation and talk to me in a calm voice.

Marshun: Allow me to calm down, and then I will talk.

Tessa: Don't let me give up on myself.

The Developmental Audit

Mark D. Freado

The Developmental Audit offers an alternative to traditional assessments that focus on pathology and disorders. It is grounded in the Circle of Courage developmental needs for Belonging, Mastery, Independence, and Generosity. When these needs are blocked, children are vulnerable. The Audit develops growth plans to help young people heal, learn, and thrive.

The Developmental Audit applies across a wide range of settings and disciplines. Schools use Audits for educational planning and behavior assessment. Social service and mental health programs employ the Audit for strength-based case evaluation and treatment planning. The Audit is also used extensively in justice settings.[38] Traditional assessments primarily address risk without regard to resilience. The Developmental Audit engages the young person and other stakeholders in the process of identifying their strengths which can be used to solve problems and find solutions.

Deep Roots and a Wide Lens

The Developmental Audit embodies values of dignity and respect in the belief that all young people have potential and promise. The Audit builds on a foundation laid by youth work pioneers who thought differently about children. Problems are seen as self-defeating coping strategies. The work of life space pioneers Fritz Redl, David Wineman, and William Morse establishes young people as the ultimate experts on their own lives.[39] That philosophy provides strong support for including young persons as primary data sources in the Audit. Youth take an active role in understanding challenges and planning for growth.

The seminal work of Urie Bronfenbrenner and Nicholas Hobbs established the importance of understanding children in the context of their social ecology of family, school, peer group, and community.[40]

As Hobbs noted, "the way one defines a problem will determine in substantial measure the strategies that can be used to solve it."[41] Careful consideration of a young person in an ecological perspective may identify particular places and times when problems occur and others where there is harmony. Morse established the importance of an "ecological scan" in order to identify sources of potential strain and support in the child's life space.[42]

When there is an aircraft accident, the authorities conduct a careful study of possible contributing factors so that steps may be taken to avoid similar tragedies. But when a young person "crashes," our systems of care lack an established protocol for purposeful inquiry. Instead, typical reactions to these human disasters attribute blame, build a thicker case file documenting deficit and failure, and call for holding the youth accountable. The Developmental Audit acknowledges the challenges these young people present and incorporates these in an objective assessment of their developmental pathways, problems, strengths, and needs in order to formulate restorative interventions.[43]

Overview of the Developmental Audit

The Developmental Audit begins with two key questions: How did this young person get to this critical situation? What might be done for positive growth? The Audit is designed to make sense out of a maze of conflicting, incomplete, and sometimes inaccurate records. Four interrelated components are part of the Developmental Audit:

Examine all available records. The goal is to identify patterns that may provide hypotheses about the function or purpose of behavior. Significant facts must be gleaned from contradictory, confusing, irrelevant, and fault-finding entries in a child's often voluminous files. The complexity of this review will vary depending on the circumstances for which the Audit is being conducted.

Scan the interpersonal ecology. The ecological model considers most problems as products of "dis-ease" in the ecology rather than "disease" in the child. An ecological map is created from conversations with the youth and others along with information from written records. Face-to-face or phone contact is considered essential. Real conversations create real information.

Identify timelines in behavior. We explore challenging events with a youth to gain a window onto the individual's private logic, motives, and coping strategies. Attention is given to behavior showing strengths and resilience as well as problems. Specific incidents are seldom isolated events but part of long-term patterns of coping behavior. There are many ways to interpret behavior so it is important to cross-check information from various sources to assess validity of data. Taking a longer view, the Audit tracks the trajectory of a child's development, following what Alfred Adler called a *life line*.[44]

Create a plan for growth. A restorative plan proposes, with the child's input and support, a corrective course of action. This considers both the youth's needs and those of the community. Particular consideration is given to the vital signs of positive youth development, namely Belonging, Mastery, Independence, and Generosity. The goal is to build inner strengths in the young person and mobilize support from significant persons in the child's ecology.

Audits also make use of relevant case information including educational, psychological, or psychiatric evaluations. Multiple sources make it possible to triangulate data for reliability and validity. As strength-based assessment instruments are becoming more available, they can be helpful tools for enhancing the Audit—for example, the Developmental Assets Profile from the Search Institute.[45] Although more specialized assessment instruments may sometimes be useful (e.g., in substance abuse or trauma treatment), the Audit still provides the basic blueprint for recommendations essential in growth planning.

Applications of the Developmental Audit

Conducting a Developmental Audit requires an attitudinal shift from deficit thinking and fault finding to discovering and supporting strengths. There are beliefs, skills, and strategies that make that possible. Since the child and others in the child's life are seen as the primary sources of information, the person conducting the audit has to have good communication and listening skills. The groundwork for those skills is the ability to connect to children and create a therapeutic alliance.[46] For children who have been hurt by adults, this is no easy matter. We do a better job of connecting when we understand the science of trauma, defense mechanisms, and the differences in the psychological world of kids who are adult-wary. A full range of trainings for gaining these skills is available as summarized in the final section on Resources.

Getting the story is one thing; being able to convey this to an audience that may be skeptical or antagonistic is another. This requires the ability to interpret, as clearly and objectively as possible, the complex big picture that surrounds an incident or pattern of problems. A goal is to enable others to set aside simplistic attitudes of blame and understand the best interests of the youth. The Audit avoids diagnostic labelling and gives a narrative of how troubling behavior is created by unmet needs, and sustained by patterns of private logic leading to self-defeating behavior. Still, there will be those who insist on consequences or punishment as the primary outcome. It is important to find methods of accountability that can promote learning and growth rather than further alienate or hurt a young person in trouble.

The Audit can be expanded or condensed to adapt to the purpose of the assessment. Further, the scope must not exceed the "skills, time, resources, and administrative support available."[47] There are three levels of Audits which serve different functions:

Level 1: Rapid Action Plan. This is a brief problem-solving alliance, working directly with a young person experiencing concern or distress. Typically, youth and adult explore the timeline of a significant here and now event. They use the Circle of Courage to identify needs and strengths and develop an immediate plan for support and encouragement. This level of Audit provides a quick resource for managing critical incidents and providing support.

Level 2: Restorative Action Plan. This is a standard tool for strength-based education, treatment, and service planning. It enhances the capacity of programs to succeed with challenging youth. By scanning the ecology of the child, sources of strain and support are pinpointed. Reviewing a series of events clarifies private logic and goals, coping behavior, and developmental pathways. This information is used to formulate a restorative plan for accountability and positive growth. Schools use this type of audit to develop Individual Education Plans and Positive Behavior Support.[48] An elaboration of the Audit for involving school teams in CLEAR Positive Behavior Planning has been developed.[49] Treatment and justice professionals use these Audits to prescribe strength-based interventions with children and families.

Level 3: Risk Assessment Plan. These highly intensive protocols are used with youth facing the most restrictive and punitive sanctions. The youth's case information and network of relationships are examined in detail. Intensive interviews gain perspectives of the young person and significant others. This rich data is integrated to identify needs, strengths, and resilience. A plan is developed to minimize risk and foster positive transformation. Use of these comprehensive Audits in forensic settings moves justice programs toward the science of positive youth development.[50] When courts consider transferring a juvenile into the adult system, the Audit must be sufficiently thorough to survive cross-examination and competing experts. In formal court proceedings, the Daubert Standard[51] for admitting expert scientific testimony applies.[a]

Conclusion

The Developmental Audit adds a valuable dimension to decision making with youth in significant and possibly life-changing circumstances. The American Psychological Association describes evidence-based practice in terms of quality research, clinical expertise, and the understanding of the individual being served. Where these lines of evidence intersect, truth emerges. The Developmental Audit is an ecological, developmental, and strength-based model of assessment. It can be summarized in terms of these resilience science principles.[52]

Connectedness. Relationships in the social ecology.

Continuity. Timelines of development and coping style.

Dignity. Respecting children by meeting growth needs.

Opportunity. Building strengths and supports so youth thrive.

---

a The trial judge rules whether expert testimony meets the Daubert standard, namely that it is based on a reliable foundation of scientific evidence relevant to the task at hand. The Daubert standard has been adopted in U.S. Federal Courts, in 32 states, and in some Canadian courts. In 2011, the Developmental Audit met this standard in the case of a 15-year-old girl charged with being an accomplice to a murder committed by a 21-year-old male companion (O'Brien, 2011).

1. Lyons, 2009, p. 99.
2. Bronfenbrenner, 1986.
3. Peterson, 2013a, p. 113.
4. Lyons, 2009.
5. Hatter, 2014.
6. Holmes, 2014.
7. Huff, cited in Larson & Brendtro, 2000, p. 42.
8. Minuchin, 1974.
9. Garfat, 2011; Small, Bellonci, & Ramsey, 2015; Blau, Caldwell, & Lieberman, 2014.
10. Cross, 2014.
11. Gray, 2011; Pilkington, 2013.
12. Masten, 2014.
13. Hatter, 2014.
14. Syvertsen, Roehlkepartain, & Scales 2012.
15. Roehlkepartain & Syvertsen, 2014, p. 14.
16. Roehlkepartain & Syvertsen, 2014, p. 16.
17. Li & Julian, 2012, p. 163.
18. Thompson & Koley, 2014.
19. Kirk & Reed-Ashcraft, 2001.
20. Seita, 2014a.
21. Brown & Seita, 2010; Seita, Mitchell, & Tobin, 1996.
22. Brown & Seita, 2010.
23. Vygotsky, 1978.
24. Seita, 2014a, p. 10-11.
25. Perry & Szalavitz, 2011.
26. Saleeby, 2012.
27. Seligman, 2011.
28. Lantieri & Goleman, 2014.
29. Hattie & Yates, 2013; Marzano & Pickering, 2010.
30. McDonald, 2013.
31. Wenger & Van Bockern, 1999.
32. Dreikurs, 1971.
33. Ashworth, 2008.
34. Ashworth et al., 2008.
35. Van Bockern, Brendtro, & Brokenleg, 2010.
36. Martin & Martin, 2012, p. 140.
37. Quigley, 2004.
38. Freado & Bath, 2014.
39. Redl & Wineman, 1957; Morse, 2008.
40. Bronfenbrenner, 2005; Hobbs 1994.
41. Hobbs, 1982, p. 182.
42. Morse, 1985.
43. Brendtro, Mitchell, Freado, & du Toit, 2012
44. Freado & Heckenliable-Gotto, 2006.
45. Search Institute, 2004.
46. Rauktis, Andrade, & Doucette, 2007.
47. Sugai & Lewis, 1999, p. 9.
48. Buffum, Mattos, & Weber, 2012.
49. Seger & Koehler, 2011.
50. Freado & Heckenlaible-Gotto, 2006; Freado & Van Bockern, 2010a, 2010b.
51. Faust, 2012.
52. Seita, Mitchell, & Tobin, 1996.

10

Transformation

*There is nothing more difficult...than to take the lead
in the introduction of a new order of things.[1]*

Niccolo Machiavelli

In *The Prince,* Machiavelli (1459-1527) described in great detail how to create and sustain change. Four centuries later, Kurt Lewin pioneered action research on the change process. Most attempts at change are short lived: after a shot in the arm, everything reverts to the previous state. Lewin identified three stages in transforming individuals, groups, and systems. These are: *unfreezing, transition,* and *refreezing.*[2]

Unfreezing involves disrupting the status quo. Until there is recognition of a problem, there is little motivation to change. Further, any change will likely create resistance, particularly if past attempts at reform have failed. Complex change often involves some outside party to assist in the process. At this stage, the goal is to encourage forces for change and respond to legitimate concerns impeding change.

Transition requires developing new thinking, values, and behavior. This is an unsettling period, since the stability of old ways is being dismantled but the new is not yet operational. An organizational example is a school that has long relied on coercive discipline but is moving toward restorative philosophies and practices.[3] In individual lives, transition is a time of neuroplasticity, designing new brain pathways and corresponding coping strategies.

Refreezing involves crystalizing new patterns so they become stable and enduring. School discipline researcher Ramon Lewis describes the failure of professional development as the "Post Guru Syndrome," where initial enthusiasm wanes without ongoing reinforcement.[4] Individual change by teaching or treatment requires sufficient dosages of practice and experience. For example, a traumatized youth needs some time to trust and become open to change, more months to develop new brain and behavior pathways, and an extended period to ensure these changes generalize. Boys Town research shows that longer lengths of treatment are more likely to create life-altering change.[5]

This chapter taps the wisdom of applied experts in the change process. We begin as our late colleague, Chris Peterson of the University of Michigan, recounts the shift of psychology from a deficit to strengths mindset. Next, veteran practitioners, Scott Larson and Kenneth Ponds, explore the challenges of changing troubled young lives. Then, James Longhurst and Juanita Capri Brown describe transformation in the mind and heart necessary to achieve racial healing and equity. Finally, Elizabeth Carey and Gary Tester challenge us to become advocates in changing systems so children and families can flourish.

The Strengths Revolution

Christopher Peterson

In compassion lies the world's true strength.[6]

Buddha

So much of what we have done in the social sciences has been problem focused. We have developed a wonderful vocabulary that explains what goes wrong with folks, and we have almost nothing to say about what can go right. There is something about the architecture of the human mind that causes us to overlook strengths—we are built to pay attention to fires, we never trust tigers.

Discovering what people do well is an excellent way to solve problems. When you paint your floor, it is best to stand on the part that does not need painting. It makes a world of difference when working with others whether your mindset is what is right versus what is wrong. We can use strengths to solve what is wrong. Here is a summary of research my colleagues and I have done on character strengths of young people.

Positive psychology is an umbrella term that describes the scientific study of what makes life most worth living. Positive psychology includes four different categories:

1. Positive psychologists are concerned with positive experiences—emotions, happiness, and the state of flow—being highly engaged in what we do.[7]

2. Positive psychology is concerned with positive traits. This includes strengths of character, like kindness, curiosity, talents, and abilities.

3. Positive psychology is concerned with relationships. If we were to reduce positive psychology to one simple sentence, it would be "other people matter."

4. Positive psychologists are beginning to explore the importance of institutions like family, schools, communities, whole nations.

Problem-focused psychology over the past century has been very important. We can help people with problems like depression, phobias, and so forth. However, this results in a very myopic view of human nature. What positive psychology intends to do is to complement and extend the focus of psychology. We know that bad things do happen in life. But if we have certain strength of character, if we have good relationships with others, these are buffers against the damaging effects of these bad life events. And this is the bottom line: the good life can be taught.

Positive psychology is rediscovering the original mission of psychology, which was to make the lives of people more fulfilling. The question, "what is the good life" has been pursued by philosophers for centuries. There are recent ancestors of positive psychology—certainly the psychologists Carl Rogers, Abraham Maslow, and Erik Erikson. And of course, there is the positive youth development movement and research on resilience and thriving. The value of positive psychology is providing an umbrella term to bring everything together and encourage us to look for connections.

My studies on optimism show that a rosy view is associated with all sorts of physical, psychological, and social benefits.[8] Happiness has positive consequences. Happy people get better grades in school, have much better relationships with other people, are healthier, and live longer. Researchers asked people in a number of cultures whether they had a good day or not. They found common factors which sound very much like the Circle of Courage. A good day was one in which they felt autonomous, competent, and connected to other people.

We know that meaning and purpose in life matters, and this includes religion. I hasten to say this is internalized religion, people who walk the walk, not just talk the talk. The heart matters more than the head in predicting the good life. As a college professor, I am told I should be teaching critical thinking. But the Danish say that critical thinking is not nearly as important in life as critical caring. So now when I teach positive psychology courses at the university, I close the door and say, "Don't tell anybody but this is a different sort of course. We are going to care about one another in this course."

Money has some small relationship to happiness. However, once we get above poverty, money makes an ever smaller contribution. If we are putting food on our table and paying our bills, and we have a choice of a couple of hours of overtime versus a couple of hours with our family, it is a no brainer; we go home to family.

I was invited to go to the University of Pennsylvania for three years to try and come up with useful tools for youth development. Various youth development programs are concerned with strengths and virtues but use different language. We do not think character is a mystery; it shows in thoughts, feelings, and actions. We see character as a subset of personality that is morally evaluative. Other characteristics like introversion and extroversion have no moral weight; they are not good or bad.

Character includes distinct strengths that people possess to different degrees. I spent about a year reading what I call character catalogs: hundreds and hundreds of lists of "these are the important strengths of a person." We came up with 24 widely-valued strengths of character. We were trying to avoid the narrow, late twentieth century bias, so we did not include ambition, celebrity, achievement, or competition. Not every imaginable character strength is on the list, but it is a good selection.

We started with focus groups in 27 high school classes in Michigan. When we said we wanted to talk to students about character, we were laughed at: "Character? They want to talk about sex and drugs and rock and roll." But because the request was so ridiculous, they let us in, and the kids talked about character. They were eloquent and passionate, particularly about self-report questionnaires. The Values in Action Inventory of Strengths (VIA survey) is available on-line at www.authentichappiness.org.

Character has a developmental trajectory, and strengths appear at different ages. Figure 1 shows the structure of character in what is known as a circumplex model. It is based on 100,000 respondents. The closer together the two strengths are, the more likely they are to co-occur with people. The axes—heart, mind, self, and others—was my interpretation. This compares to the Circle of Courage but with different labels. The Circle of Courage emerges from Native beliefs. Our data emerges from factor analysis.

In very young children, the strengths that show up are kindness, love, creativity, humor, and curiosity. Least common were honesty, gratitude, modesty, forgiveness, and open-mindedness. We do not expect a three-year-old child to be open-minded. When told to go to bed, he or she does not say, "Look at the pros and cons of the situation." There are certain strengths that adults are more likely to have than youth, such as open-mindedness or appreciation of beauty. Other strengths are more common among youth who are often more hopeful, have more teamwork, zest, perseverance, and modesty.

Strengths are interrelated. Academic achievement is produced by perseverance, but also by gratitude and love. Since kids learn in groups, interpersonal strengths predict how well they do in school. Asian education has this figured out, teaching kids to get along before they focus on formal education. It is no big surprise that they are way ahead of us. We followed Teach America teachers for two years and gauged how effective they were. An effective teacher's class advanced more than others. Three strengths predicted teacher effectiveness: zest, social intelligence, and humor.

Figure 1. Character Strengths and the Circle of Courage

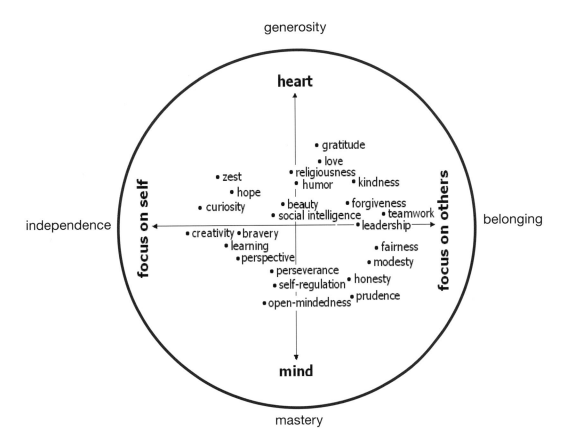

Four Factor Analysis Dimensions presented by Christopher Peterson (2008),
Roots and Wings Conference, Wayne State University, Detroit, Michigan.

We did a study with West Point and gave all of the first-year cadets the VIA survey the first week they enlisted. Commanding officers a year later gave scores of leadership effectiveness. The character strength that predicted good leadership was love. I asked the colonel in charge, "Who would have thought this would be a predictor?" He said, "What part of the band of brothers do you not understand?"

When you held your newborn, you did not say, "I hope this child goes through life and avoids a DSM diagnosis." No, you wanted your child to have health and happiness, to make a difference in the world, to have good relationships, and to someday hold his or her own child. In giving speeches about positive psychology, I often hear someone say, "What took you psychologists so long to figure out that this is what life is all about?"

Becoming Something New

Scott Larson & Kenneth Ponds

It's almost like a new you.
Like you just add a whole bunch of stuff to your brain.

Youth in Care

Discussions of transformation pervade the field of business but are rare in work with children and youth. Too often when dealing with our most difficult youth, the focus is on managing behavior and medicating disorder. While *rehabilitation* implies change, consider the definition of that term: *restoring to the original state*. But what about youth who have not experienced stable relationships? They need *transformation—becoming something new that has never before existed.*

During World War II, an international team of scientists led by Kurt Lewin sought to discover how people form and transform their character. This massive research was motivated by the fact that, for the first time in history, persons without moral conscience could use their power to wreak havoc on the whole human race. Lewin and colleagues created the science of *change theory, group dynamics*, and *conflict resolution*.

In spite of an extensive literature on creating transformational change, we too often focus on managing young people rather than helping them learn and grow. Since behavior is formed in the ecology of relationships, we can use these social bonds to help youth transform their thinking, values, and life goals. Behavior modification is a temporary fix. Instead, the goal is deep, lasting change in relational, cognitive, and spiritual domains.

Relational Change

It is said that we are wounded in relationship, but we are also healed in relationship. We are designed to live in connection with others, yet many of today's youth are alienated from parents, extended family, and community.[10] Youth who feel support from concerned adults cope better with challenges and have resilient life outcomes.

We have operated group homes for youth referred from the justice system. One night, a weekly "house meeting" focused intensively on Mike, who had been in constant conflict with adults and peers. It was not a pleasant experience, and so many difficult issues were raised, we wondered if Mike might choose to run away. When confronted about sneaking out after curfew, he denied any problems, blamed others, and reacted with explosive anger. But as staff and peers continued to show their concern, he broke down and admitted serious problem behavior he had hidden from his group and staff.

When the discussion came to an end, Mike remarked, "This was great. We need to have these talks more often!" How could he be so upbeat about such a painful meeting? Mike had experienced having the dark side of himself exposed, while still being loved. He could see that we were committed to sticking with him and solving problems. Mike no longer needed to carry the weight of his guilt or the fear of rejection. His problems were out in the open, where he could own them and receive help in changing his behavior.[11]

Cognitive Change

If I continue to think as I've always thought, I will act as I have always acted and get what I have always gotten. Adults with relational influence can encourage young people to change the way they think about what is happening to them. We demonstrate this to youth with this simple diagram of nested circles.

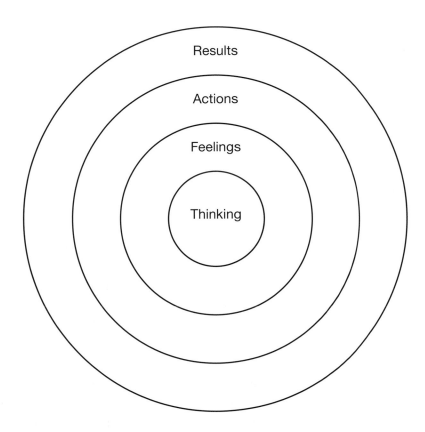

We were talking to a youth named Josh about how the way he thinks influences his feelings, which in turn determines his actions and ultimately the results he gets from others. He got the concept but was skeptical about its value in his "real world." A few hours later he had the opportunity to try it out.

Josh had gone to his job as a dishwasher at a restaurant. When he arrived, he found the kitchen stacked high with dirty dishes. He thought, *This is not how it's supposed to be! I do dishes from my shift, not the shift before me. These people are trying to play me!* Josh got angry and was about to storm out and quit when he remembered our conversation. He decided to put thinking about thinking to the test.

It took Josh a while to figure out another way to look at what seemed to be an obvious injustice. Then it hit him. *At least I'll have plenty to do to keep me busy! Usually I get bored or they let me off early because it's slow around here and then I don't get as many hours pay.* With that, he went at the dishes. Soon he was whistling and feeling good about it.

When he took his break, the manager came over to sit with him. "I meant to tell you what happened—that the dishwasher on the earlier shift became sick and was sent home. But I could see you were angry, and so I left you alone. But then you turned it around and were all happy and whistling. That blew me away. I've been over here putting together a newspaper ad to hire a cashier. I want to offer the position to you." Josh was equally blown away to see how much power he had simply by choosing to think differently about events.

Spiritual Change

> *We are not human beings having a spiritual experience.*
> *We are spiritual beings having a human experience.*[12]

> Pierre Tielhard de Chardin

Spirituality is an inner awareness which occurs when people realize they are connected with something larger than themselves.[13] Our brains are not only designed to connect with others but to find moral and spiritual meaning in life.[14] Kids in a detention center were asked if they had any hopes or dreams for their future. One responded, "No. That's why we're here." Yet each person has dreams and desires, sometimes buried deep within. These give us hope and purpose in life. Children without dreams are spiritually wounded.

The best gift we can offer young people is to help them discover their own dreams. This is the big *Yes,* which is always much stronger than the *Nos* we so often impose on youth. Stomping out old habits is not enough; we need to provide new purpose in life. One young man from our group home returned from a weeklong service project helping individuals with handicaps. He exclaimed, "I finally found the reason I was born!" Twenty years later, he continues to serve others in need in his role as assistant director in a group home for troubled youth.

How do we help nurture a young person's spiritual development so that it becomes a source of strength? While there may be extensive assessment information on a youth, we are seldom aware of the person's spiritual challenges and resources. Young people need a trusting relationship where they are free to raise deep spiritual questions. Adults who may not be confident discussing such issues can enlist another person who can address the young person's concerns.

Research on positive psychology indicates that spiritual strengths foster resilience. Times of crisis cause people to think more deeply about the meaning of life.[15] Spirituality and faith traditions can contribute to resilient outcomes among persons experiencing adversity and trauma.[16] Spirituality is a journey toward finding oneself. Spirituality is not religion, although religion can provide a supportive community in which to develop spirituality.

Finding Purpose

Troubled young people are often swirling in spiritual crisis.[17] Unless they are connected with something greater than self, they become confused about right or wrong and how to make positive life choices. Whatever image they present on the outside, they struggle with age-old questions that attend the human journey:

What is the purpose of my life? Why was I even born?

I want to do right. Why do I keep doing what is wrong?

What is really important in life?

Just knowing that many others are asking such questions makes it safe to share these concerns of the heart.

There is a natural resilience in young people who struggle to transform their lives in spite of years of adversity.[18] Lina was locked up for five years before entering our program. A high-profile gang member, she aged out of the juvenile justice system at age 21. We helped her find employment, but she struggled to cover rent and car expenses with two waitressing jobs. A big motivator was to gain custody of her son, born while she was incarcerated at age 14. One day, she told us her goal was to help other kids coming out of lock-up and just trust God with her finances. We hired her as manager of the cafe we operate with former youth at risk. Lina has made more of an impact on the lives of troubled kids than any of our other staff! She recently reached her dream, gaining custody of her nine-year-old son.

Until youth find a purpose in their lives, our work will largely be "sin management," to invoke a faith-based metaphor. Targeting what we are trying to rid ourselves of is as risky as riding a bicycle while looking backwards. Positive connections, positive thinking, and positive vision are powerful components of transformation.

Young people in spiritual crisis need the opportunity to explore their concerns in a safe, trusting relationship. These are among the deepest existential questions humans face and are a normal part of coping with life challenges. As we are able to walk with them through their spiritual storms, young people build resilience and a renewed sense of purpose in life.

Healing Hearts and Minds

James Longhurst & Juanita Capri Brown

*We must surmount the "us and them" syndrome
and learn to treat each person as part of our family.*[19]

Desmund Tutu

Many want to believe that racism is a problem of the past. Some contend that bringing up the subject of race merely serves to further polarize people. Supposedly, we should not see race since being color-blind would promote equity and justice.[20] In reality, racism and racial inequity persist on individual, organizational, and systemic levels.

Racism is an irrational commitment to ignorance.[21] It is fueled by negative emotions like hate, despair, and doubt—and at the most basic level, fear.[22] We contract and spread this prejudice in two ways: *explicitly* through culturally-learned beliefs and stereotypes; and *implicitly* at a deep and conscious level of emotional conditioning.

Governments cannot legislate away racism. Recognizing this, the W. K. Kellogg Foundation committed to the largest investment in its history to address both racial healing and racial equity.[23] While it is important to change unjust policies and practices embedded in our institutions, it is also essential to transform minds and hearts of individuals. Such healing at the personal level can lead to actions at organizational, community, and, hopefully, national levels.[24] La June Montgomery Tabron, President and CEO of the foundation, shares the philosophy of the founder, W. K. Kellogg: To help people help themselves through the practical application of knowledge and create a world in which all children thrive.[25]

Racial Healing in Action

Racial healing involves more than tolerance training, but a change in deep-seated patterns of thinking, feelings, and actions. This is the purpose of Glasswing Racial Healing sessions. The name comes from a butterfly with transparent wings, found in South American rainforests. Ecologists use the presence of this tropical gem as an indicator of high habitat quality. Glasswing provides a lens through which we can see each other clearly without the distortion of prejudice.

Two-day Glasswing sessions bring together about 25 persons led by co-trainers of diverse backgrounds. The facilitators guide participants in exploring the oftentimes painful subject of racism. Sitting in a circle as the session begins, they review the "ground rules" which ensure a safe and respectful environment. The format addresses both education of the mind and the heart. Facilitators present short modules on topics of racism: definition, pathology, forms, history, white privilege, and the oneness of the human family. Participants have the opportunity to share their personal experiences in dyads and in the full group setting. A safe environment allows those who have a story to tell to relate their experiences, and others can learn by supportive listening.

As participants share their personal narratives, the diversity of members fosters a rich experience. In segregated society, it is seldom possible to comprehend the life experiences of those unlike ourselves. Hearing these personal accounts disrupts the status quo of one's world view, creating motivation to spark change. Still, the dissonance felt by participants must be at manageable levels to be productive.

Glasswing facilitators balance the natural tension of discussing racism with an overriding sense of safety and security for participants. In this environment, people become open to listening to and empathizing with others; there is less of a need to defend oneself or one's position. There is also an increased willingness to tell one's story without fear of being judged or criticized.

The Five Shifts

Racial Healing can create profound changes in both head and heart. A typical observation is, "I feel this has been a life-altering experience." This transformation has been described as the Five Shifts:[26]

Material to Spiritual—Experiencing Connection. Consciously, or more often unconsciously, we categorize others based on past experience. One of the first characteristics we perceive is race, and we need the opportunity to see people at a deeper level. We discover what lies underneath—their hopes, fears, dreams, regrets, and memories of joy and loss. Such shared experiences link us together at the spiritual level. Gradually, we realize that we are all connected as members of one family, the human family.

Cognitive to Affective—Fostering Compassion. On a daily basis, we use our executive functions to make logical decisions and get things done. The professional world in particular tells us that our best thinking flows from using reason and not emotion. But as neurobiologist Antonio Dimasio explains, emotion and reason are intertwined.[27] In fact, emotions are essential to rational problem solving. Awareness of the feelings of self and others helps us approach problems more effectively and develop compassion for our fellow humans.

Certainty to Curiosity—Genuine Understanding. Humans prefer a predictable world in order to be able to feel secure. In racial-healing dialogues, certainty about our views hinders our ability to gain insight. Organizational behavior expert Margaret Wheatley suggests that genuine insight comes as we are able to be open about another's perspectives, even if this initially disturbs us.[28] We do not have to let go of what we believe in order to be curious about what someone else believes. Instead of shielding ourselves from divergent views, a shift to curiosity puts us on the pathway to understanding.

Solution to Transformation—Pathways to Courage. Our society places a high value on being able to fix problems. We rely on the myth that answers exist for every problem, and we are quick to seek out an expert who will tell us what to do. At other times, we try to impose our solutions on others, although biased by our own experiences and thinking. Glasswing is not training to fix problems but an opportunity to learn as we set aside our defensiveness, take risks, open up, speak out, and develop spiritual courage.

Debate to Dialogue—Listening and Learning. People have been arguing about racism for decades with little positive effect. *Debate* is an attempt to persuade or overpower—to win by finding flaws in our opponent's logic. Debates on race create anger and solidify entrenched positions. *Dialogue* involves genuine listening to avoid a rush to judgment—increasing our pause response before we jump into the conversation. We are able to learn from and be influenced by others.

Equity

If the misery of our poor be not caused by nature,
but by our social institutions, then great is our sin.[29]

Charles Darwin

While the purpose of Glasswing is to foster *racial healing*, this new-found awareness motivates individuals to promote *racial equity*. Injustice involves both deliberate and unintentional arrangements within institutions and even in the language we use to describe our differences. Centuries of invisible systems of *white privilege* serve to favor or obstruct persons based on the biological fiction of race.[30]

The Kellogg Foundation summarizes the challenge of achieving racial equity. Children of color experience many risks, but disparities in family income, health care, and access to quality education are exacerbated—and can become cross-generational—by vast inequities in neighborhood and school environments. A host of other factors include higher rates of incarceration, incidence of health problems, school failure, poverty, and disability. The need for systems-wide approaches and community empowerment is abundantly clear.[31]

Racism is also entangled with classism, elitism, sexism, and patriarchy. The failure to recognize these imbalances blinds us to oppression and impedes our ability to become more connected, informed, and effective. Equity is the quest for fairness and justice, applied with a race-sensitive lens, unleashing unlimited human potential. Among our most rewarding professional experiences has been the opportunity to train thousands of people in racial healing and equity. Those participating in this transformation abandon the distortions of prejudice and come to see themselves and others in a new light. Together, we honor and celebrate our diversity while internalizing the reality of the oneness of humankind.

Action Research

Voices for Change

Elizabeth Carey & Gary Tester

*If you are neutral in situations of injustice,
you have chosen the side of the oppressor.*[32]

Desmond Tutu

Meeting universal growth needs is the foundation of wellness, resilience, and fulfillment in life. We know what kids need, and we know what contributions we can make as professionals and citizens. But too often, organizations or systems create obstacles that make it difficult to deliver what works. Those embracing strength-based principles encounter regulations or funding restrictions based on deficit-based mindsets and bureaucratic rigidity.

Programs seeking to provide evidence-based essentials may encounter resistance from funders, whether government, insurance, or donors. Foster care payments are too meager to meet complex needs. Charter school reimbursements are contrived to contain costs instead of unleash creativity.[33] Nonprofits have to decide if they are able to provide what a young person needs or only dole out the services the funding will cover. These barriers impede the implementation of new ideas, restrict funding, and jeopardize positive outcomes.

System Failure

Social work professor, David Wineman, was an early advocate in the reclaiming youth movement. He challenged oppressive practices in education, treatment, and justice settings.[34] Students with special needs endured public humiliation, program-imposed boredom, and punitive discipline. Professionals who speak out for reform are met with "avoidance responses, which can only be characterized as a system of defense against change."[35] This can involve pious clichés: *At least the child knows that you care and understand.* Or accusations of losing objectivity: *Are you sure you are not over-identifying with your client?*[36]

Not only do systems fail too many youth; sometimes they have direct iatrogenic effects. Bessel van der Kolk defined developmental trauma as the result of *"physical, emotional, and educational neglect and maltreatment."*[37] How ironic that the very systems that could provide support may be retraumatizing our most at-risk children.

Prevention must target the ecology that creates trauma in the first place. Look at this from the perspective of child care staff in a treatment center for youth. Their daily, direct experience gives them a deep understanding of what has happened in children's lives that has caused their pain-based behaviors. This is how various systems are contributing to these problems:

1. *School:* Zero tolerance policies fuel exclusion and expulsion.

2. *Neighborhood:* Without safe after-school activities and community policing, gangs rule the dangerous streets.

3. *Social Welfare:* Policies eject families from receiving food, housing, or even quality medical services.

4. *Community Health:* Substance abuse and mental health problems decimate families without access to treatment.

5. *Child Welfare:* Lack of quality child care and family preservation services foment conflict, neglect, and abuse.

6. *Employment and Transportation:* Without work with decent pay, reliable transportation, and child care, poverty is rampant.

Striking evidence about how systems are failing our most vulnerable children has been documented by researchers from Boys Town.[38] Data indicate poor outcomes for youngsters in the child welfare system. School drop-outs are as high as 75 percent.[39] Juvenile detention rates are 6.9 times higher than in the general population,[40] and up to 80 percent of youth have mental health problems. Foster children were prescribed psychotropic drugs at five times the rate of other children.[41]

High-needs children present emotional and behavioral challenges that most foster care and school staff are simply not equipped to meet. An example is shown in the accompanying data about youth whose foster care placements were disrupted by removal for negative reasons.[42] Caregivers completed a 30-item checklist of behavior problems they encountered over the previous 24 hours. The average number of daily incidents was 5.77. This is an ill omen since most foster parents are unable to tolerate more than six problem behaviors daily.

Figure 2. Behavior Problems and Foster Care Disruption[43]

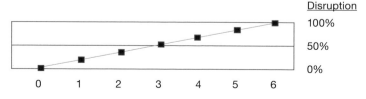

Each problem behavior reported increases the risk of failure in foster care by 17 percent.

Foster care is promoted as a less-restrictive alternative than residential group care—but in foster care as usual, serial failure of placements is the norm. In one study of 1,068 children, over half had been in seven or more placements. Whatever maltreatment might have led to removal from the family, these placement failures pile on more trauma and loss. Such children are much more likely to succeed in high-quality residential group care programs. With the proper care and treatment, most will make social, emotional, and academic gains, graduate from high school, and contribute to the community.[44]

When our systems implode on a family, children are at risk for homelessness, school truancy, substance abuse, gang involvement, and unfavorable life outcomes. We *must* see these as preventable problems. These systems are *our* systems. We created them. We pay for them. We can change them.

Leadership for Growth

Great leaders move us. They ignite our passion and inspire the best in us.[45]

Daniel Goleman

Positive change in organizations and systems is grounded in positive leadership. Kurt Lewin conducted classic studies of autocratic, laissez faire, and democratic leadership in children's groups.[46] Groups with authoritarian leaders were productive when directly controlled but spawned bullying subcultures among youth. As might be expected, permissive groups were chaotic and unproductive. Only democratic leaders were able to create a spirit of teamwork among staff and youth.

In their book, *Primal Leadership*, Goleman and colleagues described a variety of leadership styles.[47] They labelled two traditional types of leadership as *dissonant*, because these were at odds with democratic values and the neuroscience of positive emotions. A prominent traditional style was *commanding*, where most decisions have to be cleared by the person in charge. A more subtle authoritarian style was *pacesetting*, where the leader sets specific standards and holds employees accountable. While there are some situations in which authoritarian control is needed, in the long term, these approaches stifle creativity and perpetuate social inequality. Perhaps most important, they fail to tap the brain's inbuilt system of positive emotions.

Leadership Style	Leadership Goal	Circle of Courage
Affiliative	Create harmony by connecting people to one another.	Affiliative leaders meet the need for Belonging.
Coaching	Gain skills to achieve organizational and personal goals.	Coaching leaders meet the need for Mastery.
Democratic	Seek input and participation through collaboration.	Democratic leaders meet the need for Independence.
Visionary	Move people toward a shared dream of the way things could be.	Visionary leaders build shared dreams to meet the need for Generosity.

Goleman labelled the four effective leadership styles as *resonant*, since they evoke positive emotions and cultivate emotional intelligence. These are called: *affiliative, coaching, democratic,* and *visionary*.[48] Steve Van Bockern has connected these positive leadership styles with Circle of Courage needs as shown in the accompanying chart.[49] Such leadership builds personal and social competence in the staff team, which is a prerequisite for creating positive change in those we serve.

Competent and charismatic leaders are not enough; change can only endure with a competent staff. Richard DuFour calls for professional learning communities where members are committed to continual improvement in a spirit of collaboration.[50] Building a positive organizational ethos requires *teamwork primacy,* where all stakeholders are bound together by shared mission, beliefs, and goals.[51]

A leading researcher on professional development, Thomas Guskey, explains why most training rituals fail to make lasting change in staff and systems.[52] He describes five levels for evaluating the effectiveness of staff development:

1. *Participant Reaction.* Did they like the training?
2. *Participant Learning.* Did they gain knowledge and skills?
3. *Organizational Impact.* Did the agency support implementation?
4. *Implementing Learning.* Were new skills actually applied?
5. *Growth in those Served.* Did learning impact key client outcomes?

While one can gain useful data by evaluating each of these questions, which matters most? Guskey says we must plan from the bottom up, keeping the focus on the primary goals we have for our students or clients. In terms of evidence-based essentials, the most powerful measure of success is meeting universal growth needs.

Leadership in Action

Effective organizations are noted both by their stability as well as their ability to respond to ever-changing needs. We share here an example of the transformation of a juvenile court which implemented high quality treatment programs and a restorative justice model.

One of the authors began his career as a probation officer in Lucas County Juvenile Court in Toledo, Ohio. Judge Andy Devine had a vision of what courts could do to transform lives. When serious drug and alcohol problems reached epidemic proportions, the court began to fly youth and their parents to a treatment center in another state. But Judge Devine called together colleagues and said we were no longer going to send kids and families 800 miles away for treatment. Instead, the community would shoulder responsibility for addressing their needs.

The court partnered with two local hospital systems that had inpatient programs for kids with alcohol and drug problems. This was a great improvement for families, but after 45 days, the insurance money ended and services stopped. So next, the court developed its own counseling capacity by contracting with noted family therapist, Jay Haley, from the Philadelphia Child Guidance Clinic.[53] He trained a select group of probation officers and administrators in strategic and structural family therapy to support youth transitioning from treatment. This was far ahead of the traditional role of juvenile courts at that time.

Lucas County also piloted the restorative justice model, employing the power of generosity as young people gave back to the community they had harmed. Toledo has a beautiful metro-park system, and kids from the court cleared trails, trimmed trees, and planted flowers, making theirs a more beautiful city. This was a life-changing experience for children and families and changed public perceptions of the role of the youth justice system.

What was the impetus for these innovative programs? First, it was a progressive judge who redefined justice and pushed the envelope to create change. Next came a dynamic mother, fiercely advocating for her own child, who was involved in alcohol and other drugs. She helped form an organization called Parents Helping Parents. Third, a governance body, the Children's Services Board, brought together the court, mental health, education, and children's services to explore how to serve the neediest children in their systems. In sum, this was a synergy of an inspired leader, a committed parent support group, and a linkage of separate systems concerned with children and youth.

Over the years, many of these initiatives have survived by being embedded in other organizational structures. Judge Devine's model of forming a cluster of agencies is now in state law and applies across all of the counties in Ohio. This has been a process like Kurt Lewin's action research where a community solves a problem and then finds out what the next challenge might be, keeping the change process going.

Advocacy for Change

Never doubt that a small group of persons can change the world.
This is the only thing that ever has.[54]

Margaret Meade

It is imperative that we work to transform both the immediate ecology of children as well as the broader metasystem. We must become advocates at organizational, governmental, and societal levels. This is a matter of social justice. While professional voices must be heard, perhaps the most effective agents for change are young people who share personal stories about their transition from trauma to resilience.

Empowering those who are vulnerable or oppressed requires speaking truth to power. Of all the professions serving children and families, social work most directly embraces this advocacy role. The NASW code of professional ethics minces no words:

> *Social workers promote social justice and social change with and on behalf of clients. "Clients" is used inclusively to refer to individuals, families, groups, organizations, and communities. Social workers are sensitive to cultural and ethnic diversity and strive to end discrimination, oppression, poverty, and other forms of social injustice.... Social workers also seek to promote the responsiveness of organizations, communities, and other social institutions to individuals' needs and social problems.*[55]

But how can individuals change big systems? Our voices become strong when we join with other advocates to expand the impact of our actions. Talk, Tweet, Write, and Meet. We make our issue everyone's concern. We can also join advocacy movements, such as the Alliance for Strong Families and Communities. Susan Dreyfus of the Alliance observes that we must be more than providers of programs but transformational agents for change.[56]

With a goal of building resilience in our young, we reach beyond our organizations to transform communities and societies. We are all linked together on this small globe. Our challenge is to advocate for policies and practices that will impact the positive futures of children. Perhaps no person in recent times has been a more powerful force for transformation than Desmund Tutu, Nobel Peace Prize winner and Chair of the South African Truth and Reconciliation Commission. We turn to Archbishop Tutu for the final call to advocacy in words he penned for the Reclaiming Youth movement:

We must realize that it is a very, very shortsighted policy if we fail to redeem and salvage our most needy young people. We must look on children in need not as problems but as individuals with potential to share if they are given the opportunity. Even when they are really troublesome, there is some good in them, for, after all, they were created by God. I would hope we could find some creative ways to draw out of our children the good that is there in each of them.[57]

1. Machiavelli, 1513, Chapter 6.
2. Lewin, cited in Lippitt, Watson, & Westley, 1958, p. 129.
3. Ashworth et al., 2008.
4. Lewis, 2009, p. 7.
5. Thompson, Huefner, Daly, & Davis, 2014.
6. Buddha, cited in Peterson, 2013a, p. 231.
7. Csikszentmihalyi, 1990.
8. Peterson & Bossi, 1991.
9. Gold, 1999.
10. Commission for Children at Risk, 2003.
11. Larson & Brendtro, 2000.
12. de Chardin, 2010, n.p.
13. Ponds, 2014.
14. Commission for Children at Risk, 2003.
15. Peterson, 2006.
16. Wright, Masten, & Narayan, 2013.
17. Everson, 1993.
18. Brendtro & Larson, 2006.
19. Tutu, 2005, p. 124.
20. Bonilla-Silva, 2010.
21. Rutstein, 2001.
22. Du Bois, 1903.
23. Wenger, 2012.
24. Christopher, 2010.
25. Tabron with Kanani, 2014.
26. Longhurst & Brown, 2013.
27. Dimasio, 2005.
28. Wheatley, 2009.
29. Darwin, cited in Diggs, 2009, p. 112.
30. Rothenberg, 2011.
31. Kellogg Foundation, 2015.
32. Tutu, cited in Quigley, 2003, p. 8.
33. Ravitch, 2013.
34. Wineman & James, 1969.
35. Wineman & James, 1969, p. 27.
36. Wineman & James, 1969, p. 27.
37. Spinazzola, et al., 2005, p. 433.
38. Thompson, Huefner, Daly, & Davis, 2014.
39. Zorc et al., 2013.
40. Johnson-Reid, 2002.
41. GAO, 2012.
42. Chamberlain et al., 2006.
43. Chamberlain et al., 2006.
44. Thompson, Huefner, Daly, & Davis, 2014.
45. Goleman, Boyatzis, & McKee, 2013, p. 3.
46. Lewin, Lippitt, & White, 1939.
47. Goleman, Boyatzis, & McKee, 2013.
48. Goleman, Boyatzis, & McKee, 2013.
49. Van Bockern, 2011.
50. Dufour & Fullan, 2013.
51. Brendtro & Mitchell, 1983; Mitchell, 2003.
52. Guskey, 2000.
53. Richeport-Haley & Carlson, 2010.
54. Meade, cited in Sommers, 1984, p. 185.
55. NASW, 2008.
56. Dreyfus, 2014; Carey & Hollingsworth, 2013.
57. Tutu, 2005, p. 124.

Resources

Delivering the Circle of Courage Model

Derek Allen & Sarah Slamer

A global alliance of researchers and practitioners is applying evidence-based principles to build strengths in children, families, and communities.

Since 1913, Starr Commonwealth has been developing strength-based programs in the fields of education, treatment, and juvenile justice. Now in its second century, Starr is a global knowledge leader, providing research, publications, and training for all who work to strengthen children, families, and communities. The philosophical and scientific foundation for this mission is the Circle of Courage model.

Starr's global network operates through three key training institutes: Reclaiming Youth International (RYI), The National Institute for Trauma and Loss in Children (TLC), and Glasswing Racial Healing. A full range of evidence-based resources are available in areas of positive youth development, trauma-informed interventions, and diversity training. These programs are delivered through strength-based publications, seminars, skill-building training, online certification courses, and consultation (see starr.org and circleofcourage.org).

With an international board of 100 consulting editors, the quarterly *Reclaiming* journal is a forum for practice-based research on building strengths. Since 1994, the annual Black Hills Seminars have been the flagship Circle of Courage conference, bringing together practitioners and researchers from around the world. Similar events are sponsored by partner organizations in other countries. Through a network of certified trainers and consultants, the Circle of Courage model is being delivered directly to schools, youth agencies, and communities worldwide. A training-of-trainers format and online courses enable organizations to develop their own internal capacity to create reclaiming environments. As described below, each of the three programs of the Starr global network draws on a rich history.

The Circle of Courage model, which informed the Reclaiming Youth movement, began in 1988 at an international conference of the Child Welfare League of America. A presentation by Martin Brokenleg and Larry Brendtro was illustrated with the powerful art of George Bluebird, a young Native American incarcerated in a South Dakota prison. In 1990, they and Steve Van Bockern co-authored *Reclaiming Youth at Risk: Our Hope for the Future*. The model is a synergy of research on reclaiming youth, piloted at the University of Michigan and Starr Commonwealth, with the cultural wisdom of Native peoples. This strength-based philosophy now extends to all continents.

The National Institute for Trauma and Loss in Children was founded by William Steele in 1990 as a result of a wide-spread epidemic of youth suicide. Schools and agencies were seeking resources and practical strategies to address wide-spread community concerns about their children. The challenge of creating resources and working with victims of trauma led TLC to become immersed in research on trauma reactions and impacts on the developing brain. In the present day, TLC provides resources to professionals who serve traumatized individuals, families, and communities. Persons who have received this training are now working with trauma survivors worldwide.

Glasswing addresses issues related to marginalized groups excluded from belonging, emphasizing our oneness as a human family. Racism and all other forms of discrimination are destructive forces worldwide. Starr Commonwealth began work in this area in the 1990s when author and activist Nathan Rutstein introduced the process of racial healing to leaders of the organization. Beginning first with its own staff, Starr has offered these healing experiences to schools, human service organizations, faith communities, and the corporate sector. In addition to a range of formalized training opportunities, Glasswing consultants can provide evaluation and guidance in situations where schools or other organizations have experienced the crisis of hate in any of its forms. The goal of these efforts is to bring together all members of the human family, embracing the value of diversity with dignity.

The International Child & Youth Care Network

Leon Fulcher, Brian Gannon, & Thom Garfat

CYC-Net is a free international website based in South Africa providing on-line learning and networking for those who work with young people.

Before becoming a democracy, South Africa was isolated from the international community, and those working with children and youth had scant professional development resources. Accessing literature, either for practice or rudimentary training courses, was almost impossible. South Africa is a big country; child and youth care workers spread over thousands of miles felt very isolated. Nevertheless, the National Association of Child Care Workers of South Africa (naccw.org.za) had established its own print journal and benefitted from the inspiration of overseas colleagues who came to speak at conferences. This whetted appetites for further information, reading, and networking.

In the fledgling days of the internet, we were eager experimenters with this new technology, and soon started our own *intranet* for the use of staff members of the NACCW, who were emboldened to take new ideas and information to far-flung programs and courses. Written materials were made available on a primitive website; an e-mail based discussion group was introduced through which participants could wrestle with contemporary issues, problems, and controversies. A few overseas colleagues joined these discussions and soon others from around the world were "finding" us, expressing an interest, and asking to be included. This small initial network quickly swelled to fifty, then a hundred, and eventually thousands. So the International Child and Youth Care Network (cyc-net.org) was born.

A Constitution and Board of Governors were established and CYC-Net joined the World Wide Web. Our mission statement outlined these main objectives: *to promote and facilitate reading, learning, information sharing, discussion, networking, support and accountable practice amongst all who work with children, youth and families in difficulty.* This remains our focus today.

Recognizing currency variations and wealth differentials across the world community of child and youth care people and programs, the decision was made to give free access to all who used the site or participated in the discussion group. An important cornerstone of CYC-Net is that it should remain free to end-users. Many agencies, colleges, and individuals support this initiative through a process of subscription and donation, attesting to the usefulness of CYC-Net.

CYC-Net hosts thousands of daily visits to the web site. The discussion group has thousands of members and includes participants from all corners of the globe, with visitors from more than 200 countries and territories. The website offers tens of thousands of pages of reading, consisting of daily-updated news of the field, viewpoints, articles from related fields, extracts, press releases, website links, even a daily cartoon. In addition there are on-going "departments" such as a regular podcast, database searches generating reading lists on specific topics, a personality "profile" of people in the field, and an online bookshop.

The network also promotes a number of professional journals such as *Reclaiming, Relational Child and Youth Care Practice,* and *The International Journal of Social Pedagogy,* including lists of contents and abstracts, bibliographies, and full-text editorials. Visitors to this site find notices of upcoming conferences and announcements of employment positions. CYC-Net also houses the *Learning Zone Network,* with 50 modules of on-line learning on Child and Youth Care practice and Outcomes That Matter© which are being used in agency and academic training programs around the world. A special feature of the *Learning Zone* is the ability to tailor modules to meet the needs of specific groups.

Another major feature is the journal *CYC-Online,* which disseminates writings old and new, having been in continuous publication since 1999. This wealth of resources has given birth to CYC-Net Press, which makes written materials specific to the child and youth care field available worldwide in both hard copy and electronic formats.

In spite of its large international presence, CYC-Net is run by a very small, part-time, and mostly volunteer team. Brian Gannon of South Africa and Thom Garfat of Canada have served as the Founding Editors, assembling and editing much of the content. Chairman of our Board of Governors, Leon Fulcher, plays an important role in promotion and fund-raising. This international group of dedicated Board members keeps in touch with leading-edge developments impacting children of the world. You, the reader, are also invited to keep in touch regularly at www.cyc-net.org.

Contributors

Derek S. Allen, MA, Director of Program Development for the Starr Global Learning Network, Albion, Michigan.

James P. Anglin, PhD, Professor and former Director, School of Child and Youth Care, University of Victoria, Canada.

Howard Bath, PhD, former Commissioner for Children, Northern Territory, and senior international trainer for Circle of Courage, Brisbane, Australia.

Martin Brokenleg, EdD, former Professor at Augustana College and Vancouver School of Theology, Vancouver, British Columbia.

Juanita Capri Brown, MPP, Principal of Juanita Capri Brown & Associates, a social equity consulting firm, Oakland, California.

Elizabeth Carey, MSW, Executive Vice President and Chief Strategy Officer, Starr Commonwealth, Albion, Michigan.

Randy Copas, MA, Executive Director of the Albion Academy operated by Sequel Youth Services at Starr Commonwealth, Albion, Michigan.

Frank A. Fecser, PhD, CEO of the Positive Education Program, Cleveland, Ohio, and co-founder of the Life Space Crisis Intervention Institute.

Robert Foltz, PsyD, Associate Professor, The Chicago School of Professional Psychology, Chicago, Illinois.

Mark Freado, MA, MA, Counseling & Forensic Psychology, is consultant and trainer, Cal Farley's, Amarillo, Texas, and directs Reclaiming Youth projects.

Leon Fulcher, PhD, New Zealand, serves as Chairperson of the Board of Governors for CYC-Net, Cape Town South Africa.

Brian Gannon, MA, founder and editor of CYC-Net, Cape Town, and founder of the National Association of Child Care Workers of South Africa.

Thom Garfat, PhD, co-founder and co-editor of the CYC-Net, and provides training through TransformAction International, Rosemere, Quebec.

Raquel Hatter, MSW, EdD, Commissioner of the Tennessee Department of Human Services, Nashville, Tennessee.

William C. Jackson, PhD, Executive Vice President and Chief Clinical Officer, Starr Commonwealth, Detroit, Michigan.

Adrienne Brant James, MSW, President, Turtle Island Learning Circle, Member of the Mohawk Nation, Sioux Falls, SD.

Beate Kreisle, MA, founder of Jugend-Kolleg am See, a group treatment program in Moos-Bankholzem, Germany.

Caelan Kuban, LMSW, PsyD, Director of the National Institute for Trauma and Loss in Children, a program of Starr Commonwealth, Albion, Michigan.

Scott Larson, DMin, founder and president of Straight Ahead Ministries, and professor at Gordon-Conwell Theological Seminary, Boston, Massachusetts.

Erik K. Laursen, PhD, researcher on evidence-based treatment and senior international trainer for the Circle of Courage, Richmond, Virginia.

James E. Longhurst, EdD, Glasswing Racial Healing lead facilitator and director of Starr doctoral psychology intern programs, Albion, Michigan.

Tim McDonald, PhD, Director of the Catholic Education Office for Western Australia, and former professor, Edith Cowan University, Perth, Australia.

Christopher Peterson, PhD, (1950-2012), was professor of psychology at the University of Michigan and a leader of the positive psychology movement.

Kenneth Ponds, MDiv, Glasswing Racial Healing lead facilitator, and former chaplain, Starr Commonwealth, Albion, Michigan.

Richard Quigley, MEd, former President and CEO, Woodland Hills, Duluth, Minnesota, and author on positive peer empowerment.

John Seita, EdD, Associate Professor of Social Work, Michigan State University, East Lansing, Michigan, and researcher on resilience.

Sarah Slamer, MA, LPC, Assistant Director, the National Institute for Trauma and Loss in Children, Albion, Michigan.

William Steele, MSW, PsyD, founder of the National Institute for Trauma and Loss in Children, and senior training consultant, Albion, Michigan.

Thomas Tate, MA, Senior Vice President for Learning and Talent Development, Starr Commonwealth, Albion, Michigan.

Gary Tester, MRC, Executive Vice President and Senior Development Officer, Starr Commonwealth, Albion, Michigan.

Steve Van Bockern, EdD, Professor of Education and Special Education at Augustana College, Sioux Falls, South Dakota, and Dean, Reclaiming Youth.

Bibliography

Acharya, S., Shukla, S., Mahajan, S., & Diwan, S. (2010). Localization to neuroplasticity: The evolution of metaphysical neuroscience. *The Journal of the Association of Physicians of India, 60,* 38-60.

Adams, D. (1997). *Education for extinction.* Lawrence, KS: University of Kansas Press.

Addams, J. (1909). *The spirit of youth and the city streets.* New York, NY: Macmillan.

Adler, A. (1930). *The problem child.* New York, NY: W. P. Putnam's Sons.

Adler, M. (1985). *Ten philosophical mistakes.* New York, NY: Macmillan.

Aichhorn, A. (1925). *Verwahrloster Jugend.* Wien, Osterreich: Internationaler Psychoanalytischer Verlag. English translation, 1935. *Wayward youth.* New York: Viking Press.

Aichhorn, A. (1951). *Wayward youth.* London, UK: Imago. First published 1925, *Verwahrloster Jugend.* Wien, Osterreich: Internationaler Psychoanalytischer Verlag.

Ainsworth, M. (1989). Attachments beyond infancy. *American Psychologist, 44*(4), 709-716.

Ainsworth, M., Blehar, M., Waters, E., & Wall, S. (1978). *Patterns of attachment: A psychological study of the strange situation.* Hillside, NJ: Lawrence J. Erlbaum Associates.

Alexander, J. (2012). *Trauma—A social theory.* Cambridge, UK: Polity.

Amendola, M., & Oliver, R. (2014). *Anger control training, Prepare Curriculum implementation guide.* Champaign, IL: Research Press.

Amendola, M., & Oliver, M. (Eds.). (2014). *The Prepare Curriculum Implementation Guides.* Champaign, IL: Research Press.

American Psychological Association. (n.d.). The road to resilience. http://www.apa.org/helpcenter/road-resilience.aspx

American Psychological Association. (2006). *Report of the Working Group on Psychotropic Medications for Children and Adolescents.* http://www.apa.org/pi/families/resources/child-medications.pdf

American Psychological Association. (2008). Are zero tolerance policies effective in the schools? *American Psychologist, 63*(9), 852-862.

American Psychiatric Association (APA). (2013). *Diagnostic and statistical manual of mental disorders* (5th ed.). Washington, DC: Author.

Anandalakshmy, S. (2010). *Through the lens of culture: Centuries of childhood and education in India.* Chennai, India: Bala Mandir Research Foundation.

Andersen, E. (2013). *21 quotes from Henry Ford on business, leadership, and life.* http://www.forbes.com/sites/erikaandersen/2013/05/31/21-quotes-from-henry-ford-on-business-leadership-and-life/

Anderson, G., & Seita, J. (2005). Family and social factors affecting youth in the child welfare system. In N. Webb (Ed.), *Working with traumatized youth in child welfare* (pp. 67-90). New York, NY: Guilford Press.

Andrews, P., Thompson Jr., J., Amstadter, A., & Neale, M. (2012). Primum non nocere: An evolutionary analysis of whether antidepressants do more harm than good. *Frontiers in Psychology, 3,* 1-19.

Anglin, J. (2002). *Pain, normality and the struggle for congruence: Reinterpreting residential care for children and youth.* Binghamton, NY: Haworth Press.

Anglin, J. (2011). Making group home care a positive alternative, not the last resort. In K. Kufeldt & B. McKenzie (Eds.), *Child welfare: Connecting research, policy, and practice (2nd ed.)* (pp. 215-228). Waterloo, Ontario: Wilfrid Laurier University Press.

Anglin, J. (2014). Pain based behavior with children and youth in conflict. *Reclaiming Children and Youth, 22*(4), 53-55.

Anthony, E., & Cohler, B. (1987). *The invulnerable child.* New York, NY: Guilford Press.

Aries, P. (1965). *Centuries of childhood: A social history of family life.* New York, NY: Vintage.

Ashton-Warner, S. (1986). *Teacher.* New York, NY: Simon-Schuster.

Ashworth, J. (2008). *A case study of comprehensive schoolwide improvement at a high needs elementary school.* (Doctoral Dissertation). University of South Dakota, Vermillion, South Dakota.

Ashworth, J., Van Bockern, S., Ailts, J., Donnelly, J., Erickson, K., & Woltermann, J. (2008). The restorative justice center: An alternative to school detention. *Reclaiming Children and Youth, 17*(3), 22-26.

Assay, T., & Lambert, M. (1999). The empirical case for the common factors in therapy: Qualitative findings. In M. Hubble, B. Duncan, & S. Miller (Eds.), *The heart and soul of change: What works in therapy* (pp. 33-56). Washington, DC: American Psychological Association.

Athens, L. (1992). *The creation of dangerous violent criminals.* Champaign, IL: University of Illinois Press.

Augustine. (397 A.D.). *The confessions of St. Augustine.* Translated by H. Chadwick, 2009. New York, NY: Oxford Press.

Baddeley, A. (2002). Is working memory still working? *European Psychologist, 7,* 85-97.

Bandura, A. (1990). Reflections on non-ability determinants of competence. In R. Sternberg & J. Kolligian, Jr. (Eds.), *Competence considered* (pp. 315-362). New Haven, CT: Yale University Press.

Bandura, A. (1994). Self-efficacy. In V. Ramachandran (Ed.), *Encyclopedia of Human Behavior, Vol. 4* (pp. 77-81). New York, NY: Academic Press.

Bandura, A. (1997). *Self-efficacy: The exercise of control.* New York, NY: Worth Publishers.

Bandura, A. (1999). Moral disengagement in the perpetration of inhumanity. *Personality and social psychology review, 3*(3), 193-209.

Barkley, R. (2012). *Executive functions: What they are, how they work, and why they evolved.* New York, NY: Guilford Press.

Barraza, J., & Zac, P. (2009). Empathy towards strangers triggers oxytocin release and subsequent generosity. *Annals of the New York Academy of Science, 1167,* 182-189.

Barrett, H. C. (2015). *The shape of thought: How mental adaptations evolve.* New York, NY: Oxford University Press.

Bateson, M., Nettle, D., & Roberts, G. (2006). Cues of being watched enhance cooperation in a real-world setting. *Biology Letters, 2*(3), 412-414.

Bath, H. (2008). Calming together: The pathway to self-control. *Reclaiming Children and Youth, 16*(4), 44-46.

Bath, H. (2015). The Three Pillars of TraumaWise Care: Healing in the other 23 hours. *Reclaiming Children and Youth, 23*(4), 5-11.

Bauer, I., & Baumeister, R. (2011). Self-regulatory strength. In K. Vohs & R. Baumeister (Eds.), *Handbook of self-regulation: Research, theory, and applications* (pp. 64-82). New York, NY: Guilford Press.

Baumeister, R. (2011). The need-to-belong theory. In P. Van Lange, A. Kruglanski, & E. Higgins (Eds.), *Handbook of theories of social psychology, Vol. 2* (pp. 121-140).

Baumeister, R. F., DeWall, C. N., Ciarocco, N. J., & Twenge, J. M. (2005). Social exclusion impairs self-regulation. *Journal of Personality and Social Psychology, 88*(4), 589.

Baumeister, R., & Leary, M. (1995). The need to belong: Desire for interpersonal attachments as a fundamental human motivation. *Psychological Bulletin, 117,* 497-529.

Baumeister, R., Twenge, J., & Nuss, C. (2002). Effects of social inclusion on cognitive processes: Anticipated aloneness reduces intelligent thought. *Journal of Personality and Social Psychology, 83*(4), 817.

Bellonci, C., Huefner, J., Griffith, A., Vogel-Rosen, G., Smith, G., & Preston, S. (2013). Concurrent reductions in psychotropic medication, assault, and physical restraint in two residential treatment programs for youth. *Child and Youth Services Review, 35,* 1773-1779.

Belsky, J., & Pluess, M. (2009). The nature (and nurture?) of plasticity in early human development. *Perspectives on Psychological Science, 4*(4), 345-351.

Benard, B. (2004). *Resiliency: What have we learned?* San Francisco, CA: West Ed.

Benson, P. (1990). *The troubled journey: A portrait of 6th-12th grade youth.* Minneapolis, MN: Search Institute.

Benson, P. (1997). *All kids are our kids: What communities must do to raise caring and responsible children and adolescents.* San Francisco, CA: Jossey-Bass.

Benson, P., Scales, P., Hamilton, S., Sesma, A., Hong, K., & Roehlkepartain, E. (2006). PYD so far: Core hypothesis and their implications for policy and practice. *Search Institute Insights & Evidence, 3*(1), 1-13.

Benson, P., Williams, D., & Johnson, A. (1987). *The quicksilver years: The hopes and fears of early adolescents.* San Francisco, CA: Jossey-Bass.

Bergen, D. (2006). Play. In S. Feinstein (Ed.), *The Praeger handbook of learning and the brain, Vol. 2* (pp. 378-382). Westport, CT: Praeger Publications.

Berkowitz, L. (1992). *Aggression: Its causes, consequences, and control.* New York, NY: McGraw Hill.

Binet, A. (1909). *Les idées modernes sur les enfants.* Paris, France: E. Flammarion.

Blau, G., Caldwell, B., & Lieberman, R. (2014). *Residential interventions for children, adolescents, and families.* New York, NY: Routledge.

Bloom, S. (1997). *Creating sanctuary.* New York, NY: Routledge.

Bloom, S., & Farragher, B. (2011). *Destroying sanctuary: The crisis in human services delivery systems.* Oxford, UK: Oxford University Press.

Bolin, I. (1998). *Rituals of respect: The secret of survival in the high Peruvian Andes.* Austin, TX: University of Texas Press.

Bolin, I. (2006). *Growing up in a culture of respect: Child rearing in highland Peru.* Austin, TX: University of Texas Press.

Bombay, A., Matheson, K., & Anisman, H. (2009). Intergenerational trauma: Convergence of multiple processes among First Nations peoples in Canada. *Journal of Aboriginal Health, 5*(3), 6-47.

Bonilla-Silva, E. (2010). *Racism without racists: Color-blind racism and racial inequality in contemporary America.* Lanham, MD: Roman & Littlefield.

Bosco, J. (2000). Heroes and pioneers: Kindness. Available at: http://www.cyc-net.org/today2000/today000818.html

Bowlby, J. (1969/1982). *Attachment and loss, Volume 1. Attachment.* New York, NY: Basic Books.

Bradley, S. (2000). *Affect regulation and the development of psychopathology.* New York, NY: Guilford Press.

Brendtro, L., Brokenleg, M., & Van Bockern, S. (1990/2002). *Reclaiming youth at risk: Our hope for the future.* Bloomington, IN: Solution Tree.

Brendtro, L., & du Toit, L. (2005). *Response Ability Pathways: Restoring bonds of respect.* Cape Town, South Africa: Pretext.

Brendtro, L., & Hinders, D. (1990). A saga of Janusz Korzak, the king of children. *Harvard Educational Review, 60*(2), 237-246.

Brendtro, L., & Larson, S. (2006). *The resilience revolution.* Bloomington, IN: Solution Tree.

Brendtro, L., & Mitchell, M. (1983). The organizational ethos: From tension to teamwork. In L. Brendtro & A. Ness, *Re-educating troubled youth.* New York, NY: Aldine de Gruyter.

Brendtro, L., Mitchell, M., & McCall, H. (2007). Positive Peer Culture: An antidote to "peer deviance training." *Reclaiming Children and Youth, 15*(4), 200-206.

Brendtro, L., Mitchell, M., Freado, M., & du Toit, L. (2012). The Developmental Audit: From deficits to strengths. *Reclaiming Children and Youth, 21*(1), 7-13.

Brendtro, L., & Ness, A. (1983). *Re-educating troubled youth.* New York, NY: Aldine de Gruyter.

Brendtro, L., & Shahbazian, M. (2004). *Troubled children and youth: Turning problems into opportunities.* Champaign, IL: Research Press.

Briere, J., & Scott, C. (2006). *Principles of trauma therapy: A guide to symptoms, evaluations, and treatment.* Thousand Oaks, CA: Sage.

Brokenleg, M. (1998). Native wisdom on belonging. *Reclaiming Children and Youth, 7*(3), 130-132.

Brokenleg, M. (2012). Turning cultural trauma into resilience. *Reclaiming Children and Youth, 21*(3) 9-13.

Brokenleg, M., & Brendtro, L. with art by George Bluebird. (1988). *Working with Native youth in North America: Belonging, mastery, independence, and generosity.* Washington, DC: Child Welfare League of America International Conference.

Brokenleg, M., & Long, N. (2013). Problems as opportunity: Meeting growth needs. *Reclaiming Children and Youth, 22*(1), 36-37.

Bronfenbrenner, U. (1977). Toward an experimental ecology of human development. *American Psychologist, 32,* 513-531.

Bronfenbrenner, U. (1979). *The ecology of human development.* Cambridge, MA: Harvard University Press.

Bronfenbrenner, U. (1986). Alienation and the four worlds of childhood. *Phi Delta Kappan, 67*(6), 430, 432-36.

Bronfenbrenner, U. (2005). *Making human beings human: Bioecological perspectives on human development.* Thousand Oaks, CA: Sage Publications.

Brooks, C., & Roush, D. (2014). Transformation in the justice system. *Reclaiming Children and Youth, 23*(1), 42-46.

Brooks, R. (2007). The search for islands of competence: A metaphor of hope and strength. *Reclaiming Children and Youth, 16*(1), 11-13.

Brown, B. (2012). *Daring greatly: How the courage to be vulnerable transforms the way we live, love, parent, and lead.* London, UK: Penguin Books.

Brown, D. (1991). *Human universals.* Boston, MA: McGraw-Hill.

Brown, J., Roderick, T., Lantieri, L., & Aber, J. (2004). The Resolving Conflict Creatively Program: A school-based social and emotional learning program. In J. Zins, R. Weissberg, M. Wang, & H. Walberg (Eds.), *Building academic success on social and emotional learning* (pp. 151-169). New York, NY: Teacher's College Press.

Brown, W., & Seita, J. (2010). *Growing up in the care of strangers: The experiences, insights and recommendations of eleven former foster kids.* Tallahassee, FL: William Gladden Foundation.

Bryk, A., Sebring. P., Allensworth, E., Luppescu, S., & Easton, J. (2010). *Organizing schools for improvement.* Lessons from Chicago. Chicago, IL: The University of Chicago Press.

Buber, M. (1970). *I and thou.* New York, NY: Charles Scribner and Sons.

Buehler, R., Patterson, G., & Furness, J. (1966). Reinforcement of behavior in institutional settings. *Behavior, Research, and Therapy, 4:* 157-167.

Buffum, A., Mattos, M., & Weber, C. (2012). *Simplifying response to interventions: Four essential guiding principles.* Bloomington, IN: Solution Tree.

Burke, T. (1976). *I have heard your feelings.* Ann Arbor, MI: Delafield Press.

Burt, C., Jones, E., Miller, E., & Moodie, W. (1934). *How the mind works.* New York, NY: Appleton, Century, Croft.

Cajete, G. (2000). *Native science: Natural laws of interdependence.* Santa Fe, NM: Clear Light.

Calame, R., & Parker, K. (2013). *Family TIES: A family-based intervention to complement Prepare, ART, and TIES Youth Groups.* Champaign, IL: Research Press.

California Council on Youth Relations. (2007). *Transition aged youth focus groups: Youth voice and the Mental Health Services Act.* Report and recommendation. California Council on Youth Relations.

Candland, D. (1995). *Feral children and clever animals: Reflections on human nature.* New York, NY: Oxford University Press.

Cantrell, R., & Cantrell, M. (Eds.). (2007). *Helping troubled children and youth.* Memphis, TN: AREA.

Caprara, V., Barbaranelli, C., Pastorelli, C., Bandura, A., & Zimbardo, P. (2000). Prosocial foundations of children's academic achievement. *Psychological Science, 11*(4), 302-306.

Carey, E., & Hollingsworth, J. (2013). Embracing the industry of courage. In M. Mortell & T. Hansen-Turton (Eds.), *Making strategy count in the health and human services sector: Lessons learned from 20 organizations and chief strategy officers* (pp. 39-50). New York, NY: Springer Publishing.

Carter, C. (1998). Neuro-endocrine perspectives on social attachment and love. *Psycho-Neuro Immunology, 23:* 779-818.

Carter, C. (2003). Developmental consequences of oxytocin. *Physiology & Behavior, 79:* 383-397.

Carter, C. (2007). Neuropeptides and the protective effects of social bonds. In E. Harmon-Jones & P. Winkielman (Eds.), *Social neuroscience: Integrating biological and psychological explanations of social behavior* (pp. 425-437). New York, NY: Guilford Press.

Casey, B., Jones, R., & Sommerville, H. (2011). Braking and accelerating of the adolescent brain. *Journal of Research on Adolescence, 21*(1), 21-33.

Cassullo, G., & Capello, F. (2010). Back to the roots: The influence of Ian D. Suttie on British psychoanalysis. *American Imago, 67*(1), 5-22.

CDC. (2010). School connectedness: Strategies for increasing protective factors among youth. *Reclaiming Children and Youth, 19*(3), 20-24.

Cervantes, M. (1615). *Don Quixote de la Mancha.* Translated by Peter Motteux, 1930. New York, NY: Modern Library Giant.

Chamberlain, P., Price, J., Reid, J., Lansverk, K., Fisher, P., & Stoolmiller, M. (2006). Who disrupts from placement in foster and kinship care? *Child Abuse & Neglect, 30,* 409-424.

Chambers, J., & Henrickson, T. (2002). Drugships: How kids make relationships with addictive behavior. *Reclaiming Children and Youth, 11*(3), 130-134.

Chess, S., & Thomas, A. (1999). *Goodness of fit: Clinical applications, from infancy through adult life.* New York, NY: Routledge.

Christopher, G. (2010). Healing America: A funder's commitment to racial equity. *Responsive Philanthropy,* Summer, 6-9.

Churchland, P. (2011). *Braintrust: What neuroscience tells us about morality.* Princeton, NJ: Princeton University Press.

Cicchetti, D., Rogosch, F. A., & Toth, S. L. (2006). Fostering secure attachment in infants in maltreating families through preventive interventions. *Developmental Psychopathology, 18*(3), 623-649.

Cicchetti, D., & Valentino, K. (2006). An ecological-transactional perspective on child maltreatment. In D. Cicchetti & D. Cohen (Eds.), *Developmental psychology (2nd ed., Vol. 3): Risk, disorder, and adaptation* (pp. 129-201). New York, NY: Wiley.

Commission for Children at Risk. (2003). *Hardwired to connect: The new scientific case for authoritative communities.* New York, NY: Broadway Publications.

Cohen, F. (1942). *Handbook of Federal Indian law.* Ann Arbor, MI: University of Michigan Library.

Coopersmith, S. (1967). *Antecedents of self-esteem.* San Francisco, CA: Freeman.

Cory, Jr., G. (2000). *Toward consilience. The bioneurological basis of behavior, thought, experience, and language.* New York, NY: Kluwer Academic.

Cosaro, W. (2011). *The sociology of childhood.* Los Angeles, CA: Sage.

Cosgrove, L., & Krimsky, S. (2012). A comparison of DSM-IV and DSM-5 panel members' financial associations with industry: A pernicious problem persists. *PLoS Med, 9*(3), e1001190.

Coyle, D. (2009). *The talent code: Greatness isn't born. It's grown. Here's how.* New York, NY: Bantam Books.

Cozolino, L. (2006). *The neuroscience of human relationships: Attachment and the developing social brain.* New York, NY: Norton.

Crick, N., & Dodge K. (1994). A review and reformulation of social information processing mechanisms in children's social adjustment. *Psychological Bulletin, 115:* 74-101.

Cross, T. (2012). *Relational world view model.* Portland, OR: National Indian Child Welfare Association.

Cross, T. (2014). The Indian Child Welfare Act: We must still fight for our children. *Reclaiming Children and Youth, 23*(2), 23-24.

Cryder, C., Kilmer, R., Tedeschi, R., & Calhoun, L. (2006). An exploratory study of posttraumatic growth in children following a natural disaster. *American Journal of Orthopsychiatry, 76*(1), 65-69.

Csikszentmihalyi, M. (1990). *Flow: The psychology of optimal experiences.* New York, NY: Harper Perennial.

Csikszentmihalyi, M. (1996). *Creativity: The psychology of discovery and invention.* New York, NY: Harper Perennial.

Csikszentmihalyi, M., & Larson, R. (1987). Validity and reliability of the experience-sampling method. *Journal of Nervous and Mental Disease, 175:* 526-536.

Csikszentmihalyi, M., Rathunde, K., & Whalen, S. (1993). *Talented teenagers: The roots of success & failure.* Cambridge, UK: Cambridge University Press.

Csoka, A., & Szyf, M. (2009). Epigenetic side-effects of common pharmaceuticals: A potential new field in medicine and pharmacology. *Medical Hypotheses, 73:* 770-780.

Damon, W. (2004). What is PYD? *Annals of the American Academy of Political and Social Science, 591:* 13-24.

Damon, W. (2008). *The path to purpose.* New York, NY: Free Press.

Darley, J., & Batson, C. (1973). From Jerusalem to Jericho. *Journal of Personality and Social Psychology, 27:* 100-108.

Darwin, C. (1857). Letter to J. D. Hooker, Aug. 1, 1857. Published 1990 in F. Burdhard & S. Smith (Eds.), *The correspondence of Charles Darwin, Vol. 6, 1856-1857* (p. 438). Cambridge, UK: University of Cambridge.

Darwin, C. (1873). *The descent of man.* New York, NY: Appleton.

de Chardin, P. T. (2010). *Glasswing Manual.* Albion, MI: Starr Commonwealth.

Descartes, R. (1637/2008). *A discourse on the method.* [translation of the original work, 2008]. New York, NY: Oxford University Press.

Dewey, J. (1910). *How we think.* Lexington, MA: D. C. Heath.

Dewey, J. (1916). *Democracy and education.* New York, NY: Macmillan.

Dufour, R., & Fullan, M. (2013). *Cultures built to last: Systemic PLCs at work.* Bloomington, IN: Solution Tree.

Daubert Standard. (n.d.). Retrieved November 18, 2013, from Cornell University Law School Legal Information Institute: http://www.law.cornell.edu/wex/daubert_standard

Dawson, C. (2003). A study on the effectiveness of Life Space Crisis Intervention for students identified with emotional disturbances. *Reclaiming Children and Youth, 11*(4), 223-230.

Deloria, E. (1943). *Speaking of Indians.* New York, NY: Friendship Press.

Deloria, Jr., V. (2009). *C. G. Jung and the Sioux traditions: Dreams, visions, nature, and the primitive.* New Orleans, LA: Spring Journal Books.

Diamond, J. (2012). *The world until yesterday. What can we learn from traditional societies?* New York, NY: Viking Press.

Diener, E., Oishi, S., & Park, J. (2014). An incomplete list of eminent psychologists of the modern era. *Archives of Scientific Psychology, 2:* 20-32.

Diggs, T. (2009). *Counseling to empower: A philosophical shift in the way we serve our children and students.* Saarbrücken, Germany: VDM Publishing.

Digney, J. (2009). Humor and connecting with kids in pain. *Reclaiming Children and Youth, 18*(3), 54-57.

Dimasio, A. (2005). *Descartes' error: Emotion, reason, and the human brain.* New York, NY: Penguin Books.

Dishion, T., & Kavanagh, L. (2008). *Intervening in adolescent problem behavior: A family centered approach.* New York, NY: Guilford Press.

Dishion, T., McCord, J., & Poulin, F. (1999). When interventions harm: Peer groups and problem behavior. *American Psychologist, 54*(9), 755-764.

Dodge, K., Dishion, T., & Lansford, J., (Eds.). (2006). *Deviant peer influence in programs for youth: Problems and solutions.* New York, NY: Guilford Press.

Doidge, N. (2007). *The brain that changes itself.* New York, NY: Viking Press.

Dreikurs, R. (1971). *Social equality: The challenge of today.* Chicago, IL: Adler School of Professional Psychology.

Dreyfus, S. (2014). *LaSalle School enews.* http://www.lasalle-school.org/wp-content/uploads/2014/07/March-2014.pdf

DuBois, W.E.B. (1903). *The souls of black folk: Essays and sketches.* Chicago, IL: A. C. McClurg.

DuBois, W.E.B. (1909). *John Brown.* Philadelphia, PA: G. W. Jacobs.

Duckworth, A., Peterson, C., Matthews, M., & Kelly, D. (2007). Grit: Perseverance and passion for long-term goals. *Journal of Personality and Social Psychology, 92*(6), 1087-1101.

Duckworth, A., & Seligman, M. (2005). Self-discipline outdoes IQ in predicting academic performance of adolescents. *Psychological Science, 16*(12), 939-944.

Dunbar, R. (1998). The social brain hypothesis. *Evolutionary Anthropology, 6,* 178-190.

Duncan, B., Miller, S., Wampold, B., & Hubble, M. (Eds.). (2010). *The heart and soul of change, second edition: Delivering what works in therapy.* Washington, DC: American Psychological Association.

Duncan, P., Garcia, A., Frankowski, B., Carey, P., Kallock, E., Dixon, R., & Shaw, J. (2007). Inspiring healthy adolescent choices: A rationale for and guide to strength promotion in primary care. *Journal of Adolescent Health, 41*(6), 525-535.

Dweck, C. (2006). *Mindset: The new psychology of success.* New York, NY: Random House.

Eastman, C. (Ohiyesa). (1911). *The soul of the Indian.* Boston, MA: Houghton Mifflin.

Eisenberger, N. (2011). The neural basis of social pain: Findings and implications. In G. MacDonald & L. Jensen-Campbell (Eds.), *Social pain: Neuropsychological and health implications of loss and exclusion* (pp. 53-78). Washington, DC: American Psychological Association.

Eisler, R. (1998). *The chalice and the blade.* New York, NY: HarperOne.

Elder, G. (1994). Time, human agency, and social change: Perspectives on the life course. *Social Psychology Quarterly, 57*(1), 4-15.

Engel, S. (2009). Is curiosity vanishing? *Child and Adolescent Psychiatry, 48*(8), 777–779.

Enlow, M., Egeland, B., Blood, E., Wright, R., & Wright, R. (2012). Interpersonal trauma exposure and cognitive development in children to age 8 years: A longitudinal study. *Journal of Epidemiology and Community Health, 66:* 105-110.

Erikson, E. (1950/1963). *Childhood and society.* New York, NY: W. W. Norton.

Espiner, D., & Guild, D. (2010). Growing a Circle of Courage culture: One school's journey. *Reclaiming Children and Youth, 19*(2), 21-27.

Espiner, D., & Guild, D. (2015). *Rolling with resilience: Building family strengths.* Lennox, SD: Starr Commonwealth, Circle of Courage Publications.

Everson, T. (1993). *Pathways: Fostering spiritual growth among at-risk youth: The Boys Town philosophy.* Boys Town, NE: Boys Town Press.

Fahlberg, V. (1991). *A child's journey through placement.* Indianapolis, IN: Perspectives Press.

Faust, D. (2012). *Coping with psychiatric and psychological testimony.* New York, NY: Oxford University Press.

Fecser, F. (2015). Roots of psychoeducation. *Reclaiming Children and Youth, 24*(1). In press.

Feigen, S., Owens, G., & Goodyear-Smith, F. (2014). Theories of altruism: A systematic review. *Annals of Neuroscience and Psychology, 1*:1. http://www.vipoa.org/neuropsychol

Felitti, V., & Anda, R. (2010). The relationship of adverse childhood experiences to adult medical disease, psychiatric disorder, and sexual behavior: Implications for healthcare. In R. Lanius, E. Vermetten, & C. Pain (Eds.), *The impact of early life trauma on health and disease* (pp. 77-87), New York, NY: Cambridge University Press.

Ferenczi, S. (1932). In *The clinical diary of Sándor Ferenczi.* English translation, 1988. J. Dupont (Ed.). Cambridge, MA: Harvard University Press.

Ferenczi, S. (1933). The confusion of tongues between adults and children: The language of tenderness and of passion. *International Journal of Psycho-Analysis, 30*: Entire issue No. 4, 1949.

Ferenczi, S. (1934). Gedanken über das Trauma. *International Zeitschrift für Psychoanalyse, 5*(2), 5-17.

Fields, R. D. (2011). The other brain: *The scientific and medical breakthroughs that will heal our brains and revolutionize our health.* New York, NY: Simon and Schuster.

Fiske, S. (2004). *Social beings: Core motives in social psychology.* Hoboken, NJ: Wiley.

Fitzsimmons, H. (2015). *The misidentification of trauma symptoms as bipolar disorder in youth.* (Doctoral dissertation). The Chicago School of Professional Psychology, Chicago, Illinois.

Flasher, J. (1978). Adultism. *Adolescence, 13*(51), 517-523.

Flynn, J. (2012). *Are we getting smarter?* London, UK: Cambridge University Press.

Foltz, R. (2008). Medicating relational trauma in youth. *Reclaiming Children and Youth, 17*(3), 3-8.

Foltz, R., & Huefner, J. (2013). The subjective experience of being medicated in troubled youth: A sample from residential treatment. *Journal of Child and Family Studies, 23:* 752-763.

Frances, A. (2013). *Saving normal: An insider's revolt against out-of-control psychiatric diagnosis, DSM-5, big pharma, and the medicalization of ordinary life.* New York, NY: William Morrow.

Forthun, L., & McCombie, J. (2007). A preliminary outcome study of Response Ability Pathways training. *Reclaiming Children and Youth, 16*(2), 27-34.

Francis, R. (2011). *Epigenetics: The ultimate mystery of inheritance.* New York, NY: W. W. Norton.

Frankowski, B., Brendtro, L., Van Bockern, S., & Duncan, P. (2014). Strength based interviewing: The Circle of Courage. In K. Ginsburg & S. Kinsman (Eds.), *Reaching teens: Strength-based communication strategies to build resilience and support healthy adolescent development* (pp. 237-242). Elk Grove Village, IL: American Academy of Pediatrics.

Frankowski, B., Leader, I., & Duncan, P. (2009). Strength-based interviewing. *Adolescent Medicine, 20:* 22-40.

Freado, M., & Bath, H. (2014). Standing alone in judgment. *Reclaiming Children and Youth, 22*(4), 21-26.

Freado, M., & Heckenlaible-Gotto, M. (2006). Andrei's private logic: The Developmental Audit as a life line. *Reclaiming Children and Youth, 15*(3), 132-137.

Freado, M., & Van Bockern, S. (2010a). King of cool. *Reclaiming Children and Youth, 19*(1), 45-49.

Freado, M., & Van Bockern, S. (2010b). Searching for truth: Responsible decision-making with the Developmental Audit. *Reclaiming Children and Youth, 18*(4), 18-21.

Fulcher, L., & Garfat, T. (2008). *Quality care in a family setting.* Cape Town, South Africa: Pretext.

Fuller, R. (2003). *Somebodies and nobodies: Overcoming the abuse of rank.* Gabriola Island, British Columbia: New Society Publishers.

Gambone, M., Klem, A., & Connell, J. (2002). *Finding out what matters for youth: Testing key links in a community action framework for youth development.* Philadelphia, PA: Youth Development Strategies, Inc. and Institute for Research and Reform in Education.

GAO. (2012). *Concerns remain about appropriate services for children in Medicaid and foster care. GAO-13-15.* Washington, DC: Government Accountability Office.

Gardner, M., & Steinberg, L. (2005). Peer influence on risk taking, risk preference, and risky decision making in adolescence and adulthood: An experimental study. *Developmental Psychology, 41:* 625-635.

Garfat, T. (Ed.). (2011). Fresh thinking about families. *Reclaiming Children and Youth, 20*(3), 5-7.

Giacobbe, G. A., Traynelis-Yurek, E., & Laursen, E. (1994). *Strengths based strategies for children & youth: An annotated bibliography.* Richmond, VA: G & T Publishing.

Gibbs, J. (1994). Fairness and empathy as the foundation for universal moral education. *Comenius, 14:* 12-23.

Gibbs, J. (2014). *Moral development and reality: Beyond the theories of Kohlberg, Hoffman, and Haidt.* New York, NY: Cambridge University Press.

Gibbs, J., Potter, G., Goldstein, A., & Brendtro, L. (1996). Equipping youth with mature moral judgment. *Reclaiming Children and Youth, 5*(3), 156-162.

Gibbs, J., Potter, G., & Goldstein, A. (1995). *The EQUIP program: Teaching youth to think and act responsibly through a peer-helping approach.* Champaign, IL: Research Press.

Giles, J. (1975). *Positive Peer Culture in the school system.* SASSP Bulletin 59. Thousand Oaks, CA: Sage Publications.

Gilgun, J., Chalmers, M., & Kesinen, S. (2002). *The 4-D: Assessing four dimensions of youth development, belonging, mastery, autonomy, and generosity.* St. Paul, MN: Growing Home National Office.

Gilles, D. Taylor, F., Gray, C., O'Brien, L., & D'Abrew, N. (2012). *Psychological therapies for the treatment of post-traumatic stress disorder in children and adolescents.* Cochrane Database Systematic Reviews. CD006726. doi: 10.1002/14651858.CD006726.pub2.

Gilligan, C. (1993). *In a different voice: Psychological theory and women's development.* Cambridge, MA: Harvard University Press.

Ginsburg, G., Kendall, P., Sakolsky, D., Compton, S., Piacentini, J., … & Birmaher, B. (2011). Remission after acute treatment in children and adolescents with anxiety disorders: Findings from the CAMS. *Journal of Consulting and Clinical Psychology, 79*(6), 806-813.

Ginsburg, K., & Kinsman, S. (Eds.). (2014). *Reaching teens: Strength-based communication strategies to build resilience and support healthy adolescent development.* Elk Grove Village, IL: American Academy of Pediatrics.

Givens, D. (2008). *Dictionary of gestures, signs, and body language cues.* Spokane, WA: Center for Nonverbal Studies.

Glasson-Walls, S. (2004). *Learning to belong: A study of the lived experience of homeless students in Western Australia.* Master's thesis. Edith Cowan University, Perth, Australia.

Gluckman, P., & Hanson, M. (2006). *Mismatch: Why our world no longer fits our bodies.* Oxford, UK: Oxford University Press.

Golati, R. (2007). Ten poles, tribalism, and boundary spanning: The rigor-relevance debate in management research. *Academy of Management Journal, 50*(4), 775-782.

Gold, M. (1995). Charting a course: Promise and prospects for alternative schools. *Journal of Emotional and Behavioral Problems, 3*(4), 8-11.

Gold, M. (1999). *A Kurt Lewin reader. The complete social scientist.* Washington, DC: American Psychological Association.

Gold, M., & Mann, D. (1984). *Expelled to a friendlier place.* Ann Arbor, MI: University of Michigan Press.

Gold, M., & Osgood, D. W. (1992). *Personality and peer influence in juvenile corrections.* Westport, CT: Greenwood Press.

Goldstein, A., et al. (2014). *The prepare curriculum series.* Champaign, IL: Research Press.

Goleman, D. (2006). *Social intelligence.* London, UK: Hutchinson.

Goleman, D., Boyatzis, R., & McKee, A. (2013). *Primal leadership: Unleashing the power of emotional intelligence.* Boston, MA: Harvard Business School Press.

Goodheart, C. (2010). The education you need to know. *Monitor on Psychology, 41*(7), 9.

Gazzaniga, M. (2008). *Human: The science behind what makes us unique.* New York, NY: HarperCollins.

Gray, L. (2011). *First Nations 101.* Vancouver, British Columbia: Adaawx Publishing.

Greenberg, M., Weissberg, R., O'Brien, M., Zins, J., Fredericks, L., Resnik, H., & Elias, M. (2003). Enhancing school-based prevention and youth development through coordinated social, emotional, and academic learning. *American Psychologist, 58*(6 & 7), 466-474.

Greenwald, R. (2005). *Child trauma handbook: A guide for helping trauma-exposed children and adolescents.* New York, NY: Haworth Press.

Grey, P. (2013). *Free to learn: Why understanding the instinct to play will make our children happier, more self-reliant, and better students for life.* New York, NY: Basic Books.

Groos, K. (1899). *Die Spiele der Menschen.* Translated 1901 by E. Baldwin as *The Play of Man.* New York, NY: Appleton.

Gross, C. (2000). Neurogenesis in the adult brain: Death of a dogma. *Nature Review of Neuroscience, 1*(1), 67-73.

Guild, D., & Espiner, D. (2014). Strengthening resilience in families. *Reclaiming Children and Youth, 22*(4), 38-41.

Gupta, S. (2010). Cited in S. Shayon, *CNN reveals toxic America,* May 25, 2010. www.huffingtonpost.com

Guskey, T. (2000). *Evaluating professional development.* Thousand Oaks, CA: Corwin Press.

Guyatt, G., Cairns, J., & Churchill, D. (1992). Evidence-based medicine. A new approach to teaching the practice of medicine. *JAMA, 268*(17), 2420–2425.

Haidt, J. (2003). Elevation and the positive psychology of morality. In C. Keyes & J. Haidt (Eds.), *Flourishing: Positive psychology and the life well-lived* (pp. 275-289). Washington, DC: American Psychological Association.

Hall, S. (2008). Last of the Neanderthals. *National Geographic, 214*(4), 34-59.

Hall, S. (2012). Hidden treasures in junk DNA. *Scientific American.* Posted on scientificamerican.com on September 18, 2012.

Hallfors, D., Pankratz, M., & Hartman, S. (2007). Does federal policy support the use of scientific evidence of school-based prevention programs. *Prevention Science, 8*(1), 75-81.

Hamlin, J., Wynn, K., & Bloom, P. (2008). Social evaluation by preverbal infants. *Pediatric Research, 63*(3), 219.

Hanushek, E., & Raymond, M. (2005). Does school accountability lead to improved school performance? *The Journal of Policy and Management, 24,* (297-327).

Hardy, K. (2014). Healing the hidden wounds of racial trauma. *Reclaiming Children and Youth, 22*(1), 24-28.

Hart, B., & Risley, T. (1995). *Meaningful differences.* Baltimore, MD: Paul H. Brookes.

Hatter, R. (Ed.). (2014). Building family strengths. *Reclaiming Children and Youth, 23*(2) [entire issue].

Hattie, J., & Yates, G. (2014). *Visible learning and the science of how we teach.* New York, NY: Routledge.

Hauser, M. (2006). *Wild minds: What animals really think.* New York, NY: Henry Holt.

Hawkins, J., Smith, B., & Catalano, R. (2004). Social development and social and emotional learning. In J. Zins, R. Weissberg, M. Wang, & H. Walberg (Eds.), *Building academic success on social and emotional learning* (pp. 135-150). New York, NY: Teacher's College Press.

Healy, D. (2012). *Pharmageddon.* Berkeley, CA: University of California Press.

Hebb, D. (1949). *The organization of behavior: A neuropsychological theory.* New York, NY: John Wiley & Sons.

Heinrich, L., & Gullone, E. (2006). The clinical significance of loneliness: A literature review. *Clinical Psychology Review, 26:* 695-718.

Hemingway, E. (1929). *A farewell to arms.* New York, NY: Scribners.

Herringa, R., Birn, R., Ruttle, P., Burghy, C., Stodola, D., Davidson, R., & Essex, M. (2011). Childhood maltreatment is associated with altered fear circuitry and increased internalizing symptoms by late adolescence. *Current Biology, 21*(23), 19119-19124.

Herrnstein, R., & Murray, C. (1994). *The bell curve: Intelligence and class structure in American life.* New York, NY: Free Press.

Hewlett, S., & Lamb, M. (2005). *Hunter-gatherer childhoods: Evolutionary, developmental & cultural perspectives.* New Brunswick, NJ: Transaction.

Hobbs, N. (1982). *The troubled and troubling child.* San Francisco, CA: Jossey-Bass.

Hobbs, N. (1994). *The troubled and troubling child.* Cleveland, OH: American Re-EDucation Association.

Hofer, M. (1987). Early social relationships: A psycho-biologist's view. *Child Development, 48*(3), 633-647.

Hoffman, E. (1988). *The right to be human: A biography of Abraham Maslow.* New York, NY: St. Martin's Press.

Hoffman, E. (1999). *The right to be human: A biography of Abraham Maslow (2nd ed.).* New York, NY: McGraw-Hill.

Hoffman, M. (2000). *Empathy and moral development: Implications for caring and justice.* New York, NY: Cambridge University Press.

Holden, M. (2009). *Children And Residential Experiences: Creating conditions for change.* Arlington, VA: Child Welfare League of America.

Hollingsworth, J. (2014). *The Art of Resilience.* Albion, MI: Starr Commonwealth.

Holmes, J. (2014). *John Bowlby and attachment theory.* New York, NY: Routledge.

Hyman, I., & Snook, P. (2001). Dangerous schools, alienated students. *Reclaiming Children and Youth, 10*(3), 131-136.

Insel, T. (2013). *Director's blog: Transforming diagnosis.* http://www.nimh.nih.gov/about/director/2013/transforming-diagnosis.shtml

Itard, J. (1801/1962). *The wild boy of Aveyron.* New York, NY: Appleton-Century-Crofts.

Izard, C., & Ackerman, B. (2000). Motivational, organizational, and regulatory functions of discreet emotions. In M. Lewis & J. Haviland-Jones (Eds.), *Handbook of emotions, 2nd ed.* (pp. 253-264). New York, NY: Guildford Press.

Jackson, W. (2014a). The Circle of Courage: The socialization of youth in the 21st century. *Reclaiming Children and Youth, 23*(3), 16-20.

Jackson, W. (2014b). *The Circle of Courage: Childhood socialization in the 21st century.* (Doctoral dissertation). Wayne State University, Detroit, Michigan.

James, A., & Lunday, T. (2014). Native birthrights and indigenous science. *Reclaiming Children and Youth, 22*(4), 56-58.

James, S. (2011). What works in group care? A structured review of treatment models for group homes and residential care. *Child and Youth Services Review, 33*(2), 308-321.

Jenkins, R. (1954). *Breaking patterns of defeat.* Philadelphia, PA: J. P. Lippincott.

Jensen, A. (1969). How much can we boost IQ and scholastic achievement? *Harvard Educational Review, 39*(1), 1-123.

Jensen, P., Arnold, L., Swanson, J., Vitiello, B., Abikoff, H., Greenhill, L., ... & Hur, K. (2007). 3-Year Follow-up of the NIMH MTA Study. *Journal of the American Academy of Child & Adolescent Psychiatry, 46*(8), 989-1002.

Johnson, L. (2006). *A toolbox for humanity.* Bloomington, IN: Trafford Publishing.

Johnson, D., & Johnson, R. (2004). The three Cs of promoting social and emotional learning. In J. Zins, R. Weissberg, M. Wang, & H. Walberg (Eds.), *Building academic success on social and emotional learning* (pp. 40-58). New York, NY: Teacher's College Press.

Johnson-Reid, M. (2002). Exploring the relationship between child welfare intervention and juvenile corrections involvement. *American Journal of Orthopsychiatry, 72:* 559-576.

Johnston, V. (1999). *Why we feel: The science of human emotions.* Cambridge, MA: Perseus Press.

Joseph, S., & Linley, P. A. (2008). *Trauma, recovery, and growth: Positive psychological perspectives on posttraumatic stress.* New York, NY: John Wiley and Sons.

Jung, C. (1973). *Memories, dreams, reflections.* New York, NY: Pantheon Books.

Juul, K. (1981). Presentation to Starr Commonwealth, Albion, Michigan, April 1, 1981.

Juvonen, J. (2004). *Focus on the wonder years: Challenges facing the American middle school (Vol. 139).* Santa Monica, CA: Rand Corporation.

Juvonen, J., & Graham, S. (2013). Bullying in schools: The power of bullies and the plight of victims. *Annual Review of Psychology, 65:*159-185.

Kagan, J. (1971). *Personality development.* New York, NY: Harcourt Brace.

Kagan, J. (2010). *The temperamental thread: How genes, culture, time, and luck make us who we are.* New York, NY: Dana Press.

Kahneman, D. (2011). *Thinking fast and slow.* New York, NY: Farrar, Straus, & Giroux.

Kandel, E. (2007). *In search of memory: The emergence of a new science of mind.* New York, NY: W. W. Norton.

Kasser, T. (2005). Frugality, generosity, and materialism in children and adolescents. In K. Moore & L. Lippman (Eds.), *What do children need to flourish? Conceptualizing and measuring indicators of positive development* (pp. 357-373). New York, NY: Springer.

Kauffman, J. (2000). Future directions with troubled children. *Reclaiming Children and Youth, 9*(2), 126-131.

Kazdin, A., & Weisz, J. (Eds.). (2003). *Evidence-based psychotherapies for children and adolescents.* New York, NY: Guilford Press.

Kellogg Foundation. (2015). *Racial Equity.* https://www.wkkf.org/what-we-do/racial-equity

Kendall, P., Gosch, E., Furr, J., & Sood, E. (2008). Flexibility within fidelity. *Child and Adolescent Psychiatry, 47*(9), 987-993.

Key, E. (1909). *The century of the child.* New York, NY: G. P. Putnam Sons.

Keyes, C., & Haidt, J. (Eds.). (2003). *Flourishing: Positive psychology and the life well-lived.* Washington, DC: American Psychological Association.

Kidd, C., Palmeri, H., & Aslin, R. (2013). Rational snacking: Young children's decision-making on the marshmallow task is moderated by beliefs about environmental reliability. *Cognition, 126*(1), 109-114.

Kira, I., Lewandowski, L., Ashby, J, Somers, C., Chiodo, L, & Odenat, L. (2014). Does bullying victimization suppress IQ? The effects of bullying victimization on IQ in Iraqi and African American Adolescents: A traumatology perspective. *Journal of Aggression, Maltreatment & Trauma, 23*(5), 431-453.

Kirsch, I. (2010). *The emperor's new drugs: Exploding the antidepressant myth.* London, UK: Bodley Head.

Kirk, R., & Reed-Ashcraft, K. (2001). *North Carolina Family Assessment Scale (NCFAS): Research report.* Buhl, ID: National Family Preservation Network.

Kohn, A. (2006). *Beyond discipline: From compliance to community.* Alexandria, VA: ASCD Publishing.

Kok, B., Coffey, K., Cohn, M., Catalino, L., Varcharkulksemsuk, T., Algoe, S., Brantley, M., & Fredrieckson, B. (2013). How positive emotions build physical health: Perceived positive social connections account for the upward spiral between positive emotions and vagal tone. *Psychological Science, 24*(7), 1123-1132.

Koltko-Rivera, M. (2006). Rediscovering the later version of Maslow's hierarchy of needs: Self-transcendence and opportunities for theory, research, and unification. *Review of General Psychology, 10*(2), 302-317.

Konner, M. (2002). *The tangled wing.* New York, NY: Owl Books.

Kraybill, D., Nolt, S., & Weaver-Zercher, D. (2007). *Amish grace: How forgiveness transcended tragedy.* San Francisco, CA: Jossey-Bass.

Kreisle, B. (2008). *Hier läuft alles irgendwie anders. (Here everything is somehow different.)* Berlin, Germany: Pro-Business.

Kreisle, B. (2010). Punishment or self-discipline? Early roots of reform. *Reclaiming Children and Youth, 19*(3), 14-15.

Kress, C. (2014). Transformational education: The 4-H legacy. *Reclaiming Children and Youth, 23*(3), 5-9.

Kress, C., & Forrest, N. (2000). The VOICES project. *Reclaiming Children and Youth, 9*(2), 116-118.

Kuhn, T. (2012). *The structure of scientific revolutions (4th ed.).* Chicago, IL: University of Chicago Press.

Kuzawa, C., & Sweet, E. (2009). Epigenetics and the embodiment of race: Developmental origins of US racial disparities in cardiovascular health. *American Journal of Human Biology, 21*(1), 2-15.

Lantieri, L., & Goleman, D. (2014). *Building emotional intelligence: Practices to cultivate inner resilience in children.* Boulder, CO: Sounds True.

Larson, S. (2014). Transforming young lives. *Reclaiming Children and Youth, 23(*1), 19-23.

Larson, S., & Brendtro, L. (2000). *Reclaiming our prodigal sons and daughters.* Bloomington, IN: Solution Tree.

Laughlin, P., Hatch, E., Silver, J., & Boh, L. (2006). Groups perform better than the best individuals on letters-to-numbers problems: Effects of group size. *Journal of Personality and Social Psychology, 90*(4), 644-651.

Laursen, E. K. (2009). Positive youth cultures and the developing brain. *Reclaiming Children and Youth, 18*(2), 8-11.

Laursen, E. K. (2010). The evidence base of Positive Peer Culture. *Reclaiming Children and Youth, 19*(2), 37-43.

Laursen, E. K. (2014). Respectful youth cultures. *Reclaiming Children and Youth, 22*(4), 48-52.

Laursen, E. K., & Yazdgerdi, S. (2012). Autism and belonging. *Reclaiming Children and Youth, 21*(2), 44-47.

Laursen, E. K., Moore, L., Yazdgerdi, S., & Milberg, K. (2013). Building empathy and social mastery in students with autism. *Reclaiming Children and Youth, 22*(3), 19-22.

Lay, J. (2000). The person behind the file number. *Reclaiming Children and Youth, 9*(2), 68-69.

Lazarus, R., & Folkman, S. (1984). *Stress appraisal in coping.* New York, NY: Springer Publishing.

Le Bon, G. (1896). *The crowd.* New York, NY: Macmillan.

Leffert, N., Benson, P., & Roehlkepartain, J. (1997). *Starting out right: Developmental Assets for children.* Minneapolis, MN: Search Institute.

Legg, S., & Hutter, M. (2007). *A collection of definitions of intelligence.* Available at: http://arxiv.org/pdf/0706.3639.pdf

Leonhauser, M. (2012). Antipsychotics: Multiple indications drive growth. *PM 360: The Essential Resource for Pharma Marketers,* January, pp. 22-24. http://www.imshealth.com/ims/Global/Content/Corporate/Press%20Room/IMS%20in%20the%20News/Documents/PM360_IMS_Antipsychotics_0112.pdf

Lerner, R., Lerner, J., & colleagues. (2013). *The positive development of youth: Comprehensive findings from the 4-H study on positive youth development.* Medford, MA: Tufts University Institute for Applied Research in Youth Development.

Levine, P., & Kline, M. (2008). *Trauma-proofing your kids: A parents' guide for instilling confidence, joy, and resilience.* Berkeley, CA: North Atlantic Books.

Levitt, R., Janta, B., & Wegrich, K. (2008). *Accountability of teachers: Literature review.* Santa Monica, CA: RAND Corporation.

Lewin, K. (1943/1999). The process of group living. In M. Gold (Ed.), *The complete social scientist: A Kurt Lewin reader* (pp. 333-348). Washington, DC: American Psychological Association.

Lewin, K. (1943/1999). *The complete social scientist: A Kurt Lewin reader.* M. Gold (Ed.). Washington, DC: American Psychological Association.

Lewin, K. (1946). Action research and minority problems. *Journal of Social Issues, 2*(4), 34-46.

Lewin, K., Lippitt, R., & White, R. (1939). Patterns of aggressive behavior in experimentally created "social climates." *Journal of Social Psychology, 10:* 271-299.

Lewis, C. (1995). *Educating hearts and minds: Reflections on Japanese preschool and elementary education.* New York, NY: Cambridge University Press.

Lewis, R. (2009). *Understanding pupil behavior.* New York, NY: Routledge.

Lewis, T., Amini, F., & Lannon, R. (2001). *A general theory of love.* New York, NY: Random House.

Li, J., & Julian, M. (2012). Developmental relationships as the active ingredient: A unifying working hypothesis of "what works" across intervention settings. *American Journal of Orthopsychiatry, 82*(2), 157-166.

Lieberman, M. (2013). *Social: Why our brains are wired to connect.* New York, NY: Crown Publishers.

Lieberman, M., Eisenberger, N., Crockett, M., Tom, S., Pfeifer, J., & Way, B. (2007). Putting feelings into words: Affect labelling disrupts amygdala activity in response to affective stimuli. *Psychological Sciences, 18*(5), 421-428.

Liepmann, C. M. (1928). *Die Selbstverwaltung der Gefangenen [Self-governance by offenders].* Mannheim, Germany: Bernsheimer.

Lippitt, R., Watson, J., & Westley, B. (1958). *The dynamics of planned change.* New York, NY: Harcourt, Brace, & World.

Littell, J. (2010). Evidence-based practice: Evidence or orthodoxy. In B. Duncan, S. Miller, B. Wampold, & M. Hubble (Eds.), *The heart and soul of change: Delivering what works in therapy* (pp. 167-198). Washington, DC: American Psychological Association.

Lloyd, S. (2007). You know too much. *Discover,* April, 55-57.

Long, N. (2014). Disengaging from conflict cycles. *Reclaiming Children and Youth, 23*(1), 34-37.

Long, N., Fecser, F., & Brendtro, L. (2005). Life Space Crisis Intervention: New skills for reclaiming students showing patterns of self-defeating behavior. *Healing Magazine, 3*(2), 2-22.

Long, N., Wood, M., & Fecser, F. (2001). *Life Space Crisis Intervention: Talking with students in conflict.* Austin, TX: Pro-Ed.

Long, N., Fecser, F., Morse, W., Newman, R., & Long, J. (2014). *Conflict in the classroom: Successful behavior management using the psychoeducational model (7th ed.).* Austin, TX: Pro-Ed.

Longhurst, J., & Brown, J. C. (2013). The five shifts: Ensuring an environment for healing. *Reclaiming Children and Youth, 22*(1), 13-17.

Longhurst, J., & McCord, J. (2007). From peer deviance to peer helping. *Reclaiming Children and Youth, 15*(4), 194-199.

Louv, R. (2009). *Last child in the woods: Saving our children from nature-deficit disorder.* Chapel Hill, NC: Algonquin.

Luthar, S. (2006). Resilience in development: A synthesis of research across five decades. In D. Cicchetti, & D. Cohen (Eds.). *Developmental psychopathology, Vol 3: Risk, disorder, and adaptation (2nd ed.)* (pp. 739-795). Hoboken, NJ: John Wiley & Sons, Inc.

Lyons, J. (2009). *Communimetrics: A communication theory of measurement in human service settings.* New York, NY: Springer.

MacDonald, G., & Jensen-Campbell, L. (2010). *Social pain: Neuropsychological and health implications of loss and exclusion.* Washington, DC: APA.

Machiavelli, N. (1513). *The prince.* [English translation, 1962.] New York, NY: Dover.

Maier, H. W. (1982). To be attached and free: The challenge of child development. *Child Welfare, 61*(2), 67-76.

Maier, H. (1992). Rhythmicity—A powerful force for experiencing unity and personal connections. *Journal of Child and Youth Care Work, 8:* 7-13.

Malinowsky, B. (1944). *A scientific theory of culture.* Chapel Hill, NC: University of North Carolina Press.

Mandela, N. (2003). A fabric of care. In K. Asmal, D. Chidester, & W. James (Eds.), *Nelson Mandela: From freedom to the future* (pp. 416-418). Johannesburg, South Africa: Jonathan Ball Publishers.

Mandela, N. (2012). *Notes to the future: Words of wisdom.* New York, NY: Atria Books.

Manso, A., & Rautkis, M. (2011). What is the therapeutic alliance and why does it matter? *Reclaiming Children and Youth, 19*(4), 45-50.

Martin, L., & Martin, A. (2012). *Small stories: Reflections on the practice of positive youth development.* Albion, MI: Starr Commonwealth.

Martini, M., & Kirkpatrick, J. (1992). Parenting in Polynesia: A view from the Marquesas. In J. Roopnarine & D. Carter (Eds.), *Parent-child socialization in diverse cultures, Vol. 5* (pp. 199-222). Norwood, NJ: Ablex Publishers.

Marzano, R., & Pickering, D. (2011). *The highly engaged classroom.* Bloomington, IN: Solution Tree.

Maslow, A. (1943). A theory of human motivation. *Psychological Review, 50,* 370-396.

Maslow, A. (1967). *Toward a psychology of being.* New York, NY: Van Nostrand Reinhold.

Masten, A. (2014). *Ordinary magic: Resilience in development.* New York, NY: Guilford Press.

Masten, A., & Obradović, J. (2006). Competence and resilience in development. *Annals of the New York Academy of Science, 1094*: 13–27.

McCall, H. (2003). When successful alternative students "disengage" from regular school. *Reclaiming Children and Youth, 12*(2), 113-117.

McCashen, W. (2005). *The strengths approach.* Victoria, Australia: St. Luke's Innovative Resources.

McClellan, J., & Werry, J. (2000). Evidence based treatments in child and adolescent psychiatry: An inventory. *Child and Adolescent Psychiatry, 42*(12), 1388-1400.

McClelland, D., & Atkinson, J. (2012). *The achievement motive.* Whitefish, MT: Literary Licensing.

McDonald, Tim. (2013). *Classroom management: Engaging students in learning, second edition.* Melbourne, Australia: Oxford University Press.

McDougal, W. (1920). *The group mind.* New York, NY: G. P. Putnam's Sons.

McGonigal, J. (2011). *Reality is broken: Why games make us better and how they can change the world.* New York, NY: Penguin.

McHugh, P. (2006). *The mind has mountains: Reflections on society and psychiatry.* Baltimore, MD: The Johns Hopkins University Press.

McNeely, C. (2005). Connection to school. In K. Moore & L. Lippman (Eds.), *What do children need to flourish? Conceptualizing and measuring indicators of positive development* (pp. 289-303). New York, NY: Springer.

McPherson, G., Davidson, J., & Faulkner, R. (2012). *Music in our lives: Rethinking musical ability, development and identity.* Oxford, UK: Oxford University Press.

Meaney, M. (2001). Maternal care, gene expression, and the transmission of individual differences in stress reactivity across generations. *Annual Review of Neuroscience, 24:* 1161-1192.

Meaney, M. (2012). *From generation to generation: The interplay between genes and family process.* Bowen Family Center, Conference in Vancouver, British Columbia, February.

Menninger, K. (1963). *The vital balance: The life process in mental health and illness.* New York, NY: Viking Press.

Menninger, K. (1982). The church's responsibility for the homeless. In R. Gillogly (Ed.), *Sacred shelters.* Topeka, KS: The Villages.

Merker, B. (2007). Consciousness without a cerebral cortex: A challenge for neuroscience and medicine. *Behavioral and Brain Sciences, 30*(1), 63-81.

Metcalfe, J., & Mischel, W. (1999). A hot/cool system analysis of delay of gratification: Dynamics of will power. *Pscyhological Review, 106*(1), 3-19.

Meyer, I. (2003). Prejudice, social stress, and mental health in lesbian, gay, and bisexual populations: Conceptual issues and research evidence. *Psychological Bulletin, 129:* 674-697.

Mikulincer, M., & Shaver, P. (Eds.). (2010). *Prosocial motives, emotions, and behavior: The better angels of our nature.* Washington, DC: APA.

Minuchin, S. (1974). *Families and family therapy.* Cambridge, MA: Harvard University Press.

Mischel, W., & Ayduk, O. (2011). Will power in a cognitive affective processing system: The dynamics of delay of gratification. In K. Vohs & R. Baumeister (Eds.), *Handbook of self-regulation* (pp. 83-105). New York, NY: Guilford Press.

Mischel, W., Ebbesen, E., & Raskoff-Zeiss, A. (1972). Cognitive and attentional mechanisms in delay of gratification. *Journal of Personality and Social Psychology, 21*(2), 204-218.

Mitchell, M. (2003). The million dollar child. *Reclaiming Children and Youth, 12*(1), 6-8.

Mitra, S. (2013). *Build a school in the clouds.* TED talk video and transcript. http://www.ted.com/talks/sugata_mitra_build_a_school_in_the_cloud

Mitra, S., Dangwal, R., Chatterjee, S., Jha, S., Bisht, R., & Kapur, P. (2005). Acquisition of computing literacy on shared public computers: Children and the "hole in the wall." *Australasian Journal of Educational Technology, 21*(3), 407-426.

Molina, B., Hinshaw, S., Swanson, J., Arnold, L., Vitiello, B., Jensen, P., ... & MTA Cooperative Group. (2009). The MTA at 8 Years: Prospective follow-up of children treated for combined-type ADHD in a multisite study. *Journal of the American Academy of Child & Adolescent Psychiatry, 48*(5), 484-500.

Moll, J., Krueger, F., Zahn, R., Pardini, M., de Oliveria-Souza, R., & Grafman, J. (2006). Human fronto-mesolimbic networks guide decisions about charitable donation. *Proceedings of the National Academies of the Sciences, 103*(42), 15623-15628.

Montessori, M. (1912). *The Montessori method: Scientific pedagogy as applied to child education in the children's houses.* New York, NY: Frederick A. Stokes Company.

Moreno, C., Laje, G., Blanco, C., Jiang, H., Schmidt, A., & Olfson, M. (2007). National trends in the outpatient diagnosis and treatment of bipolar disorders in youth. *Archives of General Psychiatry, 64*(9), 1032-1039.

Morgan, J. (1924). *The psychology of the unadjusted school child.* New York, NY: McMillian.

Morgenthau, H. (1962). Love and power. *Commentary, 33:* 247-251.

Mullin, B., & Hinshaw, S. (2007). Emotional regulation and externalizing emotions in children and adolescents. In J. Gross (Ed.), *Handbook of emotion regulation* (pp. 523-541). New York, NY: Guilford Press.

Newmann, F., King, M., & Rigdon, M. (1997). Accountability and school performance: Implications from restructuring schools. *Harvard Educational Review, 56:* 1-17.

Morse, W. (1985). *The education and treatment of socio-emotionally impaired youth.* Syracuse, NY: Syracuse University Press.

Morse, W. (2008). *Connecting with kids in conflict: A life space legacy.* Sioux Falls, SD: Reclaiming Children and Youth & Starr Commonwealth.

Moya-Alibio, L., Herrero, N., & Bernal, M. (2010). Bases neuronales de la empatía. [The neural bases of empathy]. *Revistea de Neurología, 50*(2), 89-100.

Murphy, L., & Moriarty, A. (1976). *Vulnerability, coping, and growth.* New Haven, CT: Yale University Press.

Murray, H. (1938). *Explorations in personality.* New York, NY: Oxford University Press.

NASW. (2008). *Code of Ethics of the National Association of Social Workers.* www.socialworkers.org

Nelson, C., Fox, N., & Zeanah, C. (2014). *Romania's abandoned children.* Cambridge, MA: Harvard University Press.

Nelson, E., & Panksepp, J. (1998). Brain substrates of infant-mother attachments: Contributions of opiates, oxytocin, and norepinephrine. *Neuroscience and Behavioral Reviews, 22:* 437-452.

Newman, D. (2011). Nicholas Hobbs and schools of joy. *Reclaiming Children and Youth, 21*(1), 25-28.

Nichols, J. (1990). What is ability and why we are mindful of it. In R. Sternberg & J. Kolligian, Jr. (Eds.), *Competence considered* (pp. 11-40). New Haven, CT: Yale University.

Nisbett, R. (2004). *The geography of thought: How Asians and Westerners think differently...and why.* New York, NY: Free Press.

Nisbett, R. (2009). *Intelligence and how to get it: Why schools and cultures count.* New York, NY: W. W. Norton.

Nisbett, R., & Cohen, D. (1996). *Culture of honor: The psychology of violence in the South.* Boulder, CO: Westview Press.

Nisbett, R., Aaronson, J., Blair, C., Dickens, W., Flynn, J., Halpern, D., & Turkheimer, E. (2012). Intelligence: New findings and theoretical developments. *American Psychologist, 67*(2), 130-159.

Nunno, M., (Ed.). (2001). *Therapeutic Crisis Intervention (5th ed.), Trainer's Manual.* Ithaca, NY: Cornell University.

O'Brien, J. (2011). *In the Interest of M.D.,* JUV. 09-05, Letter Decision. Jan. 19, 2011, Hanson Co., S.Dak.

Olfson, M., Crystal, S., Huang, C., & Gerhard, T. (2010). Antipsychotic drug use by very young, privately insured children. *Journal of the American Academy of Child & Adolescent Psychiatry, 49*(1), 13-23.

Olweus, D. (1993). *Bullying at school: What we know and what we can do.* New York, NY: Wiley-Blackwell.

Oman, R., Vesely, S., McLeroy, K., Harris-Wyatt, V., Aspy, C., Rodine, S., & Marshall, L. (2002). Reliability and validity of the Youth Asset Survey (YAS). *Journal of Adolescent Health, 31*(3), 247-255.

Opp, G., & Unger, N. (2006). *Kinder stärken Kinder: Positive peer culture in der praxis.* Hamburg, Germany: Körber Stiftung.

Opp, G., Unger, N., & Teichmann, J. (2007). Together, not alone: Positive peer culture in a German school. *Reclaiming Children and Youth, 15*(4), 234-242.

Orme, N. (2003). *Medieval childhood.* New Haven, CT: Yale University Press.

Osgood, D., & Briddell, L. (2006). Peer effects in juvenile justice. In K. Dodge, T. Dishion, & J. Lansford (Eds.), *Deviant peer influence in programs for youth: Problems and solutions* (pp. 141-161). New York, NY: Guilford Press.

Osgood, D., Gruber, E., Archer, M., & Newcomb, T. (1985). Autonomy for inmates: Counterculture or cooptation? *Criminal Justice and Behavior, 12:* 71-89.

Panksepp, J., & Bivin, L. (2012). *The archaeology of the mind: Neuroevolutionary origins of human emotions.* New York, NY: W. W. Norton.

Papert, S. (1980/1993). *Mindstorms: Children, computers, and powerful ideas, second edition* (First edition, 1980). New York, NY: Basic Books.

Pasalich, D., Dadds, M., Vincent, L., Cooper, F., Hawes, D., & Brennan, J. (2012). Emotional communication in families of conduct problem children with high versus low callous-unemotional traits. *Journal of Clinical Child & Adolescent Psychology, 41*(3), 302-313.

Pascoe, E., & Richman, L. (2009). Perceived discrimination and health: A meta-analytic review. *Psychological Bulletin, 135:* 531-554.

Paul, E., Miller, F., & Paul, J. (1993). *Altruism.* Cambridge, MA: Cambridge University Press.

PDR. (2015). *Physicians' Desk Reference (69th ed.).* Montvale, NJ: PDR Network.

Pedersen, C. (2004). Biological aspects of social bonding in the roots of human violence. *Annals of the New York Academy of Science, 1036:* 106-127.

Perry, B. (2006). Applying principles of neurodevelopment to clinical work with maltreated and traumatized children: The neurosequential model of therapeutics. In N. Boyd (Ed.), *Working with traumatized youth in child welfare* (pp. 27-52). New York, NY: Guilford Press.

Perry, B. (2009). Examining child maltreatment through a neurodevelopmental lens: Clinical applications of the neurosequential model of therapeutics. *Journal of Loss and Trauma, 14*(4), 240-255.

Perry, B., & Szalavitz, M. (2007). *The boy who was raised as a dog.* Philadelphia, PA: Basic Books.

Perry, B., & Szalavitz, M. (2010). *Born for love: Why empathy is essential—and endangered.* New York, NY: William Morrow.

Pestalozzi, J. (1801). *Wie Gertrude ihre Kinder Lehrt. [How Gertrude teaches her children.)* English translation 1894 by L. Holland & T. Turner. Syracuse, NY: Swan Sonnenschein & Co.

Peter, V. (2000). *What makes Boys Town successful? A description of the 21st century Boys Town teaching model.* Omaha, NE: Boys Town Press.

Peterson, C. (2006). *A primer in positive psychology.* New York, NY: Oxford University Press.

Peterson, C. (2013a). *Pursuing the good life: 100 reflections on positive psychology.* New York, NY: Oxford University Press.

Peterson, C. (2013b). The strengths revolution: A positive psychology perspective. *Reclaiming Children and Youth, 21*(4), 7-14.

Peterson, C., & Brendtro, L. (2008). *The strength-based revolution. Roots and Wings Seminars,* Wayne State University, Detroit, Michigan, September, 2008.

Peterson, C., & Bossi, L. (1991). *Health and optimism. New research on the relationship between positive thinking and physical well-being.* New York, NY: Free Press.

Peterson, C., Maier, S., & Seligman, M. (1995). *Learned helplessness: Theory for the age of personal control.* New York, NY: Oxford University Press.

Pfeifer, D. (2011). Transforming staff through clinical supervision. *Reclaiming Children and Youth, 20*(2), 29-33.

Phelan, J. (2004). Some thoughts on using an ecosystem perspective. *CYC-Online,* issue 28, www.cyc-net.org.

Philogéne, G. (2004). *Racial identity in context: The legacy of Kenneth B. Clark.* Washington, DC: American Psychological Association.

Piaget, J. (1952). *The origins of intelligence in children.* New York, NY: The Norton Library.

Pilkington, D. (2013). *Follow the rabbit proof fence.* Brisbane, Australia: University of Queensland Press.

Pittman, K., Irby, M., Tolman, J., Yohalem, N., & Ferber, T. (2001). *Preventing problems, promoting development, encouraging engagement: Competing priorities or inseparable goals?* Washington, DC: The Forum for Youth Investment.

Ponds, K. (2014). Spiritual development with youth. *Reclaiming Children and Youth, 22*(1), 58-61.

Pope John Paul II. (1996). *Truth cannot contradict truth.* Address of Pope John Paul II to the Pontifical Academy of Sciences, Oct. 22, 1996.

Polsky, H. (1962). *Cottage six: The social system of delinquent boys in residential treatment.* New York, NY: Wiley.

Porges, S. (2011). *The polyvagal theory: Neurophysiological foundations of emotions, attachment, communication, self-regulation.* New York, NY: W. W. Norton.

Pratt, R. (2004). *Battlefield and classroom: Four decades with the American Indian, 1867-1904.* Norman, OK: University of Oklahoma Press.

Prince-Embury, S. (2007). *Resiliency scales for children and adolescents: A profile of personal strengths.* San Antonio, TX: Psych Corporation.

Provine, R. (2000). *Laughter: A scientific investigation.* New York, NY: Penguin Books.

Purkey, W., Gage, B., & Fahey, M. (1984/1993). *The Florida Key: An instrument to measure student self-concept-as-learner.* Greensboro, NC: International Alliance for Invitational Education, UNC Greensboro.

Quigley, R. (2004). Positive peer groups: Helping others meets primary developmental needs. *Reclaiming Children and Youth, 13*(3), 134-137.

Quigley, R. (2014). Empowering our children to succeed. *Reclaiming Children and Youth, 23*(1), 24-27.

Quigley, W. (2003). *Ending poverty as we know it: Guaranteeing a right to a job at a living wage.* Philadelphia, PA: Temple University Press.

Ramon y Cajal, S. (1901). *Recuerdos de Mi Vida. [Recollections of my life.* English translation 1989]. Cambridge, MA: MIT Press.

Ramon y Cajal, S. (1906). *The structure and connexions of neurons.* Nobel lecture, December 12, 1906. Oslo, Norway.

Rapoport, A. (1960). *Fights, games, and debates.* Ann Arbor, MI: University of Michigan Press.

Ratey, J. (2002). *A user's guide to the brain.* New York, NY: Vintage.

Rauktis, M., Andrade, A., & Doucette, A. (2007). Therapeutic alliance and Re-ED: Research on building positive relationships with youth. In R. Cantrell & M. Cantrell (Eds.), *Helping troubled children and youth* (pp. 327-350). Memphis, TN: American ReEducation Association.

Ravitch, D. (2013). *Reign of error: The hoax of the privatization movement and the danger to America's public schools.* New York, NY: Alfred A. Knopf.

Rawls, J. (2002). *Justice as fairness.* Cambridge, MA: Harvard University Press.

Raychaba, B. (1993). *"Pain...lots of pain." Family violence and abuse in the lives of young people in care.* Ottawa, Ontario: National Youth In Care Network.

Redl, F. (1951). Cited by Garfat, T. (1987). *Remembering Fritz Redl. International Child and Youth Care Network.* http://www.cyc-net.org/quote4/quote-2211.html

Redl, F. (1966). *When we deal with children.* New York, NY: Free Press.

Redl, F., & Wineman, D. (1951). *Children who hate.* Glencoe, IL: Free Press.

Redl, F., & Wineman, D. (1952). *Controls from within.* Glencoe, IL: Free Press.

Redl, F., & Wineman, D. (1957). *The aggressive child.* Glencoe, IL: Free Press.

Reid, J., Patterson, G., & Snyder, J. (Eds.). (2002). *Anti-social behavior in children and adolescents.* Washington, DC: American Psychological Association.

Rentoul, R. (2011). *Ferenczi's language of tenderness: Working with disturbances from the earliest years.* Lanham, MD: Jason Aronson.

Restak, R. (2013). Laughter and the brain. *The American Scholar.* https://theamericanscholar.org/laughter-and-the-brain

Rettew, D. (2013). *Child temperament: New thinking about the boundary between traits and illness.* New York, NY: W. W. Norton.

Reyna, V., & Farley, F. (2006). Risk and rationality in adolescent decision making: Implications for theory, practice, and public policy. *Psychological Science in the Public Interest, 7*(1), entire issue, 1-44.

Reyhner, J., Martin, L., Lockard, J., & Gilbert, W. (2013). *Honoring our children: Culturally appropriate approaches for teaching indigenous students.* Flagstaff, AZ: Northern Arizona University.

Rhee, S., Friedman, N., Boeldt, D., Corley, R., Hewitt, J., Knafo, A., ... & Zahn-Waxler, C. (2013). Early concern and disregard for others as predictors of antisocial behavior. *Journal of Child Psychology and Psychiatry, 54*(2), 157-166.

Richeport-Haley, M., & Carlson, J. (2010). *Jay Haley revisited.* New York, NY: Routledge.

Risch, A., & Plass, C. (2008). Lung cancer epigenetics and genetics. *International Journal of Cancer, 123*(1), 1-7.

Roehlkepartain, E., & Syvertsen, A. (2014). Family strengths and resilience: Insights from a national study. *Reclaiming Children and Youth, 23*(2), 13-18.

Rogoff, B. (2003). *The cultural nature of human development.* New York, NY: Oxford University Press.

Rothenberg, P. (2011). *White privilege: Essential readings on the other side of racism.* New York, NY: Worth Publishers.

Rousseau, J. (1762). *Émile, ou de l'éducation.* Translated by Allan Bloom (1979), *Emile,* or *On Education.* New York, NY: Basic Books.

Rutstein, N. (2001). *The racial conditioning of our children.* Albion, MI: Starr Commonwealth.

Rutter, M. (2012). Resilience as a dynamic concept. *Development and Psychopathology, 24:* 335-344.

Saleeby, D. (2012). *The strengths perspective in social work (6th ed.).* Upper Saddle River, NJ: Pearson Publishing.

Sanders, W. (2011). *Juvenile offenders for a thousand years.* Chapel Hill, NC: University of North Carolina Press.

Sarahan, N., & Copas, R. (2014). Autism assets. *Reclaiming Children and Youth, 22*(4), 34-37.

Schaps, E., Battistich, V., & Solomon, D. (2004). Community in school as key to school growth. In J. Zins, R. Weissberg, M. Wang, & H. Walberg (Eds.), *Building academic success on social and emotional learning* (pp. 189-208). New York, NY: Teacher's College Press.

Shields, J., Milstein, M., & Posner, S. (2010). Integrating RAP in public schools: Successes and challenges. *Reclaiming Children and Youth, 19*(3), 34-38.

Schoenfeld, A. (2006). What doesn't work: The challenge and failure of the What Works Clearinghouse to conduct meaningful reviews of studies of mathematics curricula. *Educational Researcher, 35:* 13-21.

Schore, A. (2003). *Affect regulation and the repair of the self.* New York, NY: W. W. Norton.

Schore, A. (2012). *The science and art of psychotherapy.* New York, NY: W. W. Norton.

Schwarz, A. (2013). The selling of attention deficit disorder. *New York Times,* Dec 15, 2013.

Schwartz, I. (1987). *Injustice for juveniles.* Lexington, MA: Lexington Books.

Search Institute. (2004). *Developmental assets profile.* Minneapolis, MN: The Search Institute.

Seery, M., Holman, E., & Silver, R. (2010). Whatever does not kill us: Cumulative lifetime adversity, vulnerability, and resilience. *Journal of Personality and Social Psychology, 99*(6), 1025-1041.

Seger, V., & Koehler, N. (2011). The CLEAR problem-solving model: Discovering strengths and solutions. *Reclaiming Children and Youth, 20*(1), 16-19.

Seita, J. (2010). Missing data: Discovering the private logic of adult-wary youth. *Reclaiming Children and Youth, 19*(2), 51-54.

Seita, J. (2014a). Family privilege. *Reclaiming Children and Youth, 23*(2), 7-12.

Seita, J. (2014b). Reclaiming disconnected kids. *Reclaiming Children and Youth, 23*(1), 28-32.

Seita, J., & Brendtro, L. (2005). *Kids who outwit adults.* Bloomington, IN: Solution Tree.

Seita, J., Mitchell, M., & Tobin, C. (1996). *In whose best interest: One child's odyssey, a nation's responsibility.* Elizabethtown, PA: Continental Press.

Seligman, M. (2006). *Learned optimism.* New York, NY: Vintage.

Seligman, M. (2011). *Flourish. A visionary new understanding of happiness and well-being.* New York, NY: Free Press.

Selye, H. (1956). *The stress of life.* New York, NY: McGraw-Hill.

Senge, P. (2006). *The fifth discipline: The art and science of the learning organization.* New York, NY: Random House.

Shenk, D. (2011). *The genius in all of us. New insights into genetics, talent, and IQ.* New York, NY: Anchor Books.

Shulevitz, J. (2013, May 27). 1 Is the deadliest number. The terrifying new science of loneliness [Special issue]. *The New Republic.*

Siegel, D. (2010). *Mindsight: The new science of personal transformation.* New York, NY: Bantam.

Siegel, D. (2012). *The developing mind: How relationships and the brain interact to shape who we are (2nd ed.).* New York, NY: Guilford Press.

Siegel, D. (2013). *Brainstorm: The power and purpose of the teenage brain.* New York, NY: Penguin.

Skiba, R. (2014). The failure of zero tolerance. *Reclaiming Children and Youth, 22*(4), 27-33.

Skogen, K. (2011). *Positive Peer Culture problem labels and juvenile delinquency: An exploratory principal components analysis and ordinary least squares regression analysis of low self-image, inconsiderate of others, and inconsiderate of self.* Thesis for Master of Arts in sociology, criminology. Missoula, MT: University of Montana.

Small, R., Bellonci, C., & Ramsey, S. (2015). Creating and maintaining family partnerships in residential treatment programs. In J. Whittaker, J. del Balle, & L. Holmes (Eds.), *Therapeutic residential care for children and youth* (pp. 156-169). London, UK: Jessica Kingsley Publishers.

Small, S., & Memmo, M. (2004). Contemporary models of youth development and problem prevention: Toward an integration of terms, concepts and models. *Family Relations, 54*(1), 3-11.

Smith, A., Chien, J., & Steinberg, L. (2014). Peers increase adolescent risk taking even when the probabilities of negative outcomes are known. *Developmental Psychology, 50*(5), 1564-1568.

Smith, B. (2012). Inappropriate prescribing. *APA Monitor on Psychology, 43*(6), 36-37.

Smith, L. (2004). A retrospective review of The Aggressive Child: An early and major exemplar of qualitative inquiry. *Qualitative Social Work, 3*(2), 221-231.

Smoller, J. (2012). *The other side of normal: How biology is providing the clues to unlock the secrets of normal and abnormal behavior.* New York, NY: HarperCollins.

Sommers, F. (1984). *Curing nuclear madness.* London, UK: Methuen Publishing.

Southard, E. (1914). The mind twist and brain spot hypotheses in psychopathology and neuropathology. *Psychological Bulletin, 11*(4), 117-130.

Spinazzola, J., Ford, J., Zucker, M., van der Kolk, B., Silva, S., Smith, S., & Blaustein, M. (2005). Survey evaluates complex trauma exposure, outcome, and intervention among children and adolescents. *Psychiatric Annals, 35*(5), 433-439.

Sroufe, L., Egeland, B., Carlson, E., & Collins, W. (2005). *The development of the person: The Minnesota study of risk and adaptation from birth to childhood.* New York, NY: Guilford Press

Stanton, M. (1993). Psychic contusion: Remarks on Ferenczi and trauma. *British Journal of Psychotherapy, 9*(4), 456-462).

Steele, W., & Kuban, C. (2013). Healing trauma, building resilience: SITCAP in action. *Reclaiming Children and Youth, 22*(4), 18-20.

Steele, W., & Kuban, C. (2014). *Working with grieving and traumatized children and adolescents: Discovering what matters most through evidence-based, sensory interventions.* Hoboken, NJ: John Wiley & Sons.

Steele, W., & Malchiodi, C. (2012). *Trauma-informed practices with children and adolescents.* New York, NY: Routledge.

Steinebach, C., Jungo, D., & Zihlmann, R. (2013). *Positive psychologie in der praxis. Anwendung in psychotherapie, beratung und coaching.* Weinheim, Deutschland: Beltz.

Sternberg, R. (1996). *Successful intelligence: How practical and creative intelligence predict success in life.* New York, NY: Plume.

Sternberg, R. (1999). The theory of successful intelligence. *Review of General Psychology, 3*: 292-316.

Sternberg, R. J., & Kolligian, J., Jr. (1990). *Competence considered.* New Haven, CT: Yale University Press.

Strenze, T. (2007). Intelligence and socioeconomic success: A meta-analytic review of longitudinal research. *Intelligence, 35*: 401-426.

Strother, M. (2007). A mind for adventure. *Reclaiming Children and Youth, 16*(1), 17-21.

Sue, D. (2010). *Micro-aggressions in everyday life: Race, gender, and sexual orientation.* New York, NY: Wiley.

Sugai, G., & Lewis, T. (1999). *Developing positive behavioral support for students with challenging behaviors.* Reston, VA: Council for Children with Behavioral Disorders.

Sugden, K., Arseneault, L., Harrington, H., Moffitt, T., Williams, B., & Caspi, A. (2010). Serotonin transporter gene moderates the development of emotional problems among children following bullying and victimization. *Child & Adolescent Psychiatry, 49*(8), 830-840.

Suttie, I. (1935). *The origins of love and hate.* [Reprinted in 2001.] London, UK: Routledge.

Sylwester, R. (2005). *How to explain a brain.* Thousand Oaks, CA: Corwin Press.

Syvertsen, A. K., Roehlkepartain, E. C., & Scales, P. C. (2012). *The American family assets study.* Minneapolis, MN: Search Institute. www.search-institute.org/research/family-strengths

Szyf, M., McGowan, P., Turecki, G., & Meaney M. (2010). The social environment and the epigenome. In C. Worthman, P. Plotsky, D. Schechter, & C. Cummings (Eds.), *Formative experiences: The interaction of caregiving, culture, and developmental psychobiology* (pp. 53-81). Boston, MA: Cambridge University Press.

Tabron, L. with Kanani, R. (2014). An interview with La June Montgomery Tabron of the W. K. Kellogg Foundation. *Forbes,* http://www.forbes.com/sites/rahimkanani/2014/03/15/an-interview-with-la-june-montgomery-tabron-of-the-w-k-kellogg-foundation/

Tagore, R. (1924/2007). To teachers. In *The English Writings of Rabindranath Tagore* (Vol. 4) (pp. 703-708). New Delhi, India: Atlantic Publishers and Distributors.

Tancredi, L. (2005). Hard-wired behavior: *What neuroscience reveals about reality.* New York, NY: Cambridge University Press.

Tangney, J. (2001). Constructive and destructive aspects of shame and guilt. In A. Bohart & D. Stipek (Eds.), *Constructive and destructive behavior: Implications for family, school, and society* (pp. 127-145). Washington, DC: American Psychological Association.

Tate, T., Copas, R., & Wasmund, W. (2012). *Partners in empowerment: A practitioner's guide to implementing peer group treatment models.* Albion, MI: Starr Commonwealth.

Taussig, H., & Culhane, S. (2010). Childhood emotional abuse and the attachment system across the life cycle: What theory and research tell us. *Journal of Aggression, Maltreatment & Trauma, 19*(1), 52-74.

Taylor, S. (2002). *The tending instinct: How nurturing is essential to who we are and how we live.* New York, NY: Holt.

Taylor, S., & Gonzaga, G. (2007). Affilliative responses to stress: A social neuroscience model. In E. Harmon-Jones & P. Winkielman (Eds.), *Social neuroscience: Integrating biological and psychological explanations of social behavior* (pp. 454-473). New York, NY: Guilford Press.

Teicher, M., Anderson, S., Polcari, A., Anderson, C., Navalta, C., & Kim, D. (2003). The neurobiological consequences of early stress and childhood maltreatment. *Neuroscience & Behavioral Reviews, 27*: 33-44.

Terr, L. (1991). Childhood traumas: An outline and overview. *American Journal of Psychiatry, 148*(1), 10-20.

Thapa, A., Cohen, J., Higgins-D'Alessandro, A., & Guffey, S. (2012). School climate research summary. National School Climate Center, *School Climate Brief, 3.* http://www.schoolclimate.org/climate/documents/policy/sc-brief-v3.pdf

The C. elegans Sequencing Consortium. (1998). Genome sequence of the nematode C. elegans: A platform for investigating biology. *Science, 282:* 2012-2018.

The ENCODE Project Consortium. (2012). An integrated encyclopedia of DNA elements in the human genome. *Nature, 489*(7414), 57-74.

Thomann, C., & Carter, A. (2009). Social and emotional development theories. In J. Benson & M. Haith (Eds.), *Social and emotional development in infancy and early childhood* (pp. 420-428). San Diego, CA: Academic Press.

Thompson, R., Huefner, J., Daly, D., & Davis, J. (2014). *Why quality foster care is good for America's at-risk kids: A Boys Town initiative.* Omaha, NE: Boys Town.

Thompson, R., & Koley, S. (2014). Engaging families in in-home family intervention. *Reclaiming Children and Youth, 23*(2), 19-22.

Thorsborne, M. (2013). *Implementing restorative practice in schools: A practical guide to transforming school communities.* London, UK: Jessica Kingsley Publications.

Tileston, D. (2006). Self-efficacy. In S. Feinstein (Ed.), *The Praeger handbook of learning and the brain, Vol. 2* (pp. 431-434). Westport, CT: Praeger Publications.

Trieschman, A., Whittaker, J., & Brendtro, L. (1969). *The other 23 hours: Child-care work with emotionally disturbed children in a therapeutic milieu.* Piscataway, NJ: Transaction.

Turkheimer, E., Blair, C., Sojourner, A., Protzko, J., & Horn, E. (2012). *Gene environment interaction for IQ in a randomized clinical trial. Unpublished manuscript.* Department of Psychology, University of Virginia, Charlottesville.

Tutu, D. (2005). Our hope for the future. *Reclaiming Children and Youth, 14*(2), 124.

Twenge, J., Baumeister, R., Tice, D., & Stucke, T. (2001). If you can't join them, beat them: Effects of social exclusion on aggressive behavior. *Journal of Personality and Social Psychology, 81*(6), 1058-1069.

Twenge, J., Baumeister, R., DeWall, C., Ciarocco, N., & Bartels, J. (2007). Social exclusion decreases prosocial behavior. *Journal of Personality and Social Psychology, 92*(1), 56-66.

Twenge. J., Catanese, K., & Baumeister, R. (2002). Social exclusion causes self-defeating behavior. *Journal of Personality and Social Psychology, 83*(3), 606-615.

Tyler, T., Rasinski, K., & Spoddick, N. (1985). Influence of voice on satisfaction with leaders: Exploring the meaning of process control. *Journal of Personality and Social Psychology, 48*(1), 72-81.

Ungar, M. (2007). *Playing at being bad: The hidden resilience of troubled teens.* Toronto, Canada: McClelland and Stewart.

Van Bockern, S. (2011). Intentional schools: Living in the moment. *Reclaiming Children and Youth, 20*(1), 6-9.

Van Bockern, S., Brendtro, L., & Brokenleg, M. (2010). *Circle of Courage tool kit for elementary schools.* Lennox, SD: Reclaiming Youth International.

Van Bockern, S., & McDonald, T. (2012). Creating Circle of Courage Schools. *Reclaiming Children and Youth, 20*(4), 13–17.

Vandenberghe, L., & Costa Prado, F. (2009). Law and grace in Saint Augustine: A fresh perspective on mindfulness and spirituality in behaviour therapy. *Mental Health, Religion & Culture, 12:* 587-600.

van der Kolk, B. (2003). The neurobiology of childhood trauma and abuse. *Child and Adolescent Psychiatric Clinics of North America, 12*(2), 293-317.

van der Kolk, B. (2005). Developmental trauma disorder: Toward a rational diagnosis for children with complex trauma histories. *Psychiatric Annals, 33*(5), 401-408.

van der Kolk, B. (2014). *The body keeps score: Brain, mind, and body in the healing of trauma.* New York, NY: Viking.

van der Kolk, B., McFarlane, A., & Weisaeth, L. (2007). *Traumatic stress: The effects of overwhelming experience on mind, body, and society.* New York, NY: Guilford Press.

VanderVen, K. (2009). Why focusing on control backfires: A systems perspective. *Reclaiming Children and Youth, 17*(4), 8-12.

Vilakazi, H. (1993). Rediscovering lost truths. *Journal of Emotional and Behavioral Problems, 1*(4), 37.

Villa, R., & Thousand, J. (2000). *Restructuring for caring and effective education.* Baltimore, MD: Brookes.

Vorrath, H., & Brendtro, L. (1985). *Positive peer culture.* Hawthorne, NY: Aldine Publishing.

Vrlicka, P. (2013). Evolution of the "social brain" in humans: What are the benefits and costs of belonging to a social species? *Huffington Post Science.* Available at: http://www.huffingtonpost.com/pascal-vrticka/human-social-development_b_3921942.html

Vygotsky, L. (1978). *Mind in society: The development of higher psychological processes.* Cambridge, MA: Harvard University Press.

Wachtel, T. (2003). Restorative justice in everyday life: Beyond the ritual. *Reclaiming Children and Youth, 12*(2), 82-87.

Wallach, M., & Wallach, L. (1983). *Psychology's sanction for selfishness: The error of egoism in theory and therapy.* New York, NY: Freeman.

Wampold, B., & Imel, Z. (2015). *The great psychotherapy debate. The evidence for what makes psychotherapy work.* New York, NY: Routledge.

Warneken, F., & Thomasello, M. (2006). Altruistic helping in young infants. *Science, 311*(5765), 1301-1303.

Way, D. (1993). I just have a half heart. *Journal of Emotional and Behavioral Problems, 2*(1), 4-5.

Wenger, L., & Van Bockern, S. (1999). Educational best practice or malpractice? Our choice. *Reclaiming Children and Youth, 7*(4), 212-216, 223.

Wenger, M. (2012). *Racial equity resource guide.* Battle Creek, MI: W. K. Kellogg Foundation.

Werner, E. (2012). Risk, resilience, and recovery. *Reclaiming Children and Youth, 21*(1), 18-23.

Werner, E., & Smith, R. (1982). *Vulnerable but invincible: A longitudinal study of resilient children and youth.* New York, NY: McGraw Hill.

Werner, E., & Smith, R. (1992). *Overcoming the odds: High risk children from birth to adulthood.* Ithaca, NY: Cornell University Press.

Werry, J. (2013). Fifty years in child and adolescent psychiatry. *Reclaiming Children and Youth, 22*(2), 25-30.

Wexler, B. (2006). *Brain and culture.* Cambridge, MA: Massachusetts Institute of Technology.

Wheatley, M. (2002). *Turning to one another: Simple conversations to restore hope to the future.* San Francisco, CA: Berrett-Koehler.

Whewell, W. (1847). *The philosophy of inductive sciences.* London, UK: Parker.

White, R. (1959). Motivation reconsidered: The concept of competence. *Psychological Review, 66*(5), 297-333.

Whiting, J., & Seita, J. (2008). The perspective of the consumer: Foster children tell us what they need. In R. Lee & J. Whiting (Eds.), *Foster care therapist handbook: Relational approaches to the children and their families* (pp. 63-84). Washington, DC: CWLA Press.

Wilker, K. (1921). *Der Lindenhof.* Translated into English in 1993 by Stephan Lhotzky. Sioux Falls, SD: Augustana College.

Willner, A., Braukmann, C., Kirigin, K., Fixsen, D., Philips, E., & Wolf, M. (1970). The training and validation of youth-preferred social behaviors of child-care personnel. *Journal of Applied Behavior Analysis, 10*(2), 219-230.

Wilson, D., Gottfredson, D., & Najaka, S. (2001). School-based prevention of problem behaviors: A meta-analysis. *Journal of Quantitative Criminology, 17:* 247-242.

Wilson, E. O. (1998). *Consilience: The unity of knowlege.* New York: Alfred A. Knopf.

Wilson, H. (2014). Turning off the school to prison pipeline. *Reclaiming Children and Youth, 23*(1), 49-53.

Wineman, D., & James, A. (1969). The advocacy challenge to schools of social work. *Social Work, 14*(2), 23-32.

Winnicott, D. (1965). *The maturational processes and the facilitating environment: Studies in the theory of social development.* New York, NY: International Universities Press.

Wolins, M., & Wosner, Y. (1982). *Revitalizing residential settings: Problems and potential in education, health, rehabilitation, and social service.* San Francisco, CA: Jossey-Bass.

Wood, M., Davis, K., Swindle, F., & Quirk, C. (1995). *Developmental Therapy-Developmental Teaching: Fostering social-emotional competence in troubled children and youth.* Austin, TX: Pro-Ed.

Woodland Hills Youth. (2008). Voices of youth: "Don't let me give up." *Reclaiming Children and Youth, 17*(1), 10-11.

Wright, M., Masten, A., & Narayan, A. (2013). Resilience processes in development: Four waves of research on positive adaptation in the context of adversity. In S. Goldstein & R. Brooks (Eds.), *Handbook of resilience in children* (pp. 15-37). New York, NY: Springer.

Zeigarnik, B. (1927). Das Behalten von erledigten und unerledigten Handlungen. [The memory of completed and uncompleted tasks.] *Psychologische Forschung, 9:* 1-85.

Zimbardo, P. (2007). *The Lucifer effect: Understanding how good people turn evil.* New York, NY: Random House.

Zorc, C., O'Reilly, A., Matone, M., Long, J., Watts, C., & Rubin, D. (2013). The relationship of placement experience to school absenteeism and changing schools in young school-age children in foster care. *Child and Youth Services Review, 35:* 826-833.

Index

About the Authors

Larry K. Brendtro, PhD, is a licensed psychologist and Dean of the Starr Global Learning Network, Albion, Michigan. He served fourteen years as president of Starr Commonwealth and taught in the area of children's behavior disorders at the University of Illinois, The Ohio State University, and Augustana College. He is founding editor of the journal *Reclaiming,* and with colleagues has authored numerous books on positive learning and treatment environments. Dr. Brendtro has been a member of the U.S. Coordinating Council on Juvenile Justice and Delinquency during three administrations and trains professionals worldwide.

Martin L. Mitchell, EdD, has served at Starr Commonwealth for 45 years including twelve years as the President and CEO. He has experience as a youth care worker, educator, program executive, and has written, taught, and consulted extensively on issues related to children, families, and communities. He has provided national leadership on racial healing and has served on numerous nonprofit boards including the Alliance for Strong Families and Communities. Dr. Mitchell has led Starr's international initiatives including the Starr Global Learning Network which serves professionals and policy leaders worldwide.